"Music is, what Music is for You".
- Damian Hermann

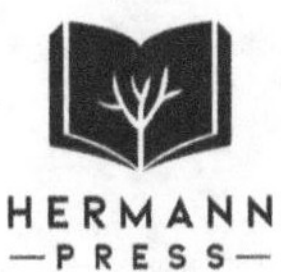

HERMANN
—PRESS—

Welcome

Your journey through musical scales, the essential
Foundation for understanding harmony and
Enhancing creativity.

This *step-by-step* guide serves you the most essential, and
Valuable music information about scales and inversions,
In a very practical and simple way.

Consistency is key and with just a couple of minutes each day
You will get the most out of this book.

Now is your time

INSTRUCTIONS

Each scale presented in this book adheres to a consistent structure.
One has the option, to begin with either the left or right hand first. Typically, the left hand will accompany the melody performed by the right hand. A well-developed base knowledge is essential and therefore serves as the very first step.

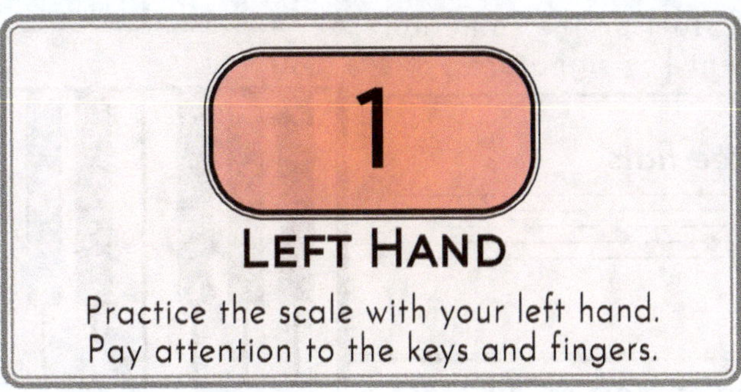

Practice the scale with your left hand.
Pay attention to the keys and fingers.

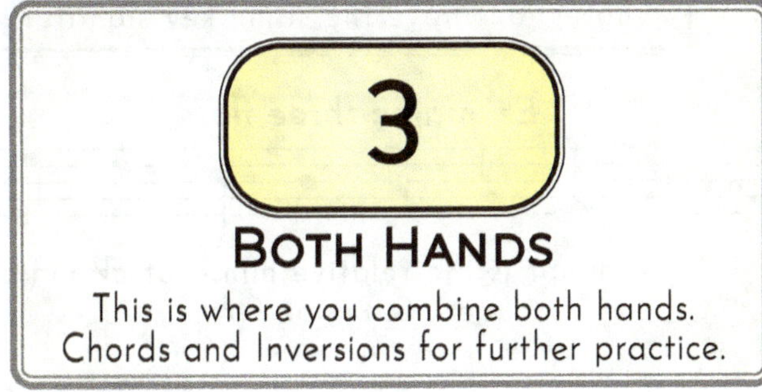

Practice the scale with your right hand.
Try different tempos and be creative.

This is where you combine both hands.
Chords and Inversions for further practice.

NOTES OF THE SCALE:

These seven notes build the scale. A major scale follows the pattern of whole and half steps: W-W-H-W-W-W-H. A minor scale follows the pattern: W-H-W-W-H-W-W, creating a different emotinal tone.

KEY SIGNATURE:

How many "accidentals" (sharps or flats) does the key have. Accidentals, sharps(#), and flats(b) modify the pitch of a note, raising (sharp) or lowering (flat) it by a half step from its natural state. A key signature has either sharps or flats, never both.

ORDER OF SHARPS & FLATS:

Sharp and flat symbols follow this order when written on the clef. For example, five sharp key signature has (F#,C#,G#,D#,A#) written on the clef in this order. Although, when playing the scale this order can be different.

RELATIVE KEY:

A relative key has the same notes as its relative major or minor.
For example Aminor is the relative minor of Cmajor, they have the same key signature. They also have the same notes, however, in a different order.

PRACTICE TIPS:

Use a metronome for practicing in different tempos.
Legato: Notes are played smooth and connected without breaks between notes.
Staccato: Notes are played short and crisp and as detached as possible (*Machine gun sound*).

THE LEFT & RIGHT HAND FOLLOW THIS PATTERN OF DEFINITIONS
AND STEPS THROUGHOUT ALL KEYS.

RELATIVE KEYS

C major: *no sharps or flats*

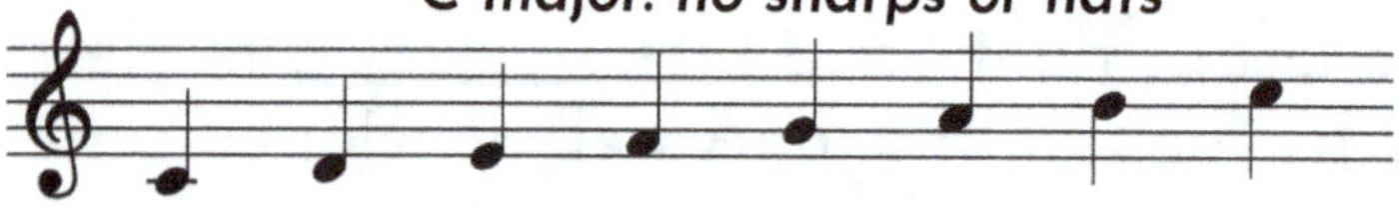

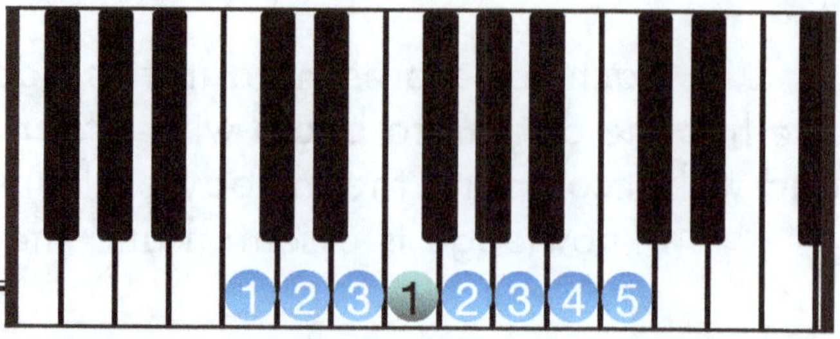

C major and C minor start on the same note, but have different key signatures.

C minor: *three flats*

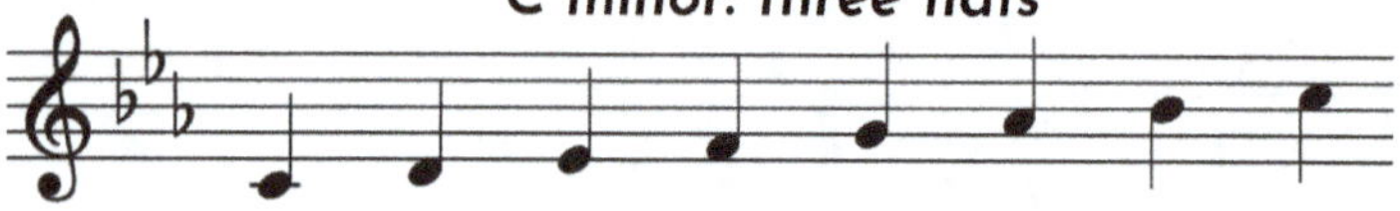

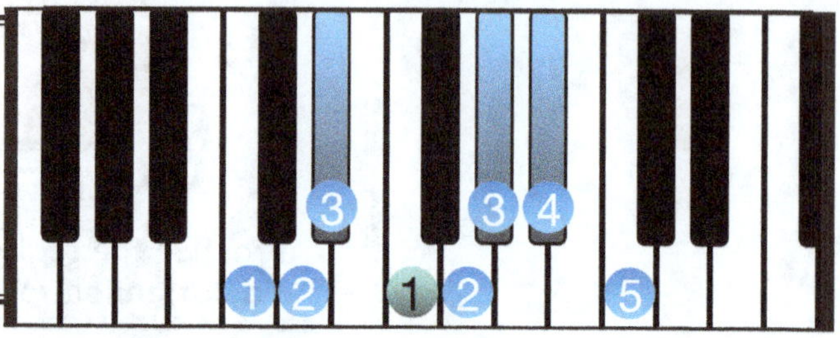

C minor and E♭ major start on different notes, but have the same key signature.

E♭ major: *three flats*

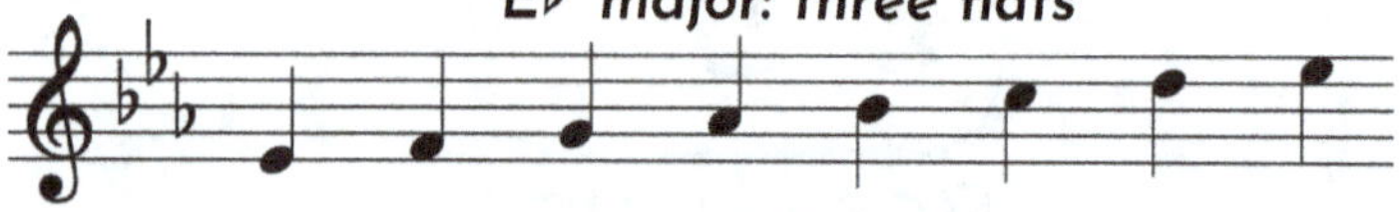

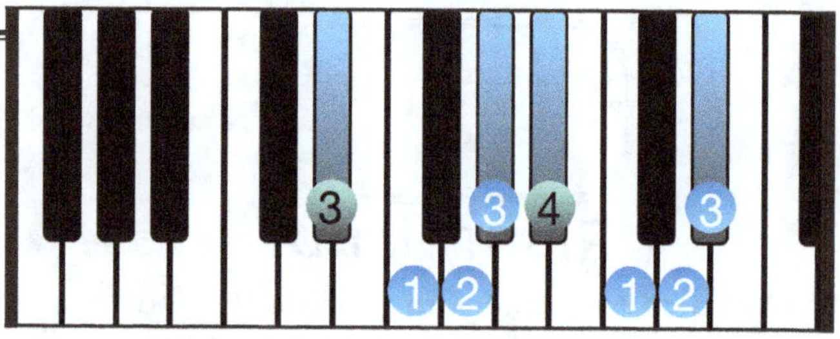

C minor is the relative minor of E♭ major.
see - Circle of Fifths p.7

ENHARMONIC SCALES

Major and Minor keys always follow the same half-step and whole-step rhythm.
See Major Keys and Scales (*page 5*).
So, for example, whether you begin a Minor scale on E flat or D sharp, you will always follow the same rhythm, playing the same piano keys as you go up the scale.
E♭ and D♯ share the same column in the *Circle of Fifths* (*page 7*).

E♭ minor: *six flats*

D♯ minor: *six sharps*

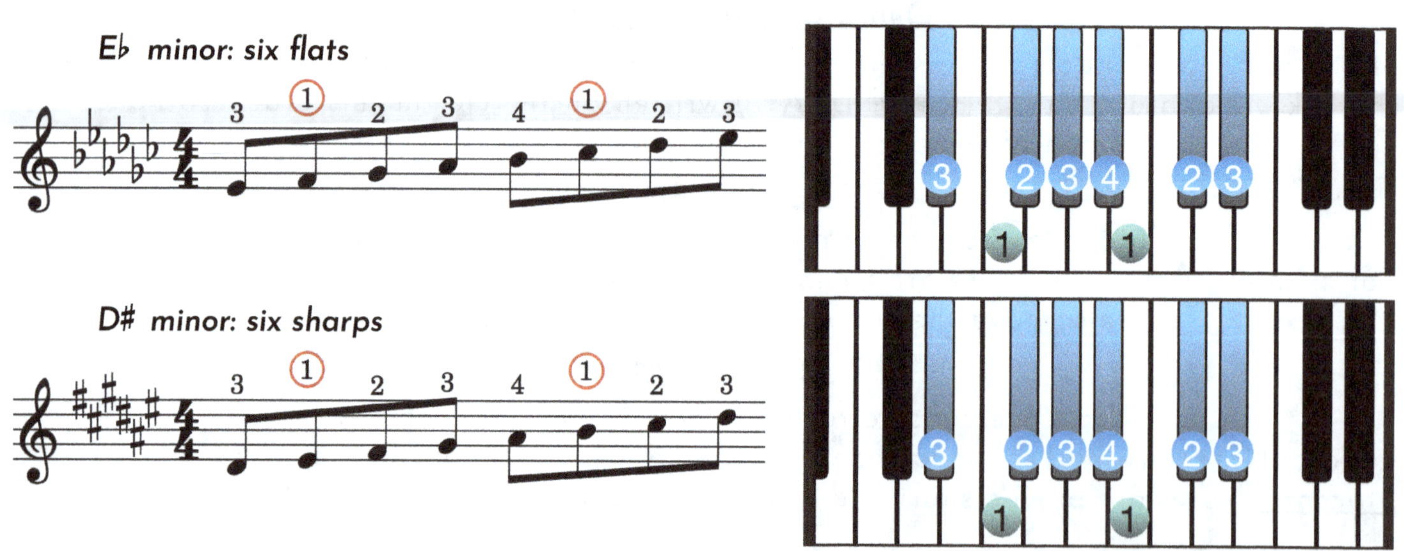

Both scales have the same layout on the keys, which makes them enharmonic.
However, the notes have different names and are written differently.

MAJOR & NATURAL MINOR KEYS

Comparing Major and Minor Scale Patterns

Minor Scale Pattern (natural):   W   H   W   W   H   W   W

Major Scale Pattern (natural):   W   W   H   W   W   W   H

W = Whole   **H** = Half
   Step   Step

Notice that the pattern for minor scales overlaps with the pattern for major scales.
The minor scale starts a half step plus a whole step lower than the major scale pattern, so
a relative minor is always three half steps lower than its relative major.
A minor has the same key signature as C major since C is a minor third higher than A.

**Example
The key of 'A'**

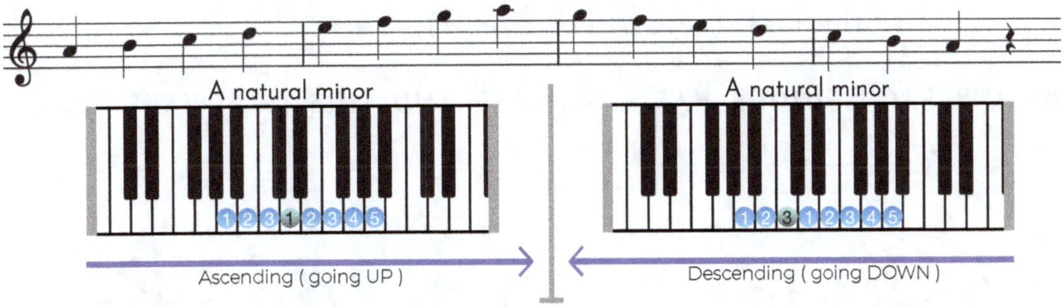

NATURAL MINOR SCALE

- *see graphic above:*
Minor Scale Pattern
(natural)

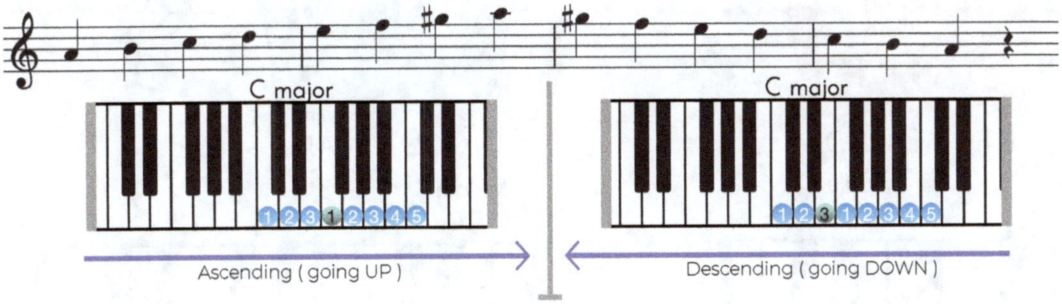

MAJOR SCALE

- *see graphic above:*
Major Scale Pattern
(natural)

Exercise I

Rewrite each scale fom the
Figure as an <u>ascending</u>
natural minor scale.

*Grand staff on page 102
(solution to exercise on p. 103)*

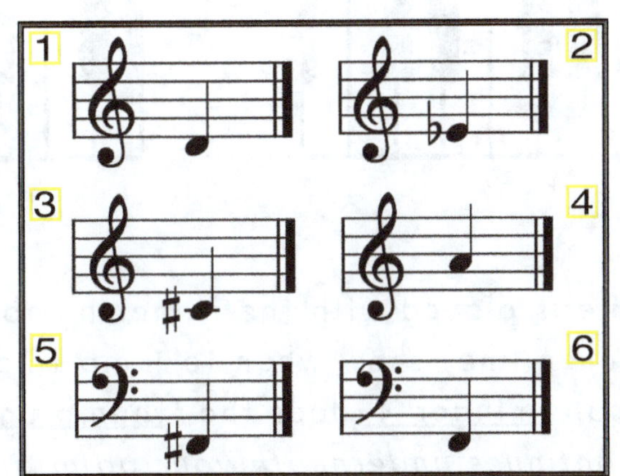

Exercise II

Rewrite each scale fom the
Figure as a <u>descending</u>
major scale..

*Grand staff on page 102
(solution to exercise on p. 103)*

Major and natural Minor scales follow the same step pattern, just starting in a different place.

Notes of the Scale:	**C major** 1 Octave Both Hands	Key Signature:
C, D, E, F, G, A, B		No Flats / No Sharps

In music an Octave is the distance between two musical notes that have the same letter name (*latin: octo = eight*).

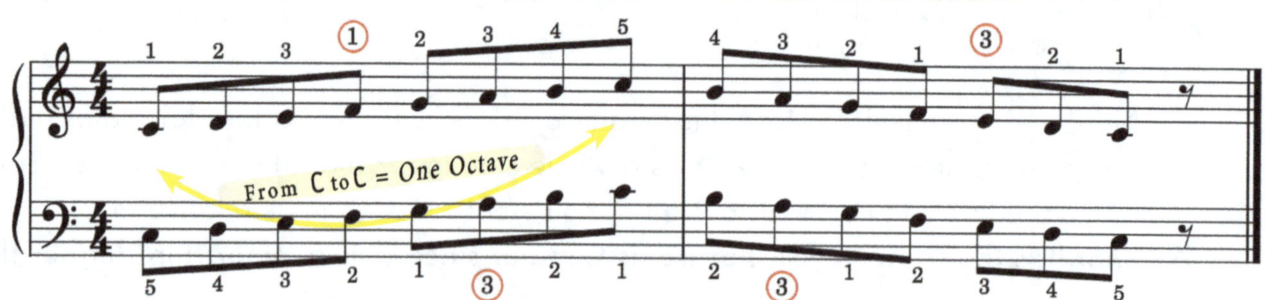

Above you have the notes on the staff. Note 8 completes the Octave, in this example a 'C'. The "Notes of the scale" box follows the written order on the clef. (*repeating after 7*)

AS SHOWN BELOW EACH FINGER HAS A NUMBER AND THIS IS ALWAYS TRUE

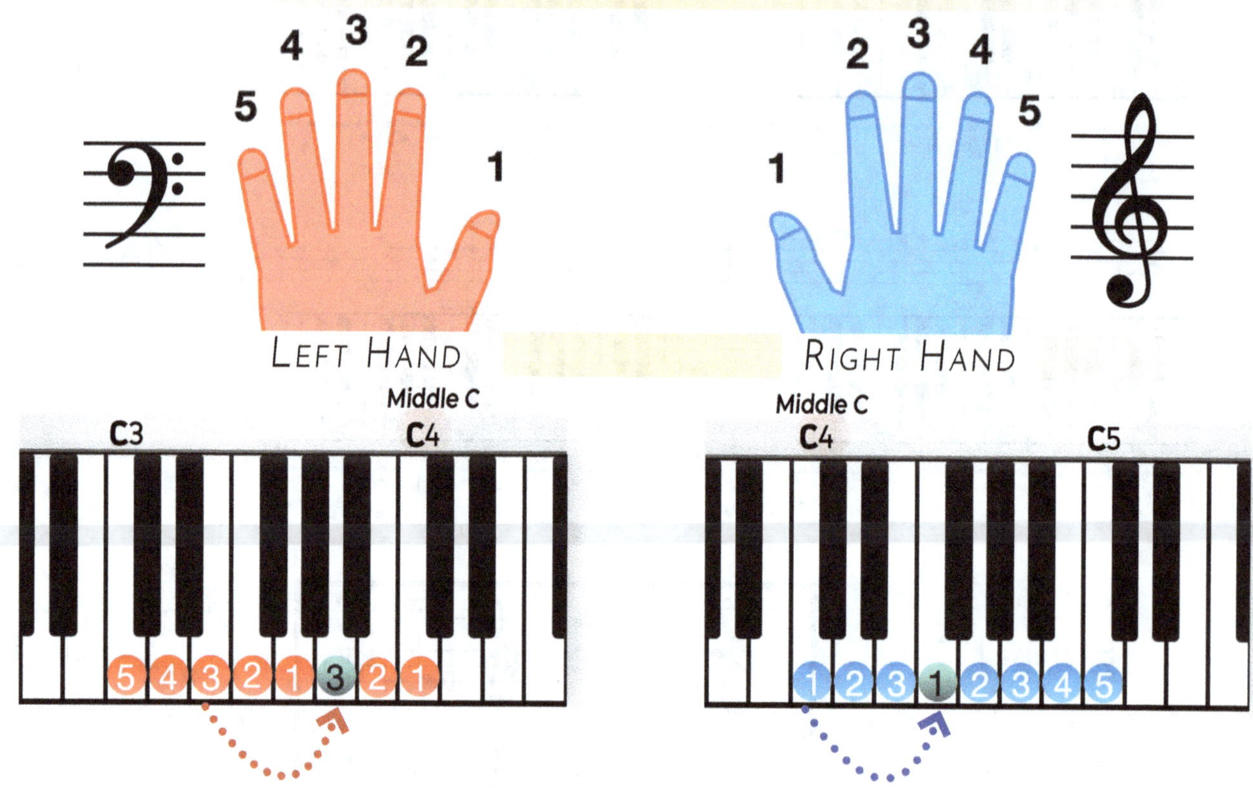

The scale is played with the finger number attached to it. Arrows (broken line) show when to jump fingers. Use <u>finger '3'</u> to continue the scale. <u>Finger '1'</u> does the "<u>thumb under</u>" (*A technique where your thumb continues underneath your palm and plays the next note*).

ASCENDING (*GOING UP, LEFT TO RIGHT*), DESCENDING (*GOING DOWN, RIGHT TO LEFT*)

PAGE LAYOUT

Circle of Fifths

The Circle of Fifths is a graphic representation of the relationships between the 12 major and minor keys. A _relative minor key exists for every major key._ Imagine each key as a different city on the map. For every city (or major key), there's a smaller city nearby that's closely related to it (this is the relative minor key). These major and minor keys are special friends because they share the _same set of notes,_ just in a different order.

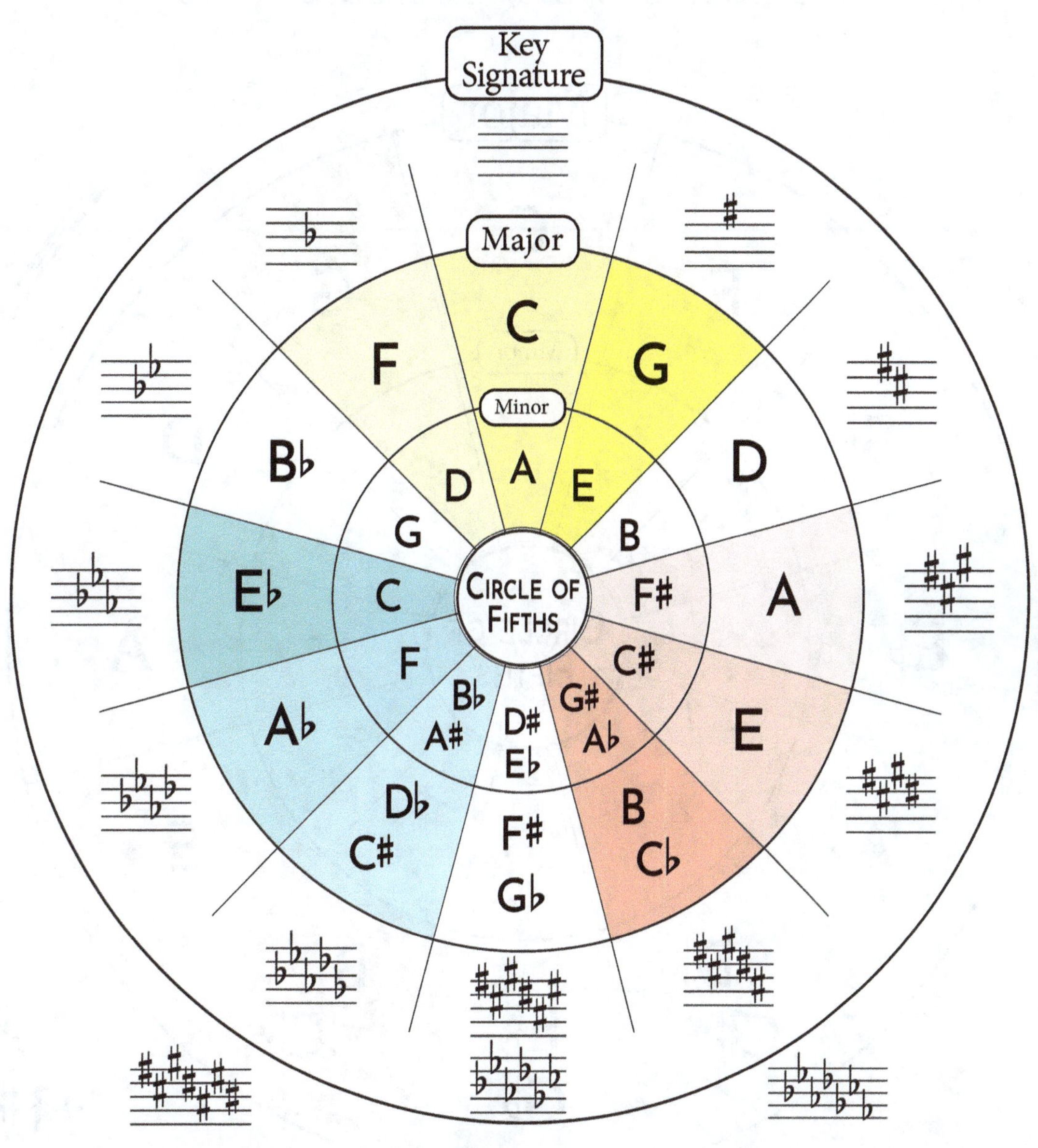

<u>ORDER OF FLATS (KEY SIGNATURE)</u>

Bb, Eb, Ab, Db, Gb, Cb, Fb

<u>ORDER OF SHARPS (KEY SIGNATURE)</u>

F#, C#, G#, D#, A#, E#, B#

Major Scales

Moving **CLOCKWISE**

C major (no sharps) ---> C# major (7 sharps)

Key signature

(Number of sharps, Increase # +1)
(Number of flats, Decrease ♭ -1)

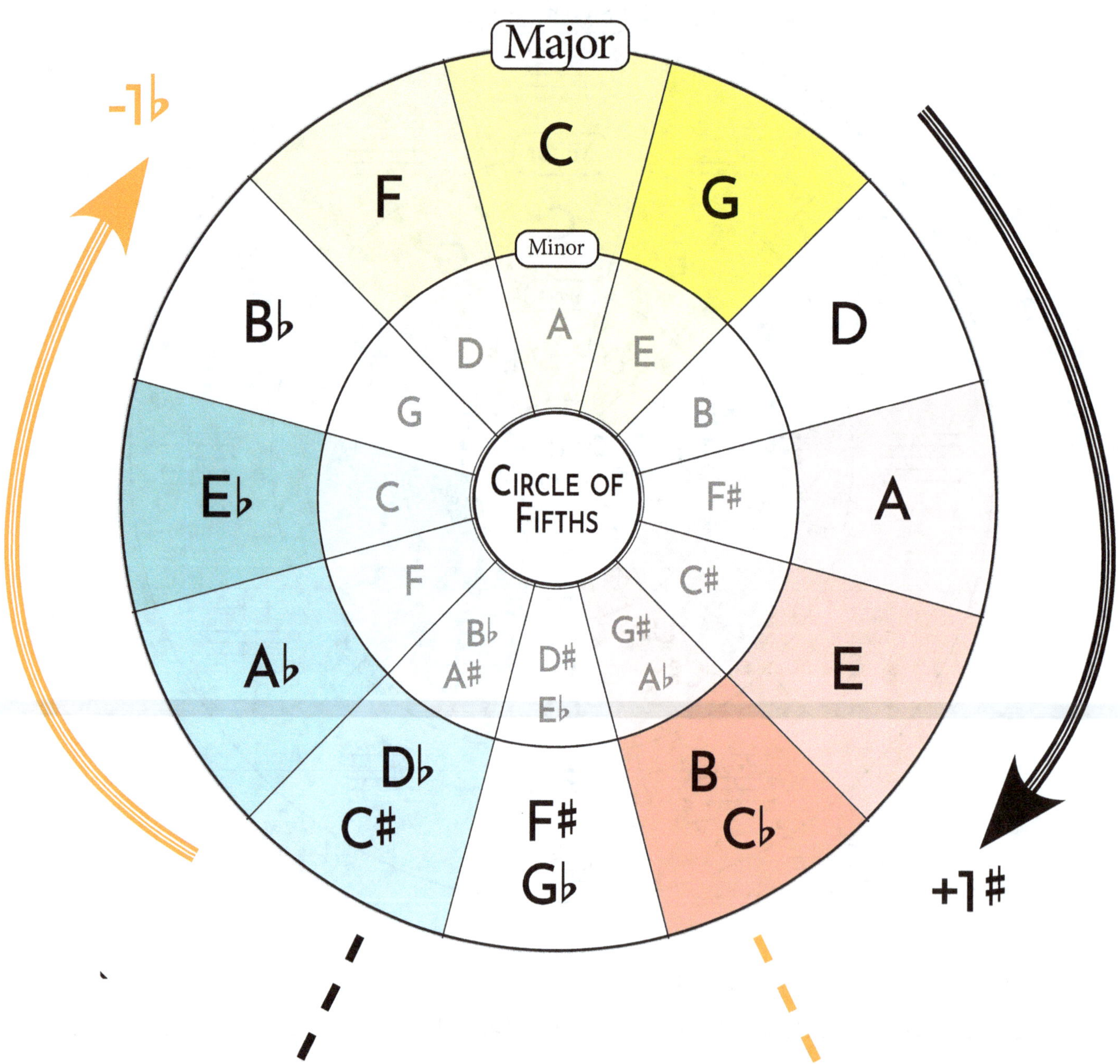

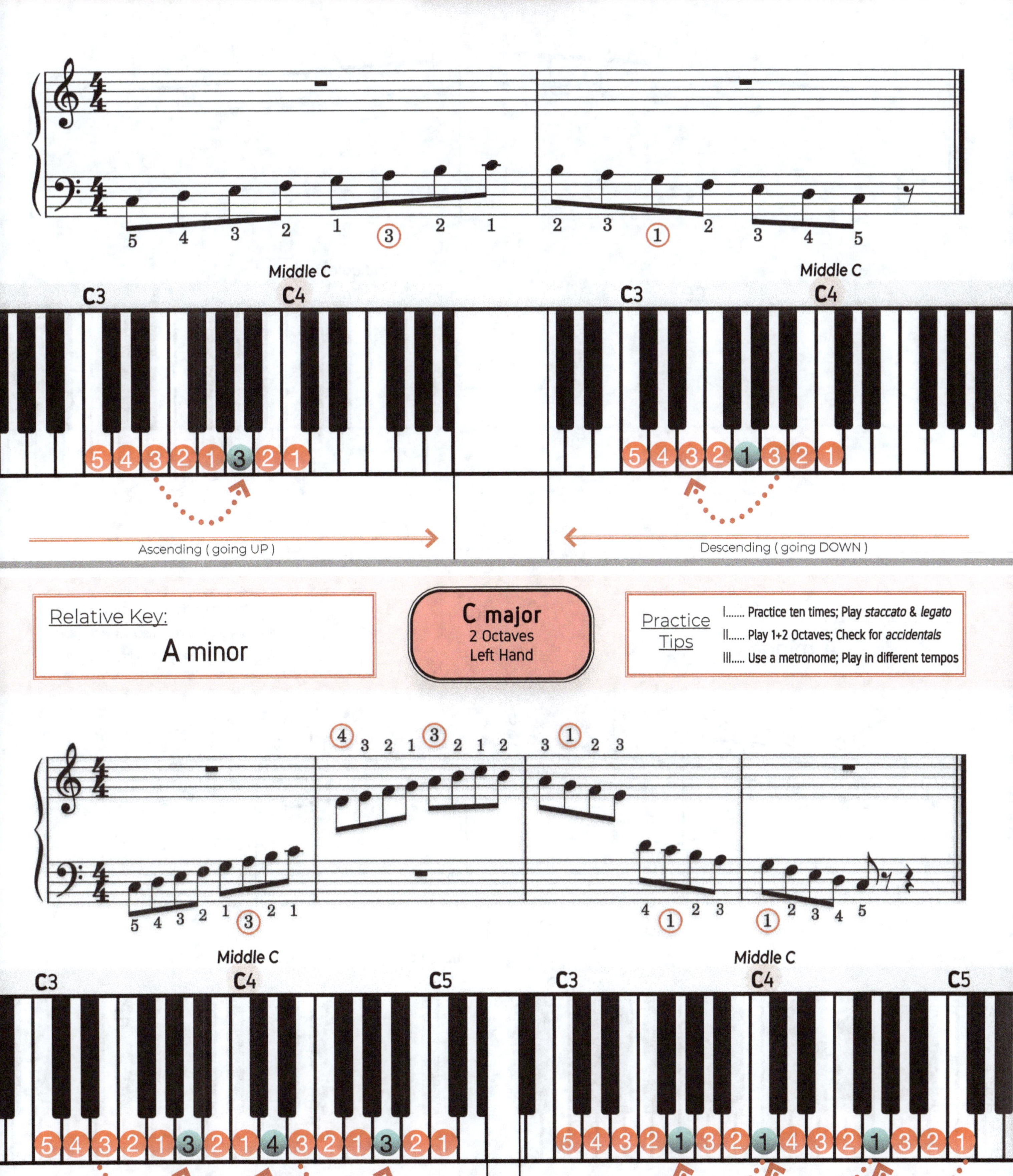

Notes of the Scale:
C, D, E, F, G, A, B
C major
1 Octave
Left Hand
Key Signature:
No Flats / No Sharps
5 4 3 2 1 3 2 1
2 3 1 2 3 4 5
Middle C
C3
C4
C3
Middle C
C4
5 4 3 2 1 3 2 1
5 4 3 2 1 3 2 1
Ascending (going UP)
Descending (going DOWN)
Relative Key:
A minor
C major
2 Octaves
Left Hand
Practice Tips
I....... Practice ten times; Play staccato & legato
II...... Play 1+2 Octaves; Check for accidentals
III..... Use a metronome; Play in different tempos
4 3 2 1 3 2 1 2
3 1 2 3
5 4 3 2 1 3 2 1
4 1 2 3
1 2 3 4 5
Middle C
C3
C4
C5
C3
Middle C
C4
C5
5 4 3 2 1 3 2 1 4 3 2 1 3 2 1
5 4 3 2 1 3 2 1 4 3 2 1 3 2 1
Ascending (going UP)
Descending (going DOWN)

Notes of the Scale:

C, D, E, F, G, A, B

Key Signature:

No Flats / No Sharps

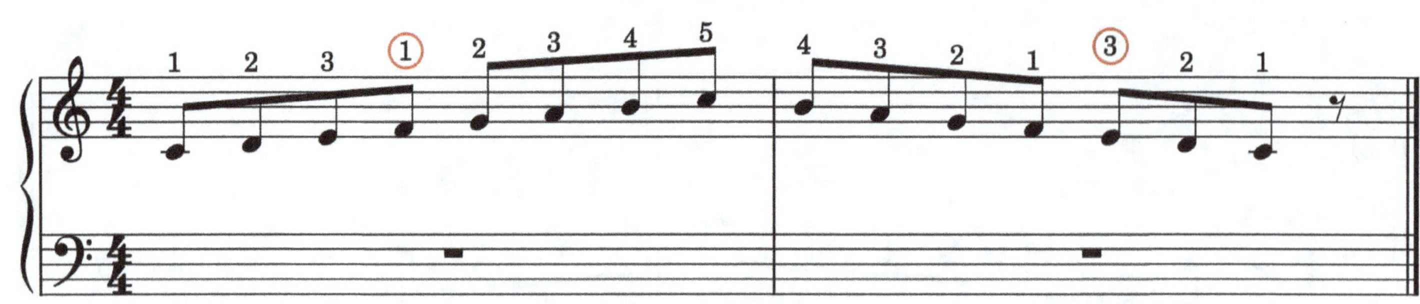

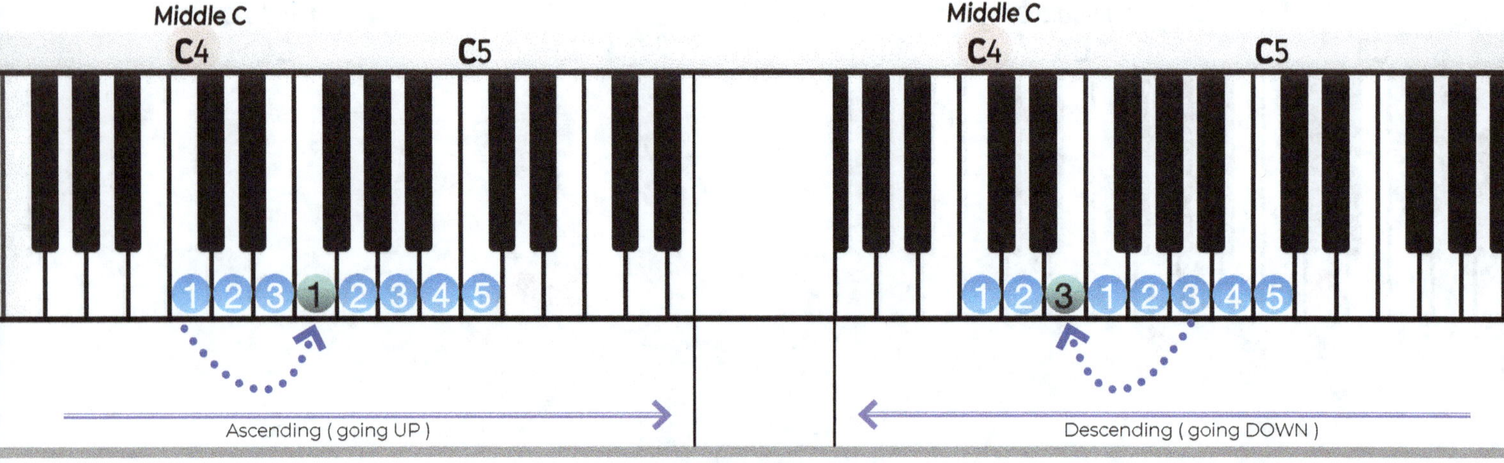

Relative Key:

A minor

C major
2 Octaves
Right Hand

Practice Tips

I...... Practice ten times; Play *staccato* & *legato*
II...... Play 1+2 Octaves; Check for *accidentals*
III..... Use a metronome; Play in different tempos

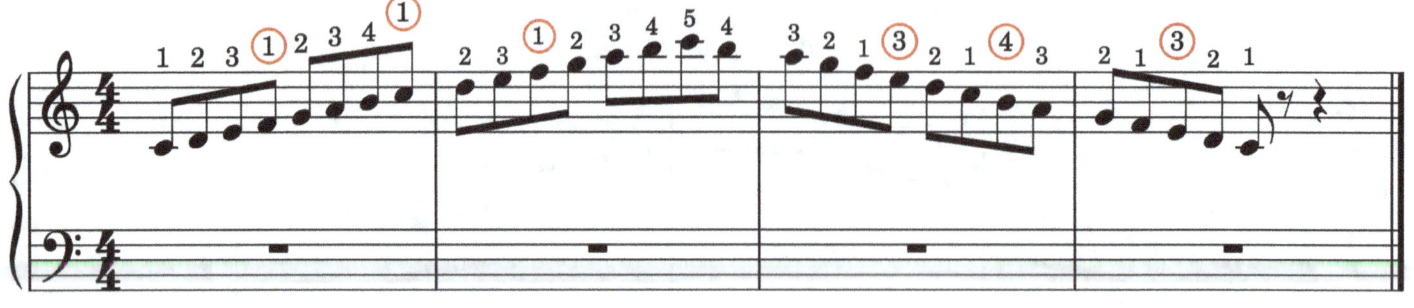

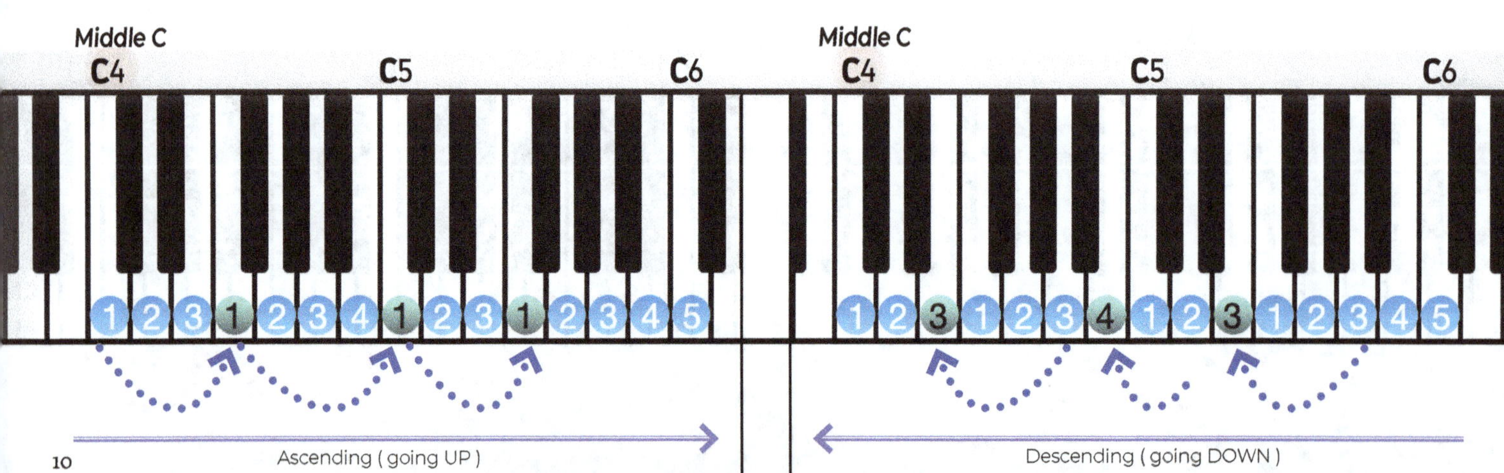

Notes of the Scale:	**C major**	Key Signature:
C, D, E, F, G, A, B	1 Octave / Both Hands	No Flats / No Sharps

Middle C — **C4** ... **C5**

Right Hand

1 2 3 1 2 3 4 5

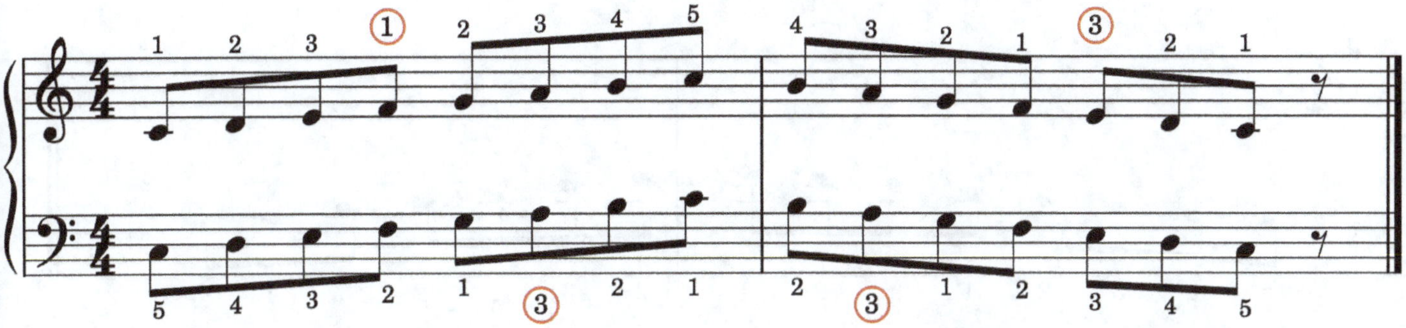

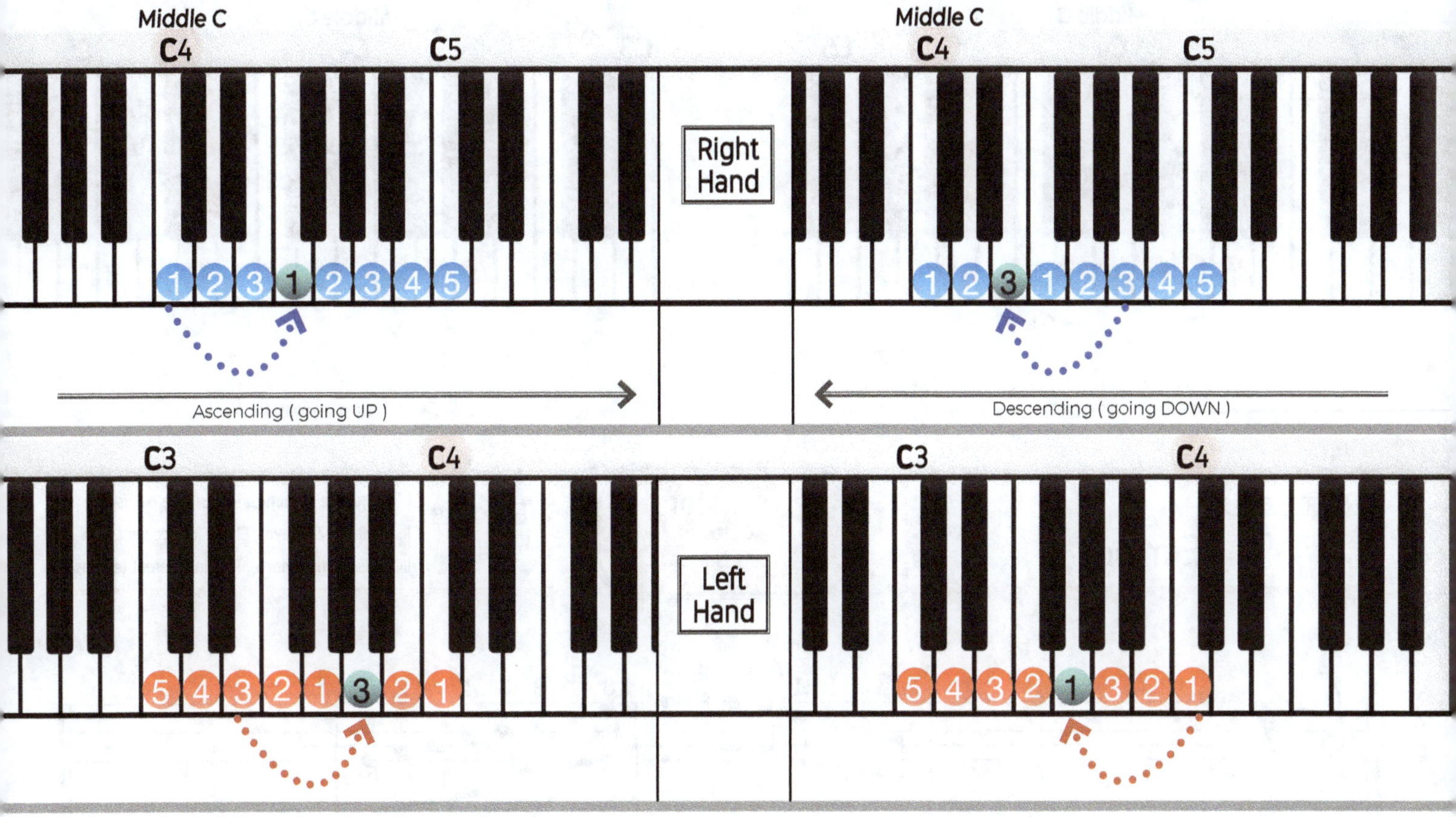

Ascending (going UP)

1 2 3 1 2 3 4 5

Descending (going DOWN)

C3 ... **C4**

Left Hand

5 4 3 2 1 3 2 1

5 4 3 2 1 3 2 1

Basic Chord:		**C major**	Inversion: *(different note at the bottom of the chord)*
C major chord (**C, E, G**)	*The root note of the* **C** *major scale is* **C**	Chords & Inversions	**1**st **Inversion** ---> **E** as bottom note
---> **C** is the root note			**2**nd **Inversion** ---> **G** as bottom note

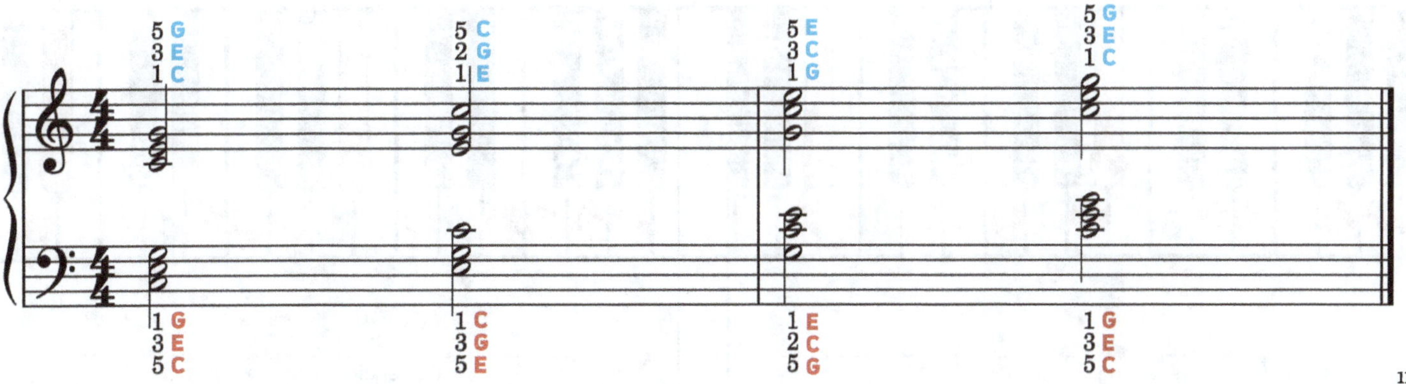

Notes of the Scale:
G, A, B, C, D, E, F#

G major
1 Octave
Left Hand

Key Signature:
One Sharp (F#)

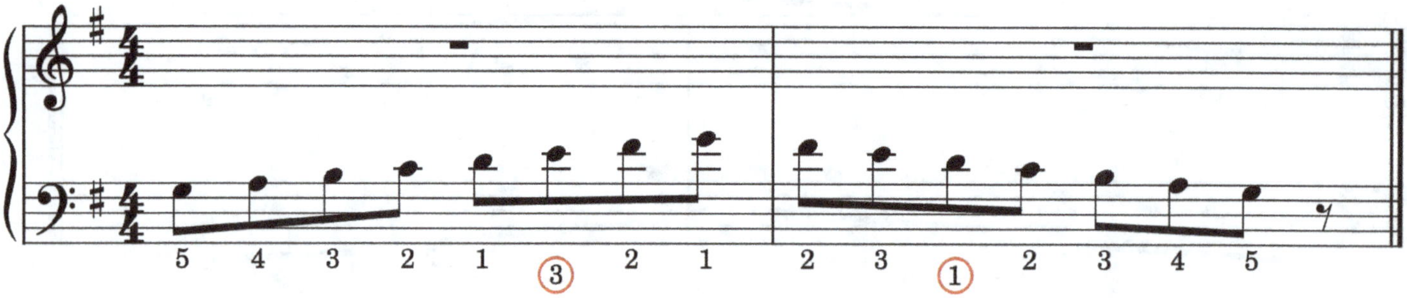

5 4 3 2 1 3 2 1   2 3 1 2 3 4 5

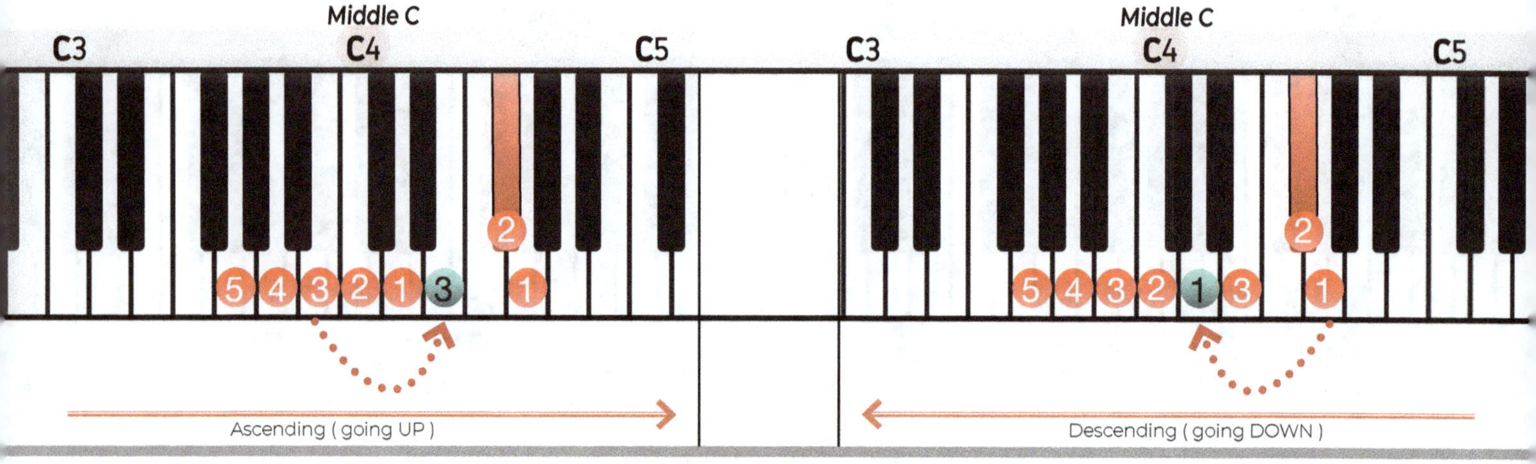

C3   Middle C   C4   C5   C3   Middle C   C4   C5
5 4 3 2 1 3   1   5 4 3 2 1 3   1
2   1   2   1
Ascending (going UP)   Descending (going DOWN)

Relative Key:
E minor

G major
2 Octaves
Left Hand

Practice Tips
I....... Practice ten times; Play staccato & legato
II..... Play 1+2 Octaves; Check for accidentals
III..... Use a metronome; Play in different tempos

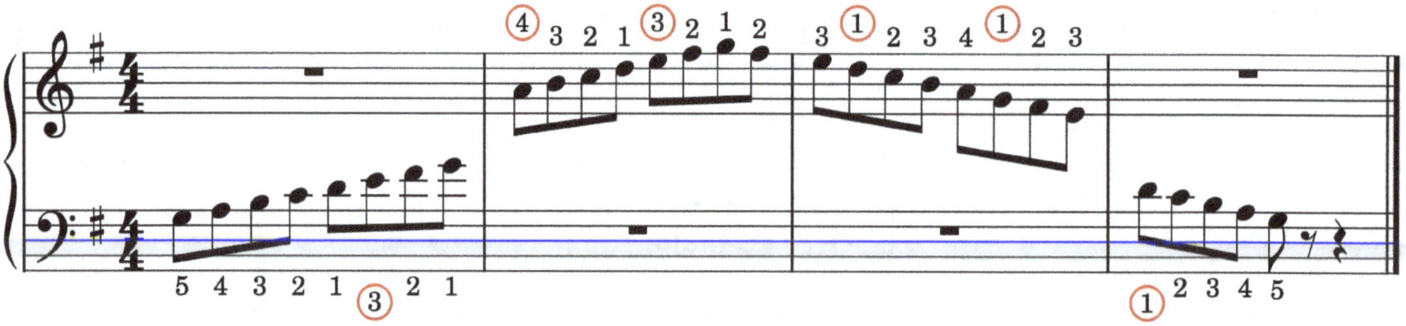

4 3 2 1 3 2 1 2   3 1 2 3 4 1 2 3
5 4 3 2 1 3 2 1   1 2 3 4 5

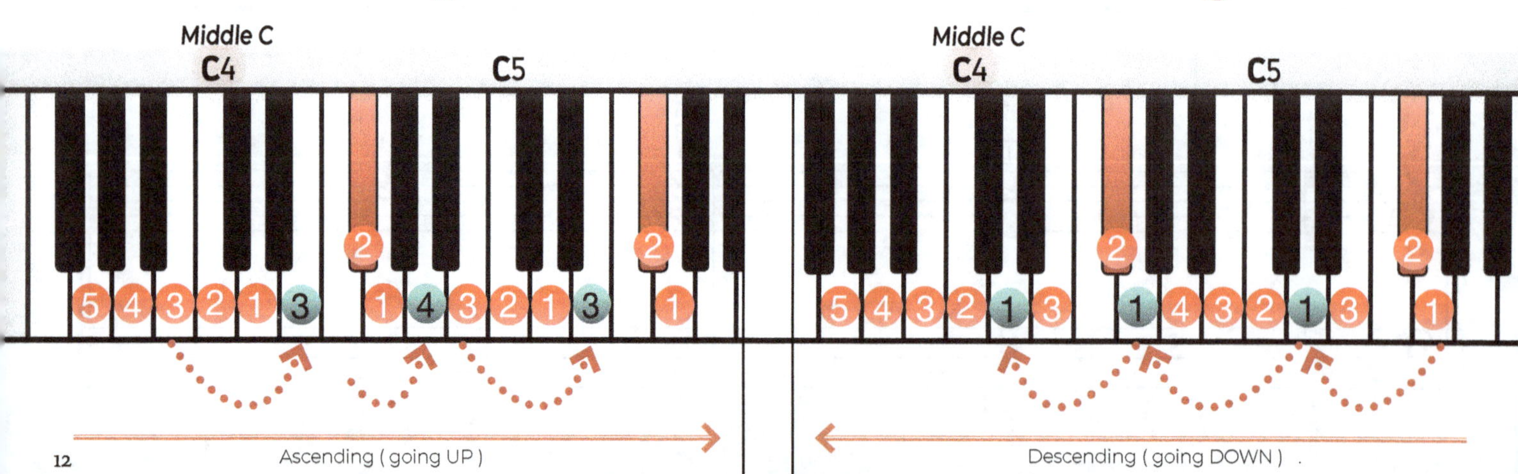

Middle C   C4   C5   Middle C   C4   C5
5 4 3 2 1 3   1 4 3 2 1 3   1
2   2   2   2
5 4 3 2 1 3   1 4 3 2 1 3   1
Ascending (going UP)   Descending (going DOWN)

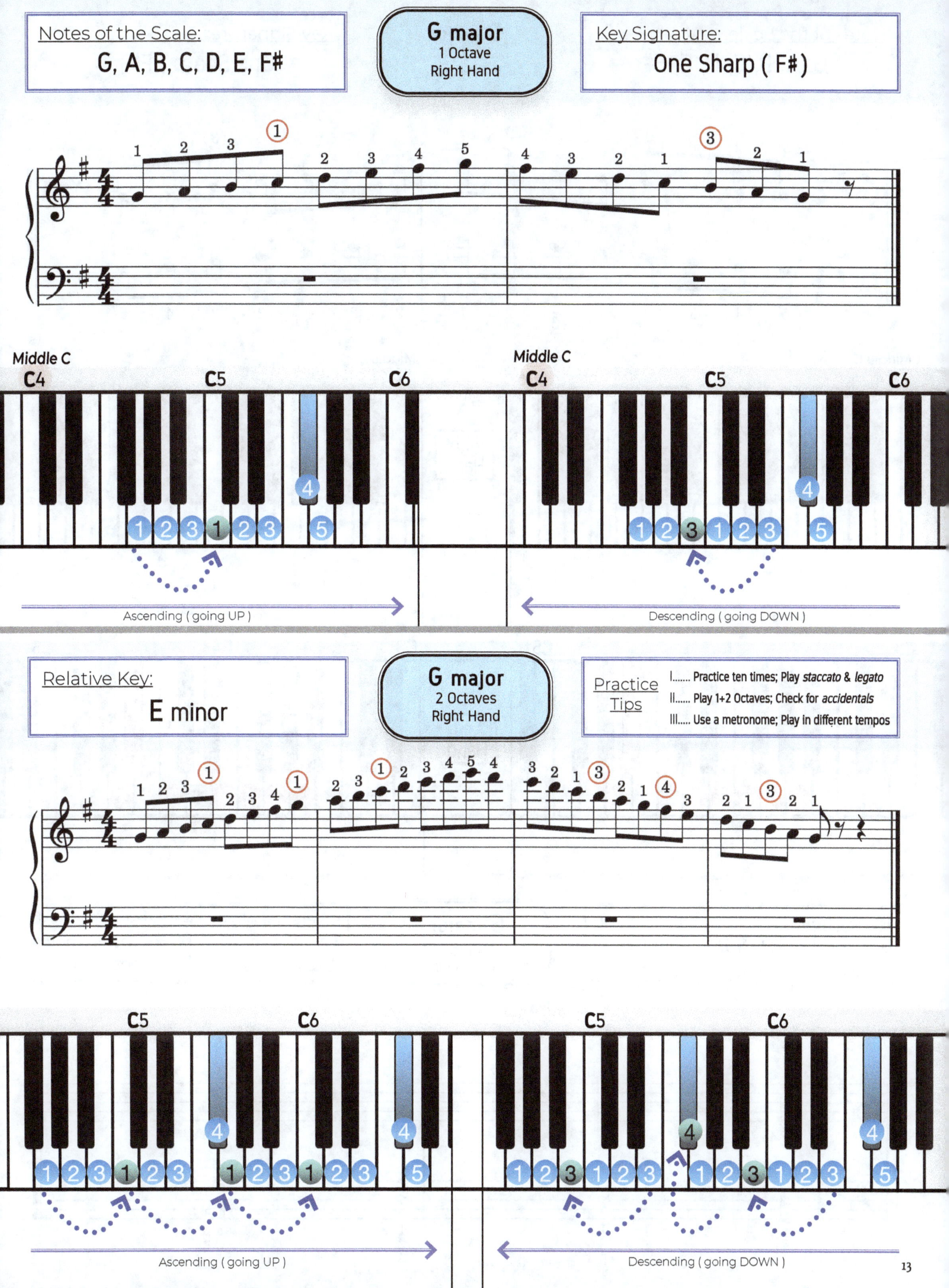

Notes of the Scale:
G, A, B, C, D, E, F#
G major
1 Octave
Right Hand
Key Signature:
One Sharp (F#)
Middle C
C4
C5
C6
Middle C
C4
C5
C6
1 2 3 1 2 3 5
1 2 3 1 2 3 5
4
4
Ascending (going UP)
Descending (going DOWN)
Relative Key:
E minor
G major
2 Octaves
Right Hand
Practice Tips
I....... Practice ten times; Play staccato & legato
II....... Play 1+2 Octaves; Check for accidentals
III..... Use a metronome; Play in different tempos
C5
C6
C5
C6
1 2 3 1 2 3 1 2 3 1 2 3 5
1 2 3 1 2 3 1 2 3 1 2 3 5
4
4
4
4
Ascending (going UP)
Descending (going DOWN)
13

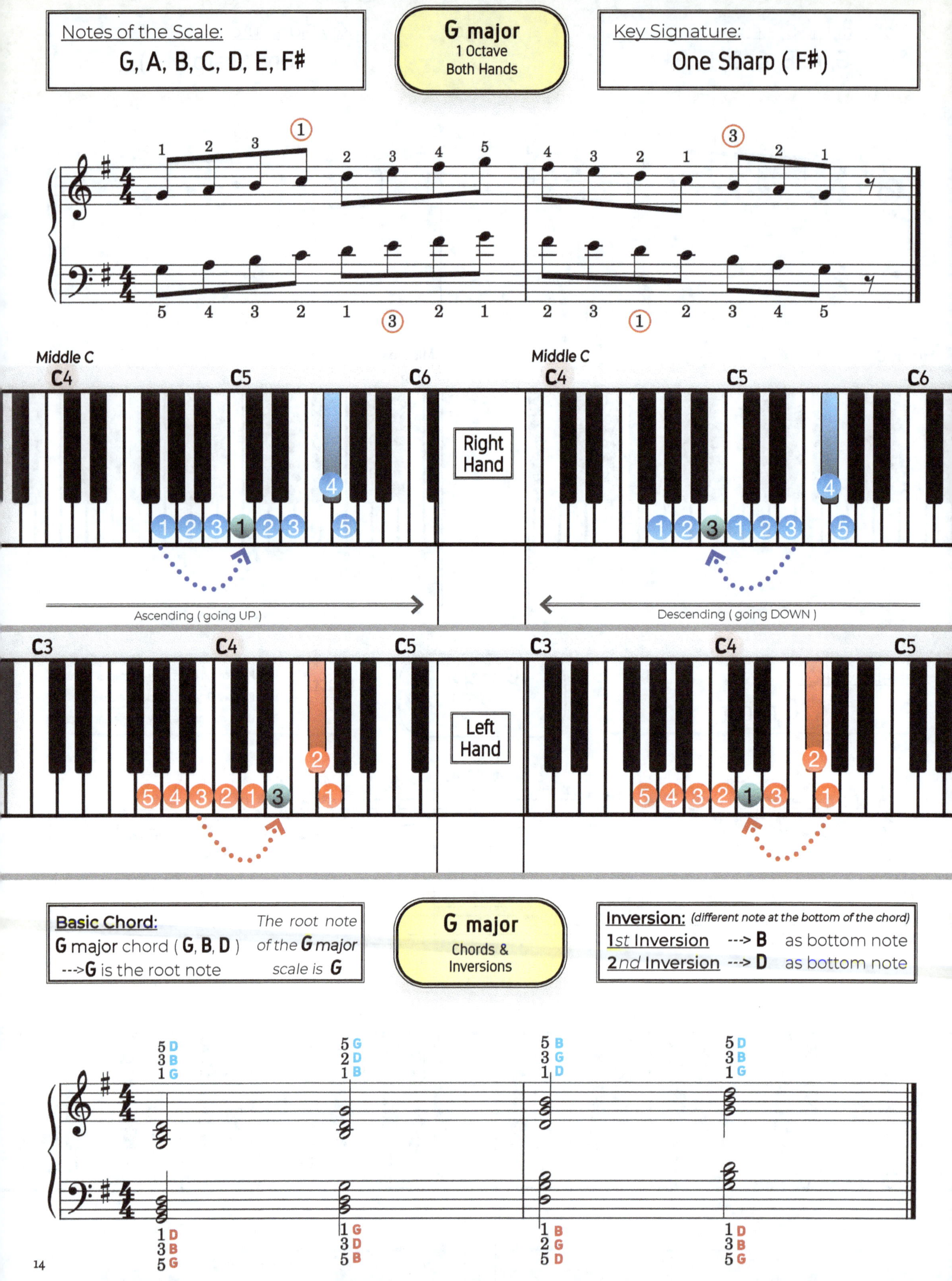

Notes of the Scale:
G, A, B, C, D, E, F#
G major
1 Octave
Both Hands
Key Signature:
One Sharp (F#)
Middle C
C4
C5
C6
Right Hand
Ascending (going UP)
Descending (going DOWN)
C3
C4
C5
Left Hand
Basic Chord:
G major chord (G, B, D)
--->G is the root note
The root note of the G major scale is G
G major
Chords & Inversions
Inversion: (different note at the bottom of the chord)
1st Inversion ---> B as bottom note
2nd Inversion ---> D as bottom note

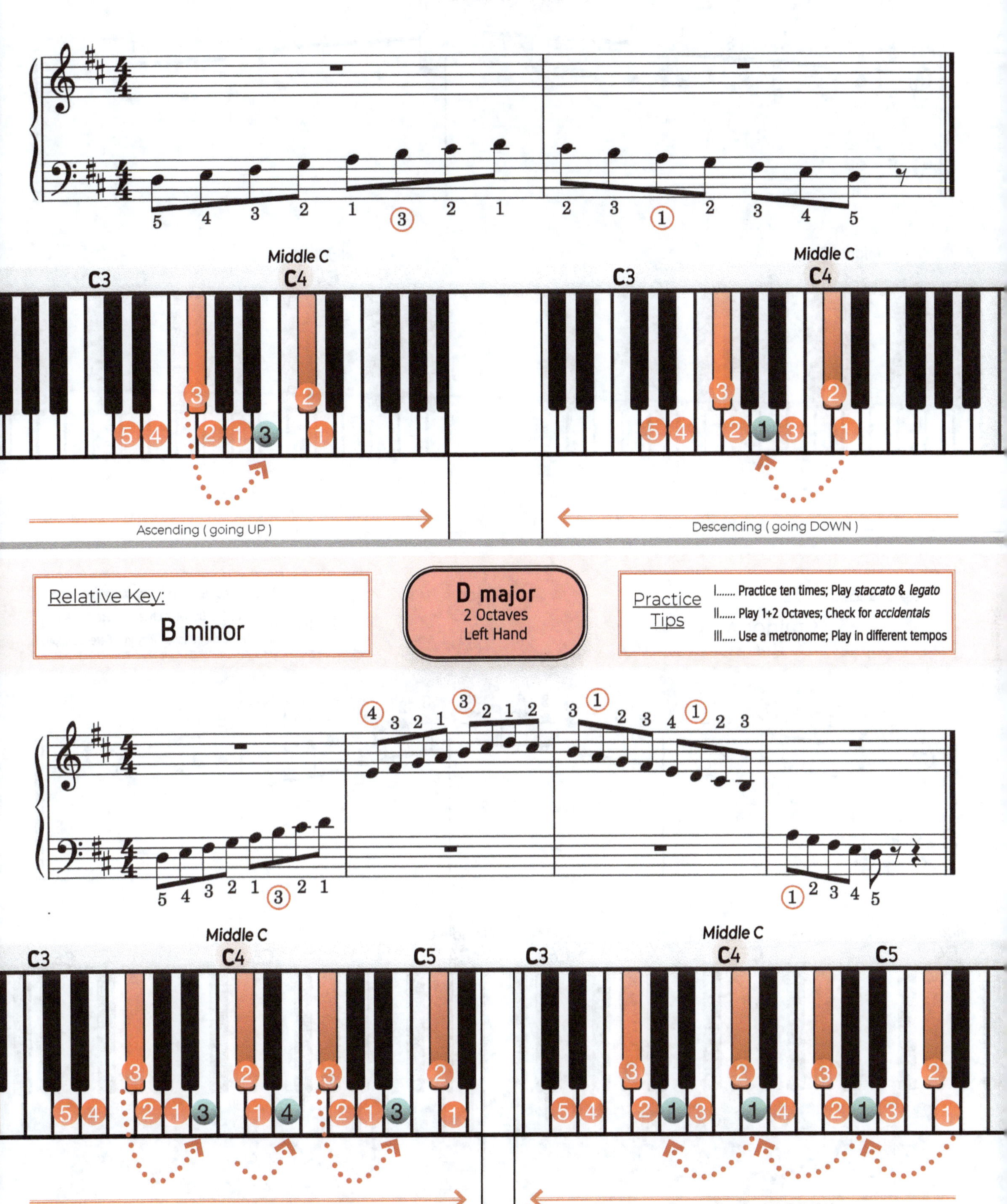

Notes of the Scale:
D, E, F#, G, A, B, C#
D major
1 Octave
Left Hand
Key Signature:
Two Sharps (F#, C#)
Middle C
C4
C3
5 4 3 2 1 3 2 1
2 3 1 2 3 4 5
3 2 1
5 4 2 1 3
2 1 3 1
5 4 2 1 3
Ascending (going UP)
Descending (going DOWN)
Relative Key:
B minor
D major
2 Octaves
Left Hand
Practice Tips
I....... Practice ten times; Play staccato & legato
II...... Play 1+2 Octaves; Check for accidentals
III..... Use a metronome; Play in different tempos
4 3 2 1 3 2 1 2
3 1 2 3 4 1 2 3
5 4 3 2 1 3 2 1
1 2 3 4 5
Middle C
C4
C5
C3
C5
C3
C4
Middle C
3 2 1 2 1 4 3 2 1 3 1
5 4 2 1 3 1 4 2 1 3 1
3 2 3 2 1 4 3 2 1 3 1
5 4 2 1 3 1 4 2 1 3 1
Ascending (going UP)
Descending (going DOWN)
15

Notes of the Scale:
D, E, F#, G, A, B, C#

D major
1 Octave
Right Hand

Key Signature:
Two Sharps (F#, C#)

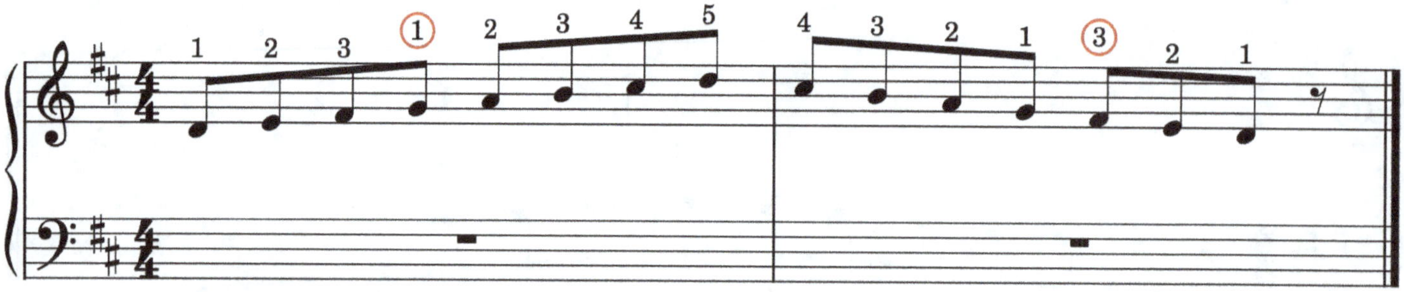

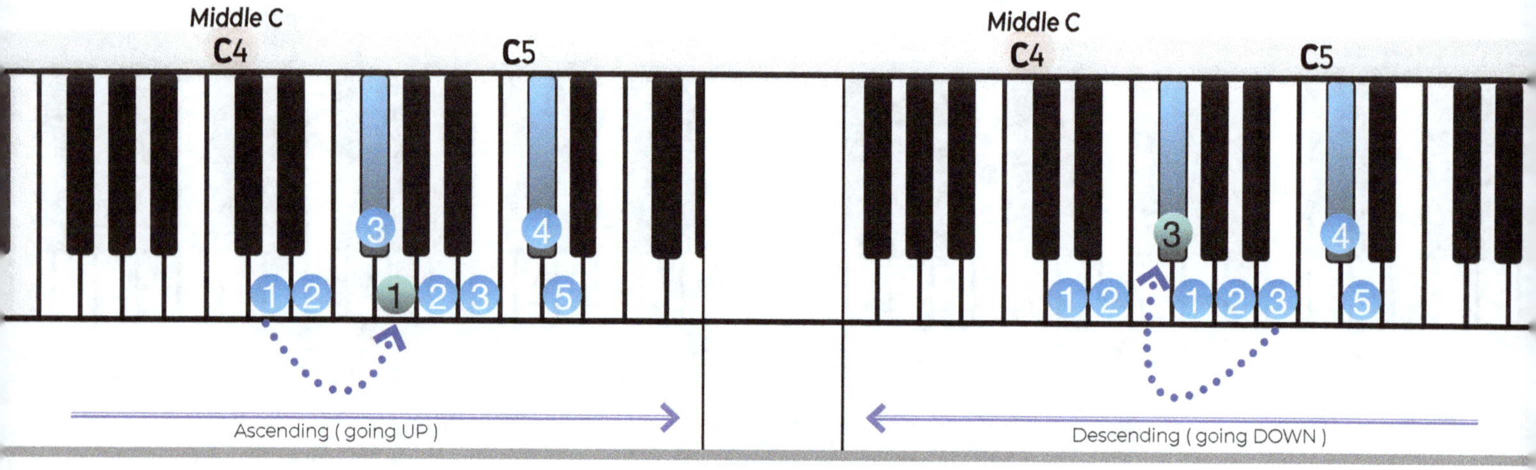

Middle C
C4
C5

Ascending (going UP)
Descending (going DOWN)

Middle C
C4
C5

Relative Key:
B minor

D major
2 Octaves
Right Hand

Practice Tips
I...... Practice ten times; Play staccato & legato
II...... Play 1+2 Octaves; Check for accidentals
III..... Use a metronome; Play in different tempos

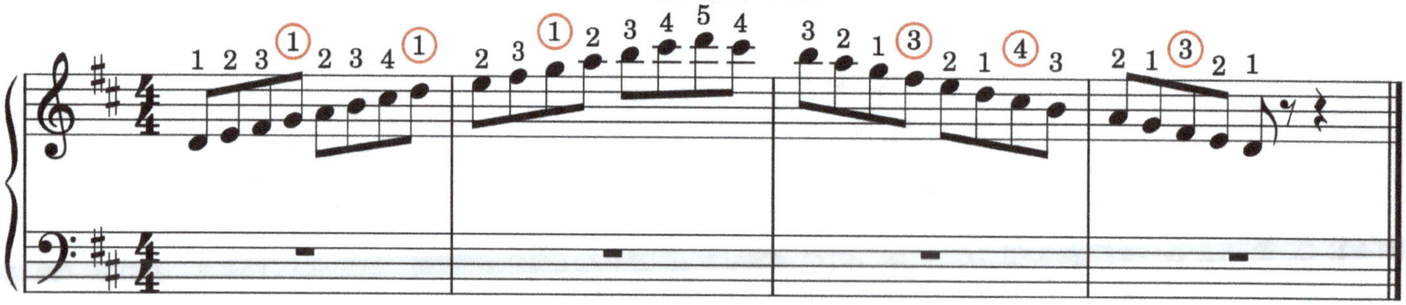

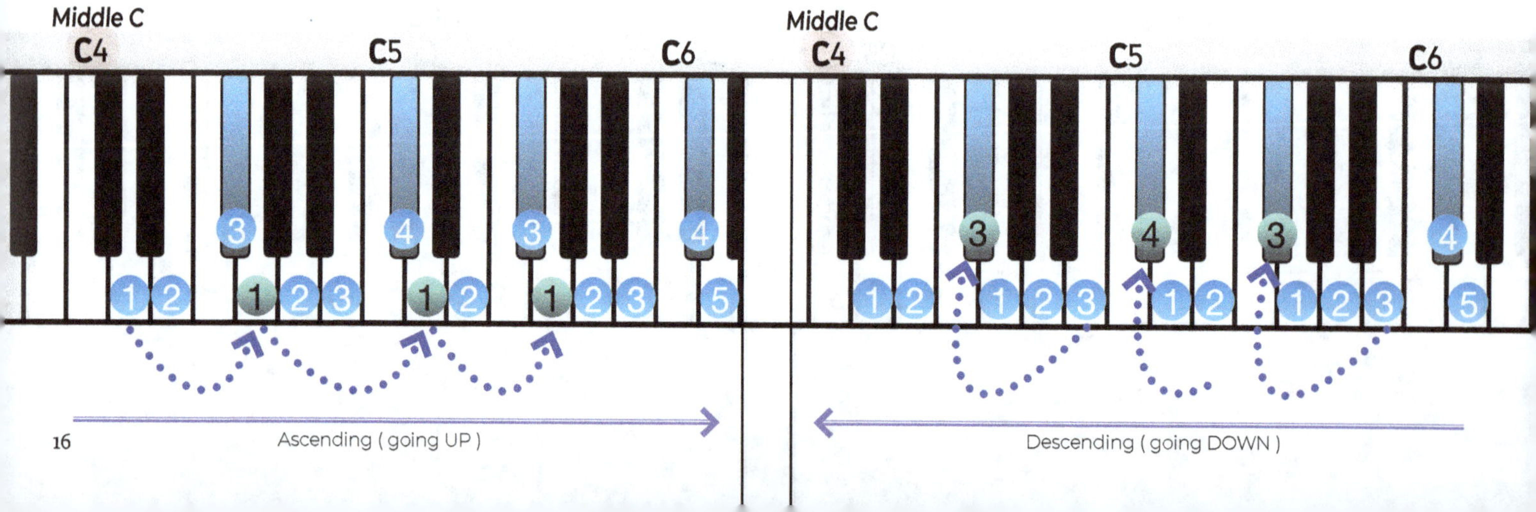

Middle C
C4
C5
C6

Middle C
C4
C5
C6

Ascending (going UP)
Descending (going DOWN)

Notes of the Scale:
D, E, F#, G, A, B, C#

D major
1 Octave
Both Hands

Key Signature:
Two Sharps (F#, C#)

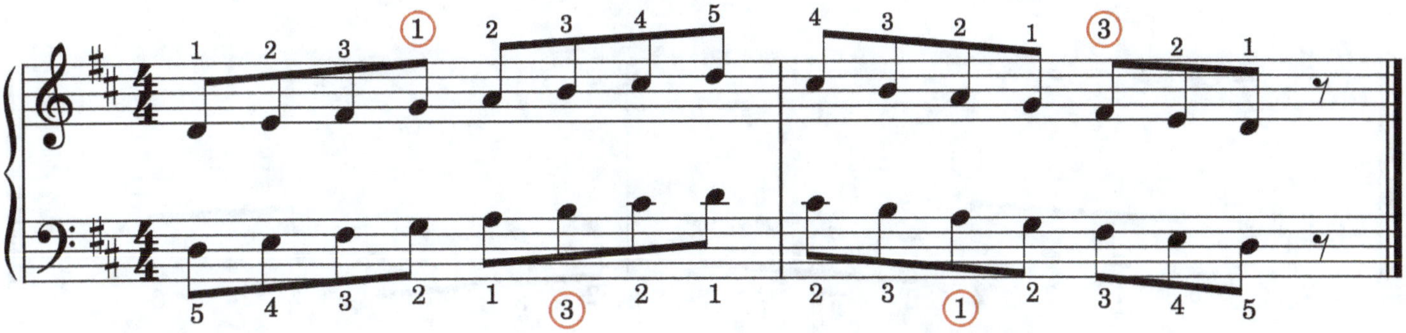

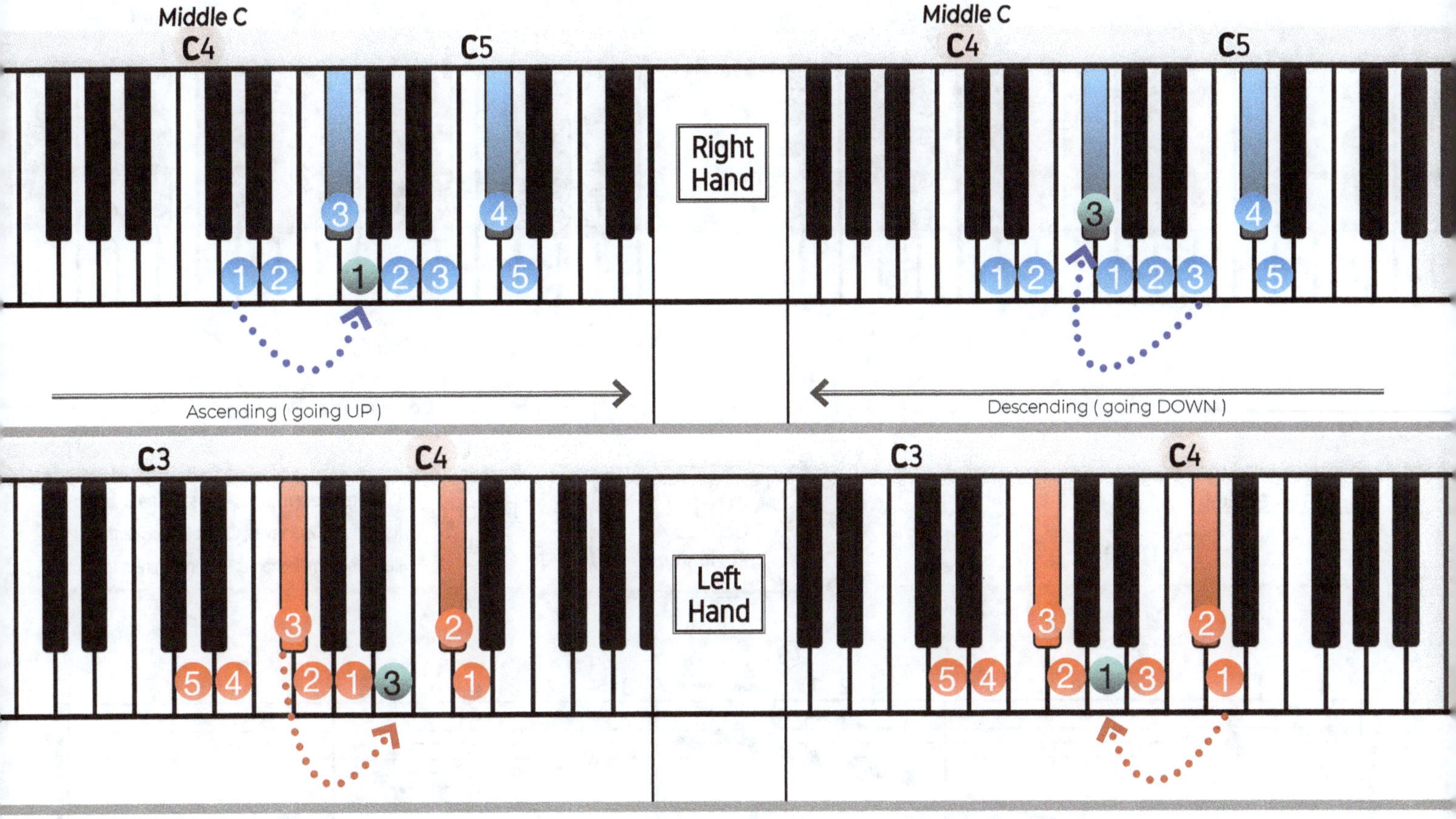

Middle C
C4
C5
Right Hand
Ascending (going UP)
Descending (going DOWN)

C3
C4
Left Hand

Basic Chord:
D major chord (D, F#, A)
---> D is the root note

The root note of the D major scale is D

D major
Chords & Inversions

Inversion: (different note at the bottom of the chord)
1st Inversion ---> F# as bottom note
2nd Inversion ---> A as bottom note

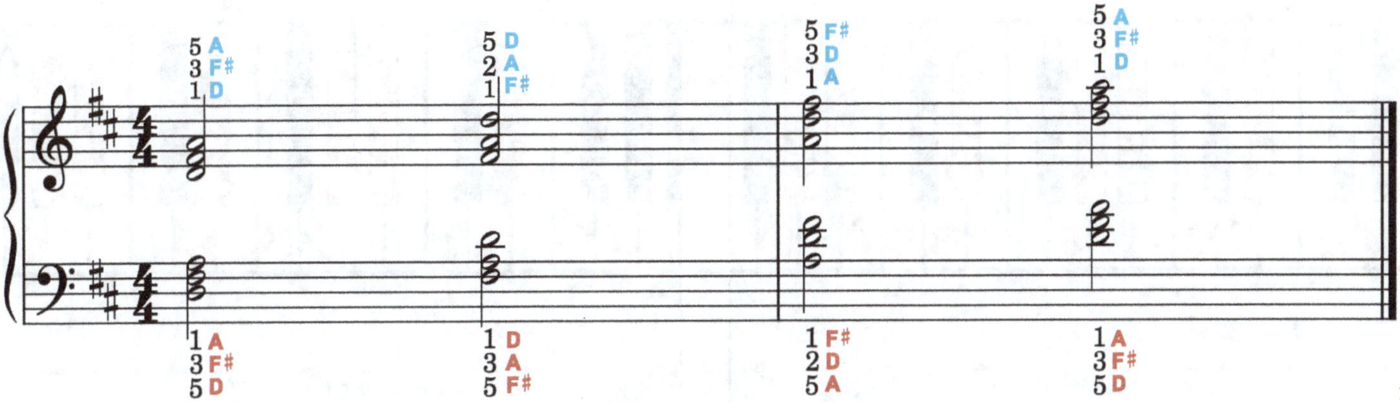

5 A
3 F#
1 D

5 D
2 A
1 F#

5 F#
3 D
1 A

5 A
3 F#
1 D

1 A
3 F#
5 D

1 D
3 A
5 F#

1 F#
2 D
5 A

1 A
3 F#
5 D

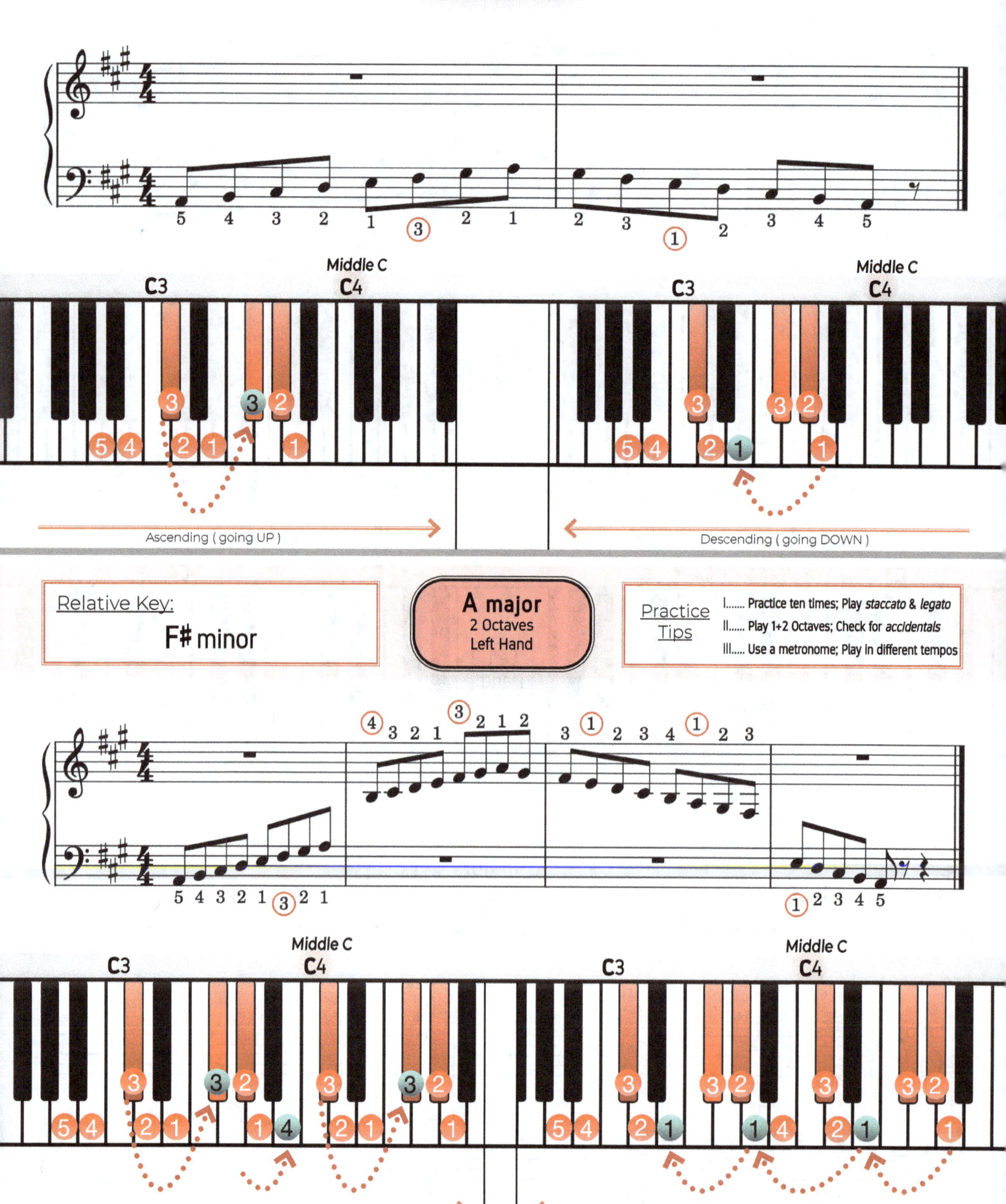

Notes of the Scale:
A, B, C#, D, E, F#, G#
A major
1 Octave
Left Hand
Key Signature:
Three Sharps (F#,C#,G#)
Middle C
C3
C4
C3
Middle C
C4
Ascending (going UP)
Descending (going DOWN)
Relative Key:
F# minor
A major
2 Octaves
Left Hand
Practice Tips
I....... Practice ten times; Play staccato & legato
II...... Play 1+2 Octaves; Check for accidentals
III..... Use a metronome; Play in different tempos
Middle C
C3
C4
C3
Middle C
C4
Ascending (going UP)
Descending (going DOWN)

Notes of the Scale:
A, B, C#, D, E, F#, G#

A major
1 Octave
Right Hand

Key Signature:
Three Sharps (F#, C#, G#)

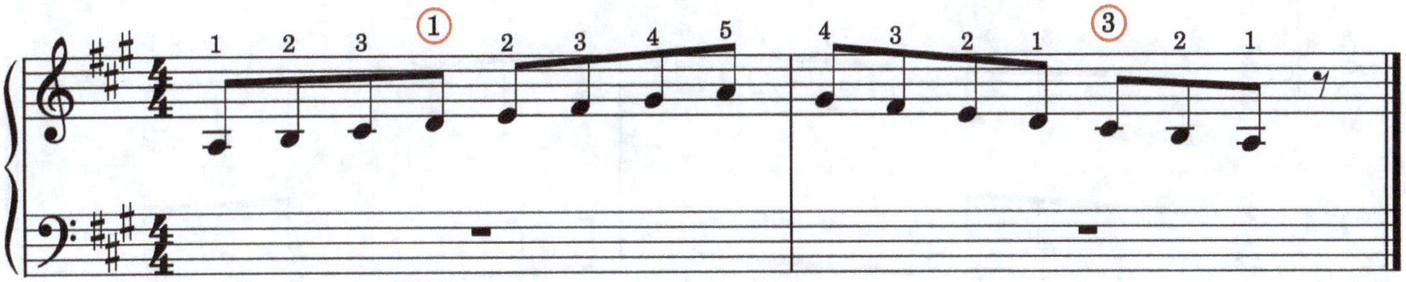

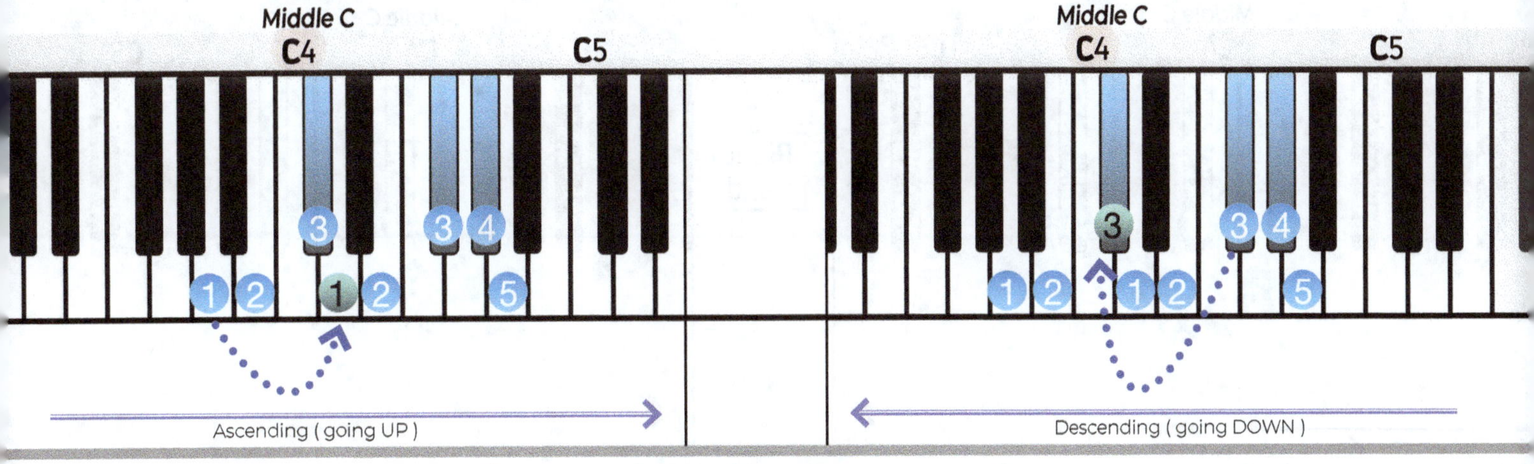

Middle C
C4
C5
Middle C
C4
C5

Ascending (going UP)
Descending (going DOWN)

Relative Key:
F# minor

A major
2 Octaves
Right Hand

Practice Tips
I....... Practice ten times; Play staccato & legato
II...... Play 1+2 Octaves; Check for accidentals
III..... Use a metronome; Play in different tempos

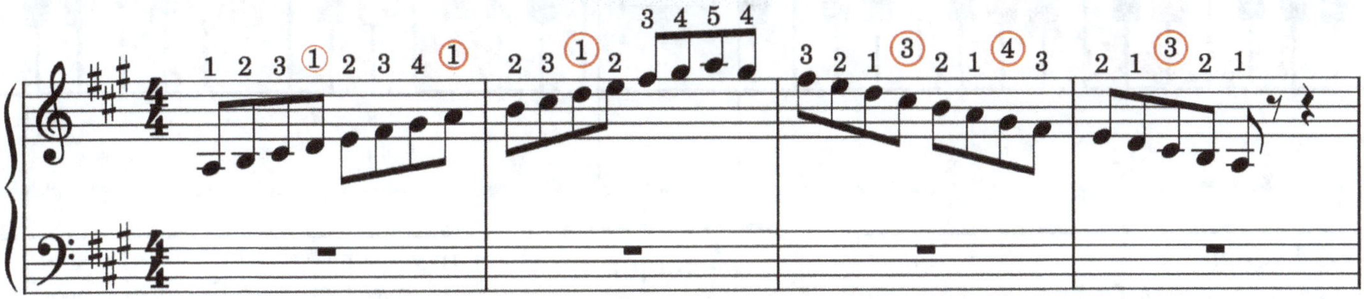

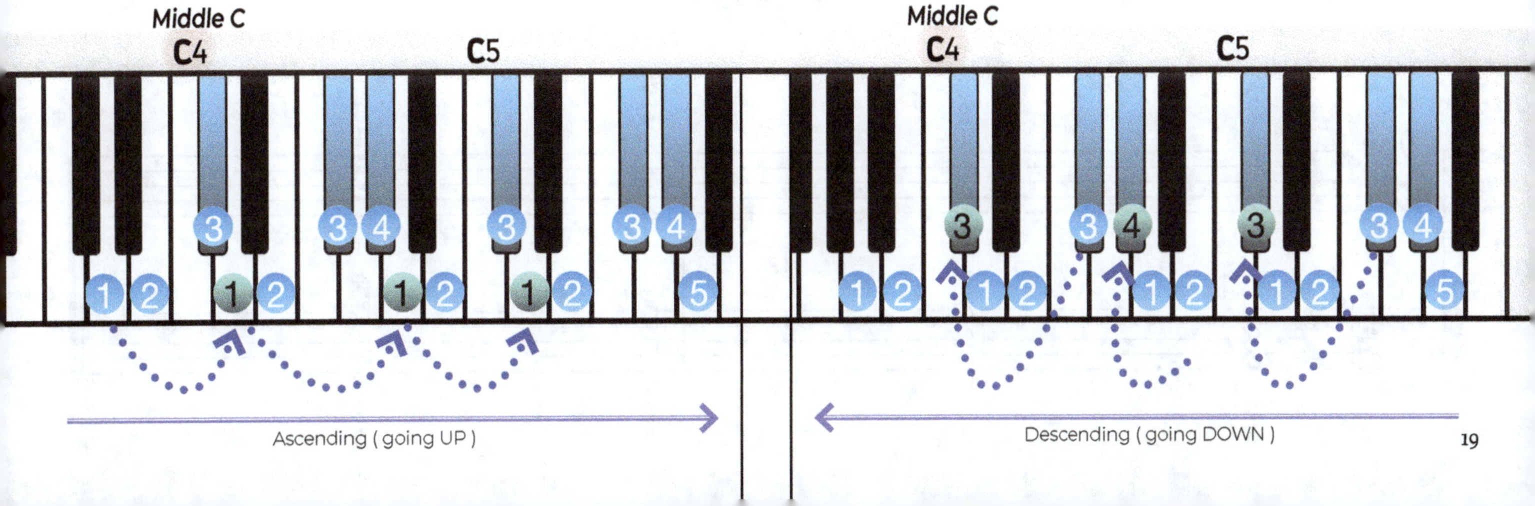

Middle C
C4
C5
Middle C
C4
C5

Ascending (going UP)
Descending (going DOWN)

Notes of the Scale:
A, B, C#, D, E, F#, G#

A major
1 Octave
Both Hands

Key Signature:
Three Sharps (F#, C#, G#)

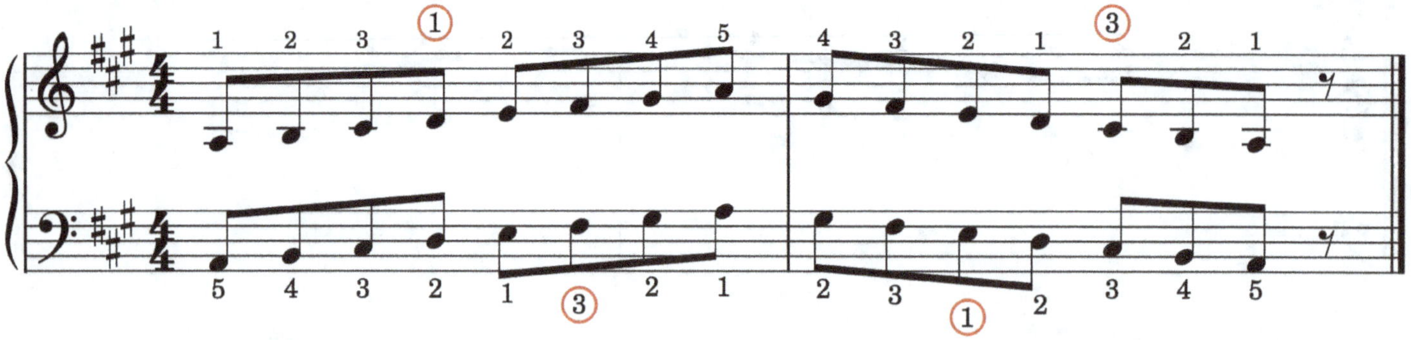

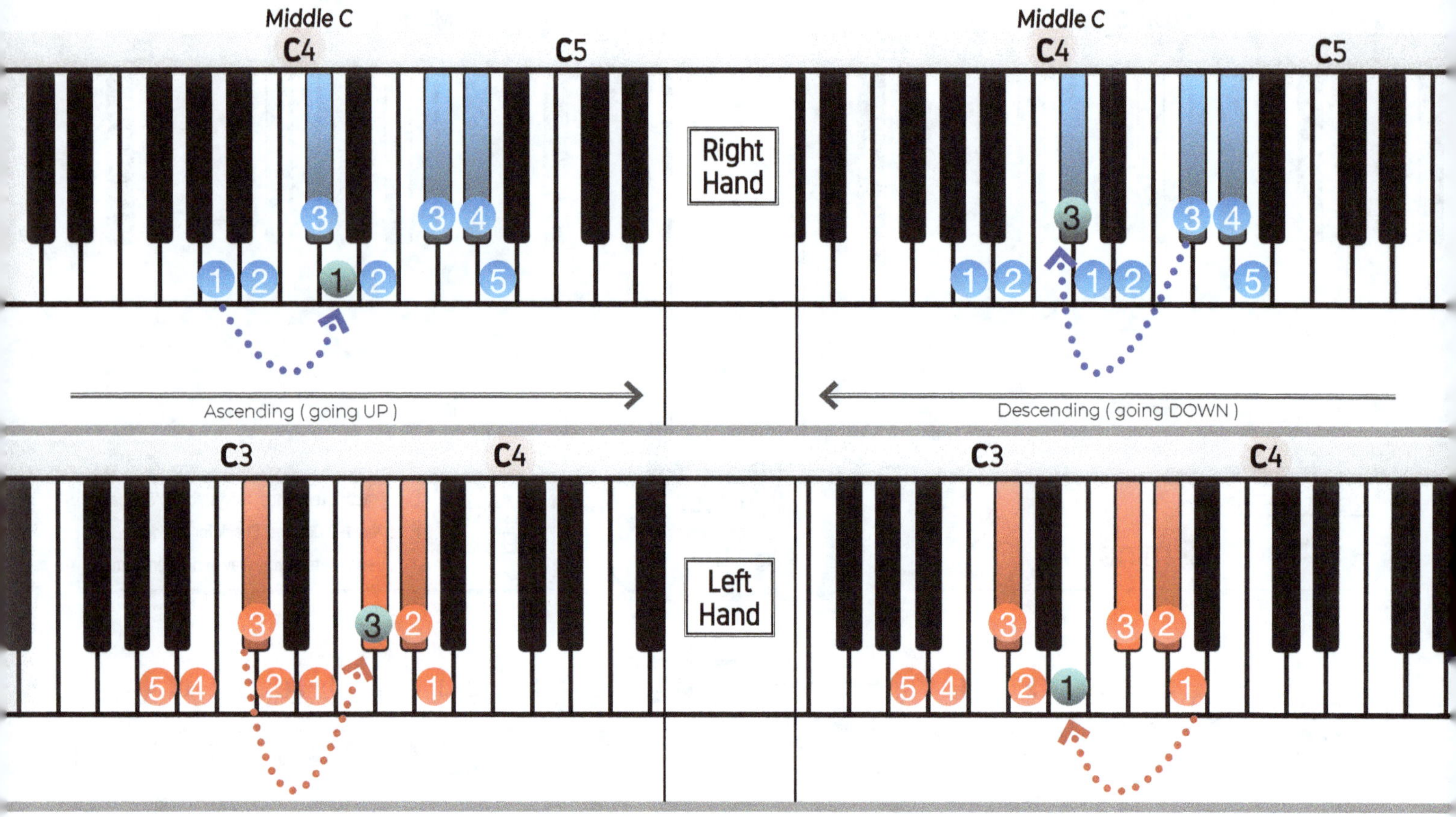

Middle C
C4
C5
Right Hand
C5

Ascending (going UP)
Descending (going DOWN)

C3
C4
Left Hand
C3
C4

Basic Chord:
A major chord (A, C#, E)
--->A is the root note
The root note
of the A major
scale is A

A major
Chords &
Inversions

Inversion: (different note at the bottom of the chord)
1st Inversion ---> C#   as bottom note
2nd Inversion ---> E   as bottom note

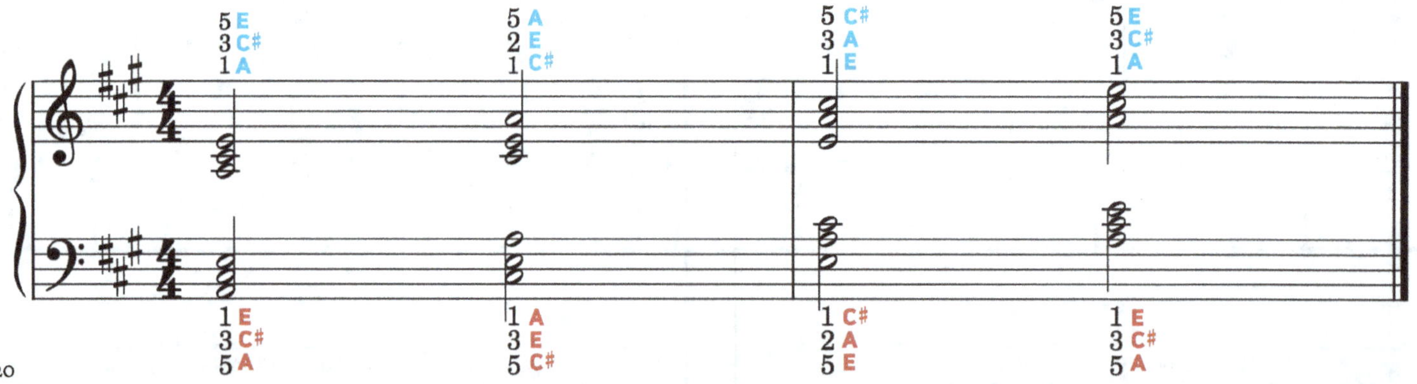

Notes of the Scale:
E, F#, G#, A, B, C#, D#
E major
1 Octave
Left Hand
Key Signature:
Four Sharps (F#, C#, G#, D#) 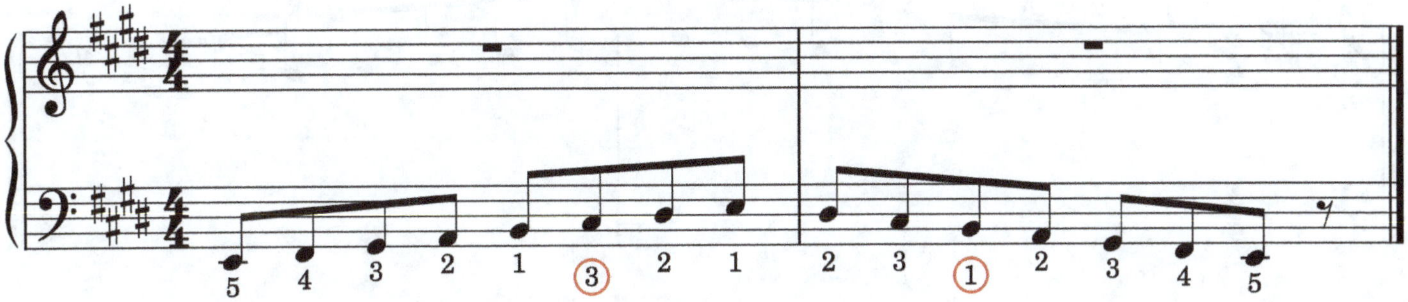 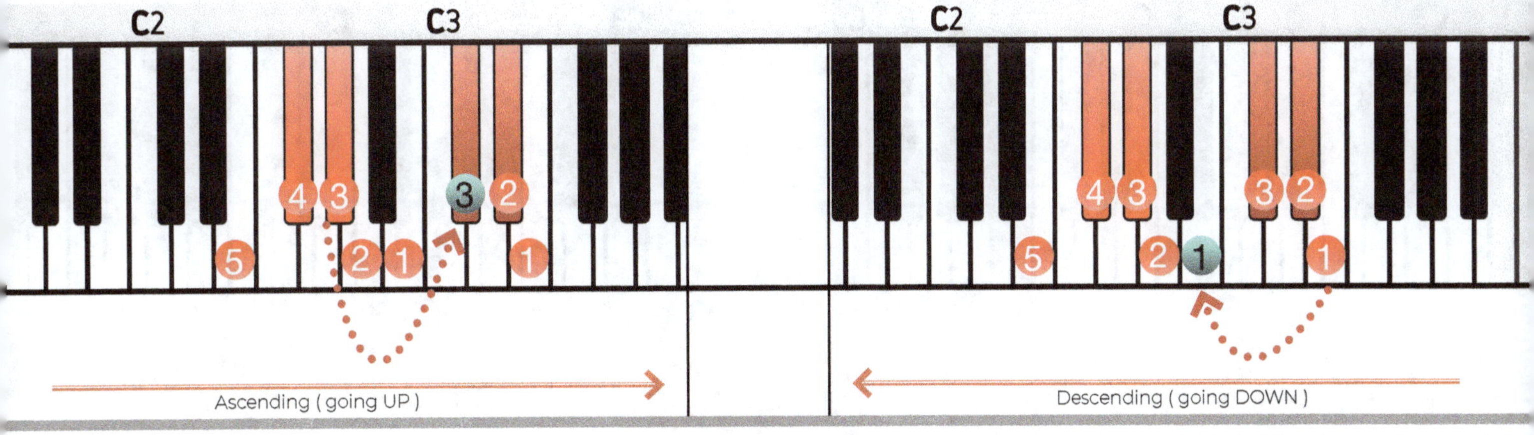
C2
C3
C2
C3
5 4 3 2 1 3 2 1
2 3 1 2 3 4 5
4 3 5 2 1 3 2 1
5 4 3 2 1
Ascending (going UP)
Descending (going DOWN)
Relative Key:
C# minor
E major
2 Octaves
Left Hand
Practice Tips
I....... Practice ten times; Play staccato & legato
II...... Play 1+2 Octaves; Check for accidentals
III..... Use a metronome; Play in different tempos
5 4 3 2 1 3 2 1   4   3 2 1 3 2 1 2   3 1 2 3 4 1 2 3   1 2 3 4 5
Middle C
C3
C4
Middle C
C3
C4
4 3 5 2 1 3 2 4 3 2 1 3 2 1
4 3 5 2 1 3 2 4 3 2 1 3 2 1
Ascending (going UP)
Descending (going DOWN)

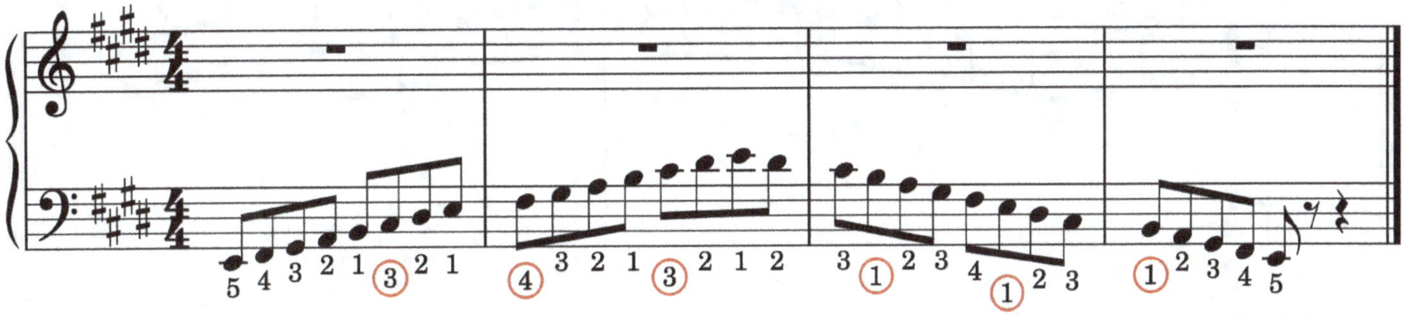

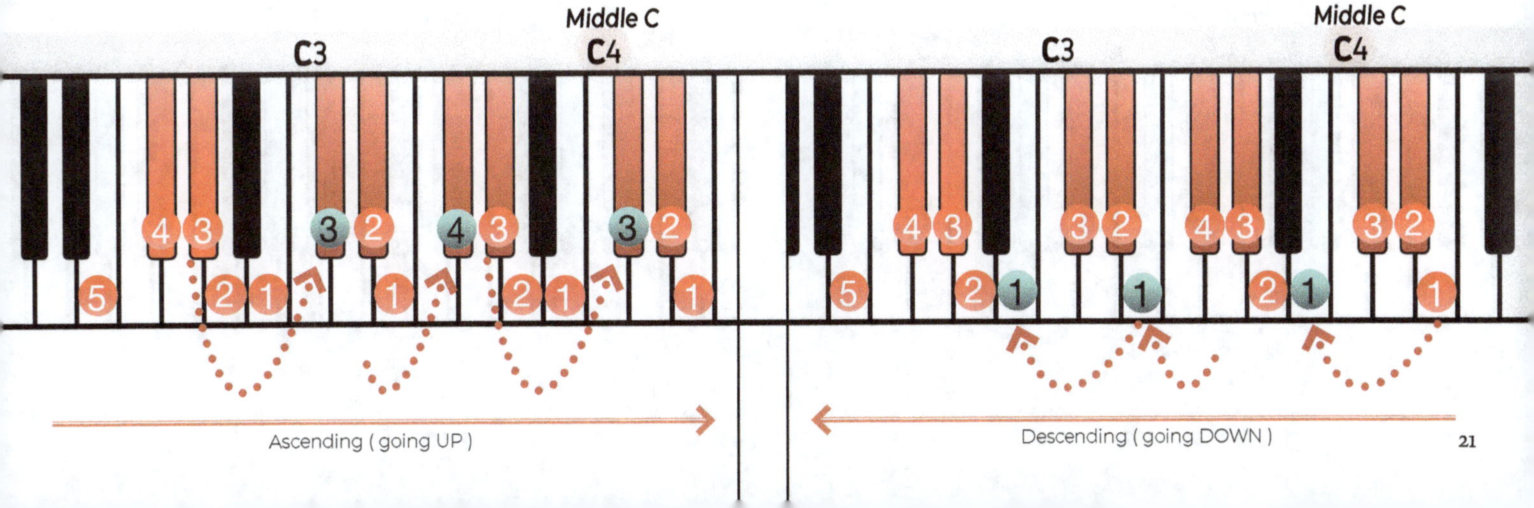

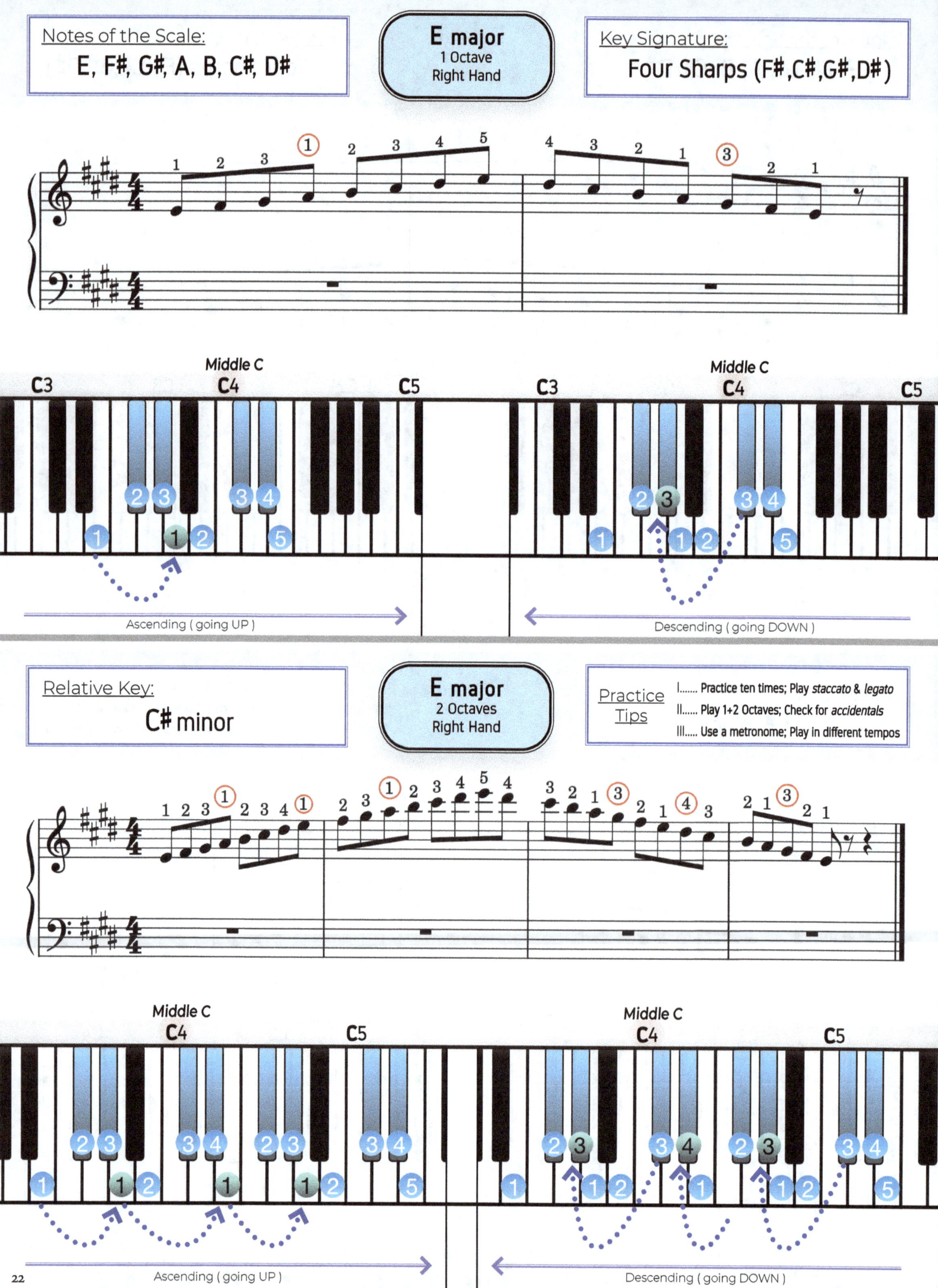

Notes of the Scale:
E, F#, G#, A, B, C#, D#
E major
1 Octave
Right Hand
Key Signature:
Four Sharps (F#,C#,G#,D#)
Middle C
C3
C4
C5
C3
Middle C
C4
C5
Ascending (going UP)
Descending (going DOWN)
Relative Key:
C# minor
E major
2 Octaves
Right Hand
Practice Tips
I...... Practice ten times; Play staccato & legato
II...... Play 1+2 Octaves; Check for accidentals
III..... Use a metronome; Play in different tempos
Middle C
C4
C5
Middle C
C4
C5
Ascending (going UP)
Descending (going DOWN)
22

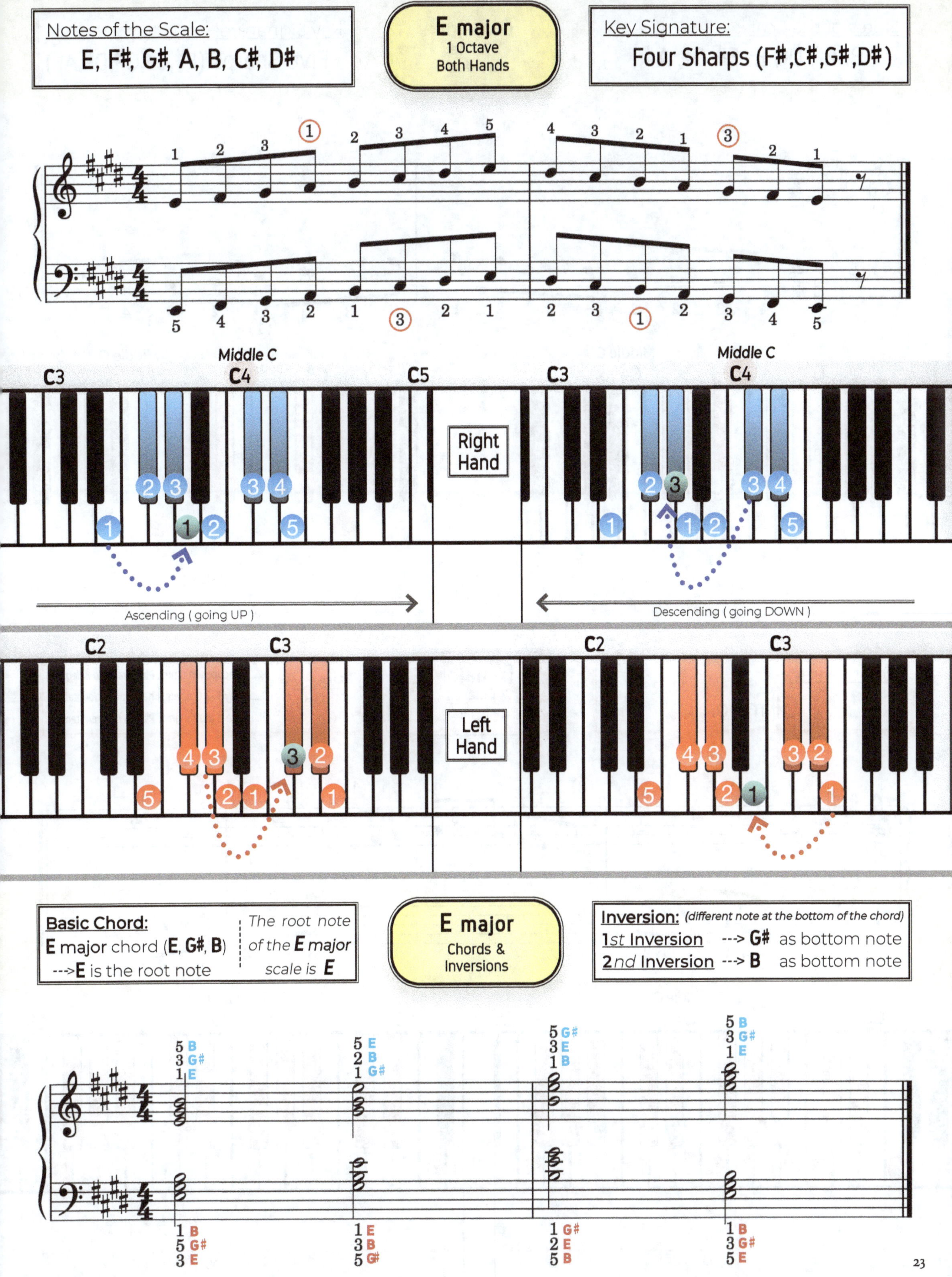

Notes of the Scale:
E, F#, G#, A, B, C#, D#

E major
1 Octave
Both Hands

Key Signature:
Four Sharps (F#, C#, G#, D#)

Middle C
C3
C4
C5
Right Hand
Ascending (going UP)
Descending (going DOWN)

C2
C3
Left Hand

Basic Chord:
E major chord (E, G#, B)
--->E is the root note

The root note of the E major scale is E

E major
Chords & Inversions

Inversion: (different note at the bottom of the chord)
1st Inversion ---> G# as bottom note
2nd Inversion ---> B as bottom note

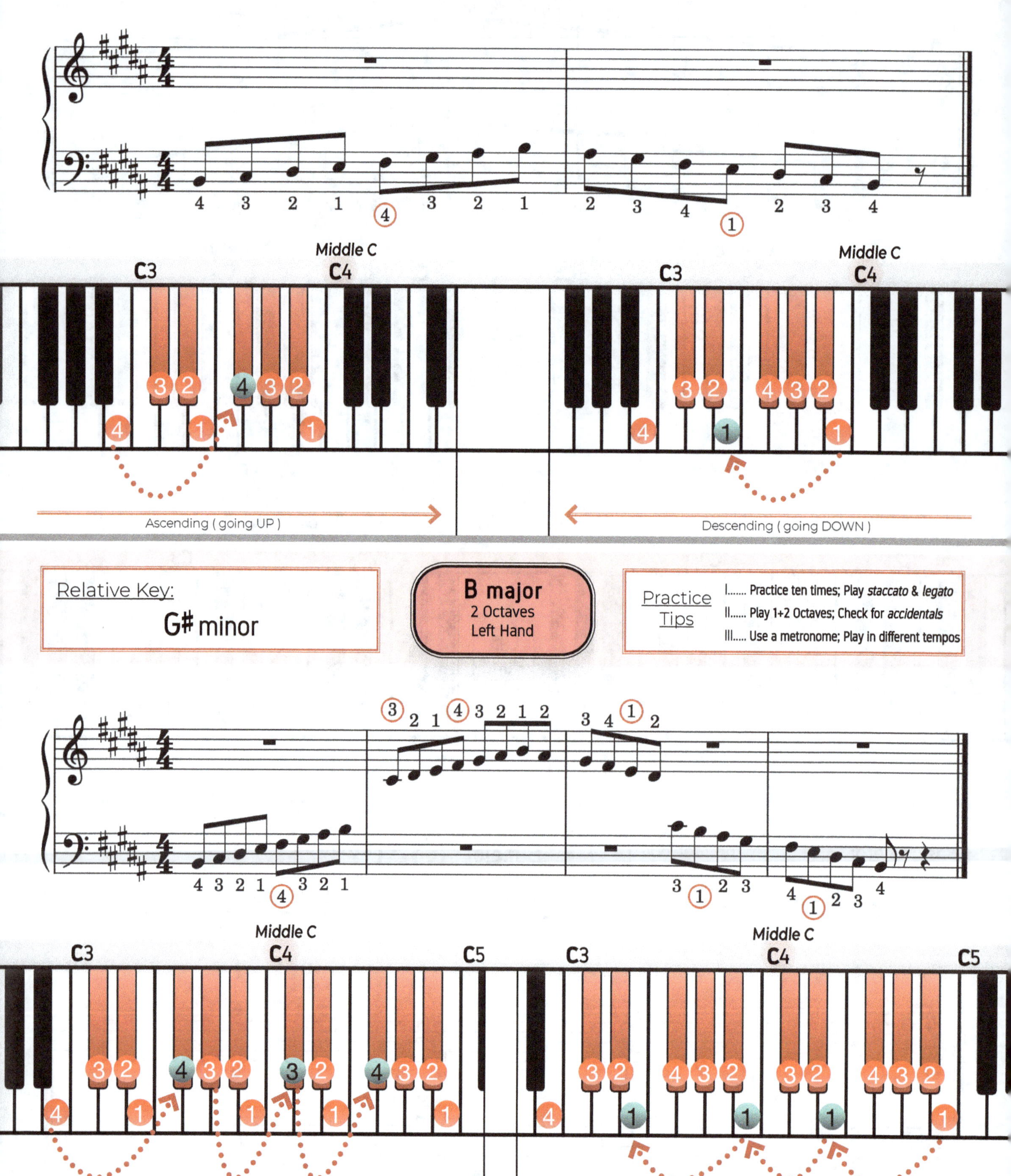

Notes of the Scale:
B, C#, D#, E, F#, G#, A#

B major
1 Octave
Left Hand

Key Signature:
Five Sharps (F#,C#,G#,D#,A#)

4 3 2 1
4 3 2 1
2 3 4
1

Middle C
C4
C3

3 2 4 3 2
4 1 1

Middle C
C4
C3

3 2 4 3 2
4 1 1

Ascending (going UP)
Descending (going DOWN)

Relative Key:
G# minor

B major
2 Octaves
Left Hand

Practice Tips
I....... Practice ten times; Play staccato & legato
II...... Play 1+2 Octaves; Check for accidentals
III..... Use a metronome; Play in different tempos

3 2 1 4 3 2 1 2
3 4 1 2

4 3 2 1 4 3 2 1
3 1 2 3
4 1 2 3 4

Middle C
C4
C3
C5

3 2 4 3 2 3 2 4 3 2
4 1 1 1 1

Middle C
C4
C3
C5

3 2 4 3 2 3 2 4 3 2
4 1 1 1 1

Ascending (going UP)
Descending (going DOWN)

Notes of the Scale:
B, C#, D#, E, F#, G#, A#

B major
1 Octave
Right Hand

Key Signature:
Five Sharps (F#,C#,G#,D#,A#)

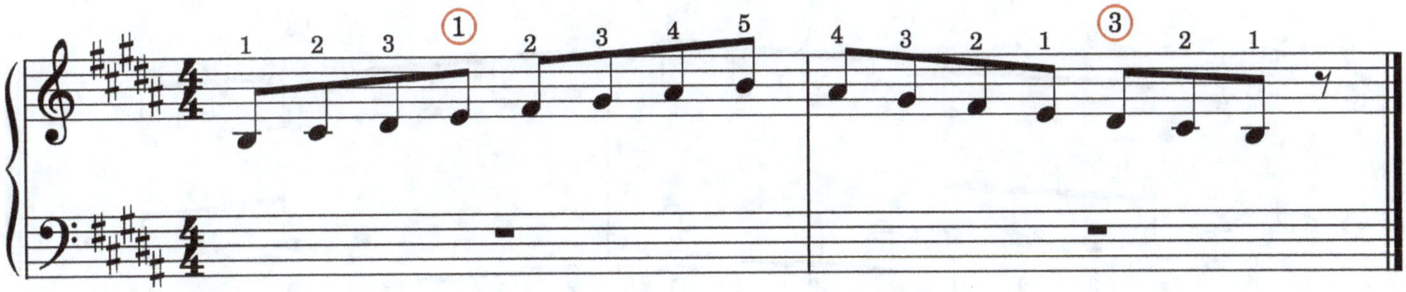

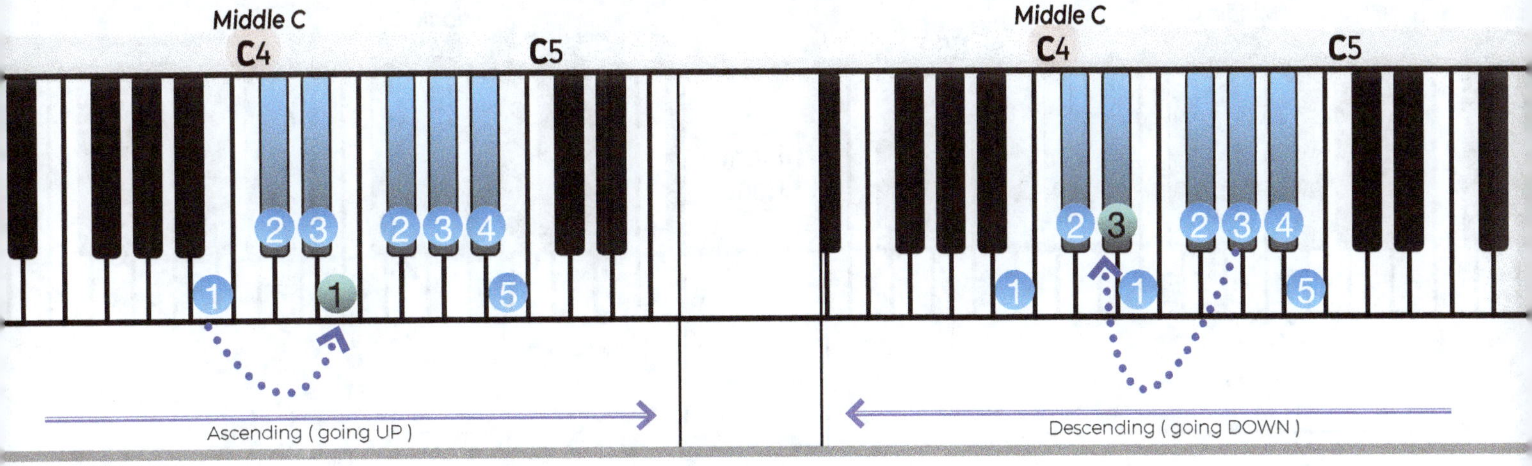

Middle C
C4
C5
2 3 2 3 4
1 1 5
Ascending (going UP)

Middle C
C4
C5
2 3 2 3 4
1 1 5
Descending (going DOWN)

Relative Key:
G# minor

B major
2 Octaves
Right Hand

Practice Tips
I....... Practice ten times; Play staccato & legato
II...... Play 1+2 Octaves; Check for accidentals
III..... Use a metronome; Play in different tempos

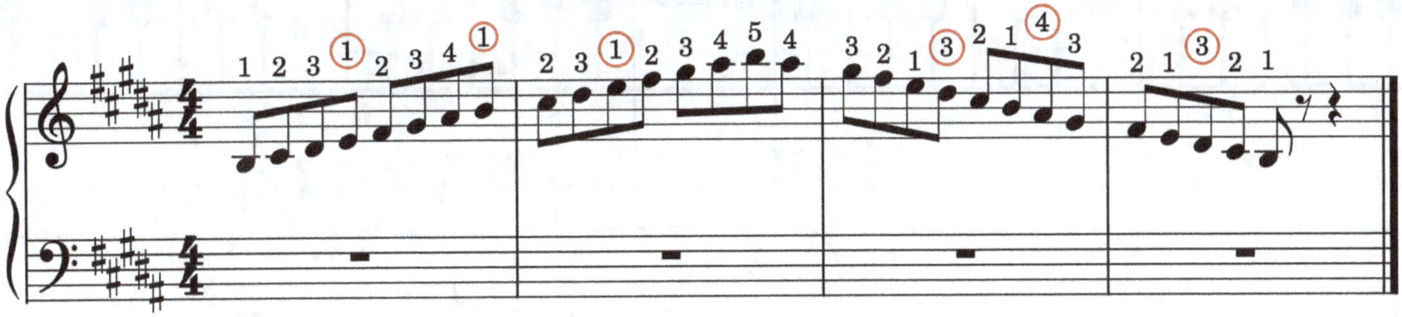

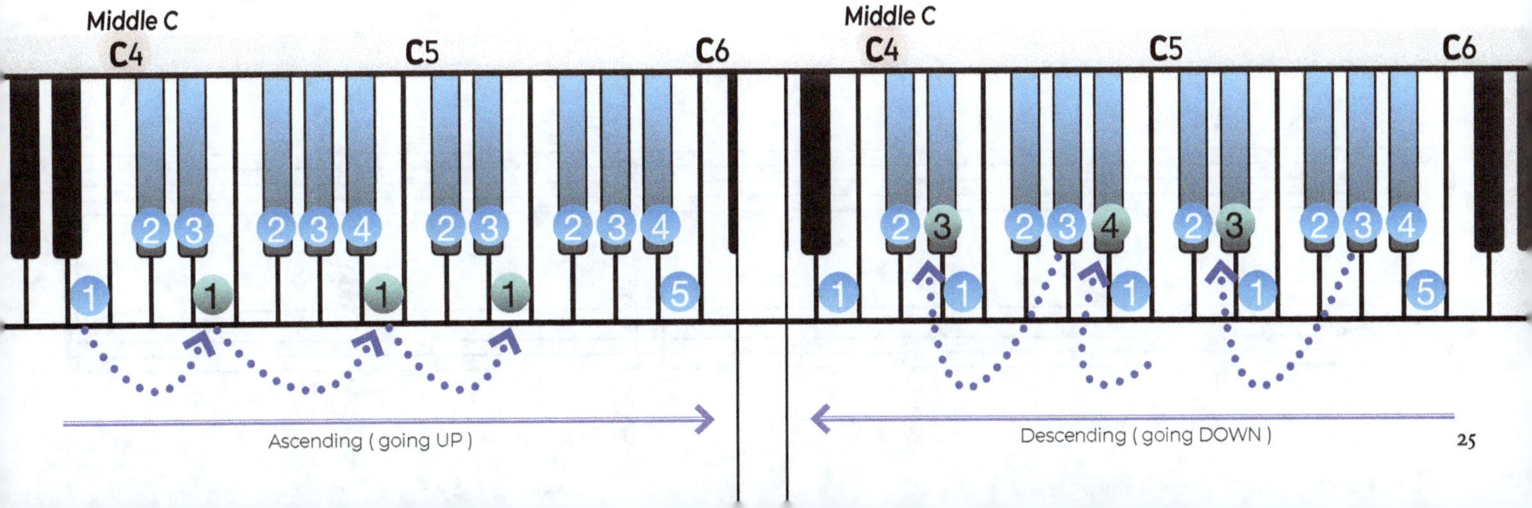

Middle C
C4
C5
C6
Ascending (going UP)

Middle C
C4
C5
C6
Descending (going DOWN)

Notes of the Scale:
B, C#, D#, E, F#, G#, A#

B major
1 Octave
Both Hands

Key Signature:
Five Sharps (F#,C#,G#,D#,A#)

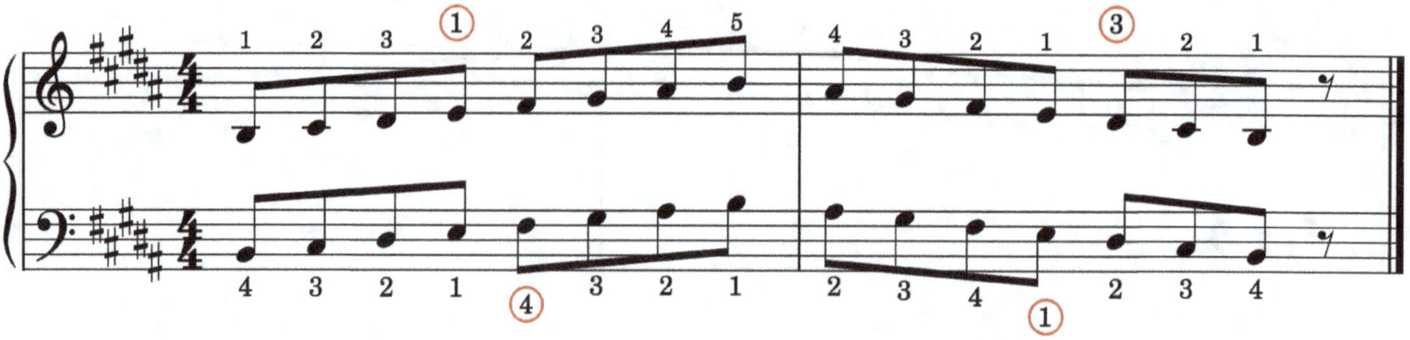

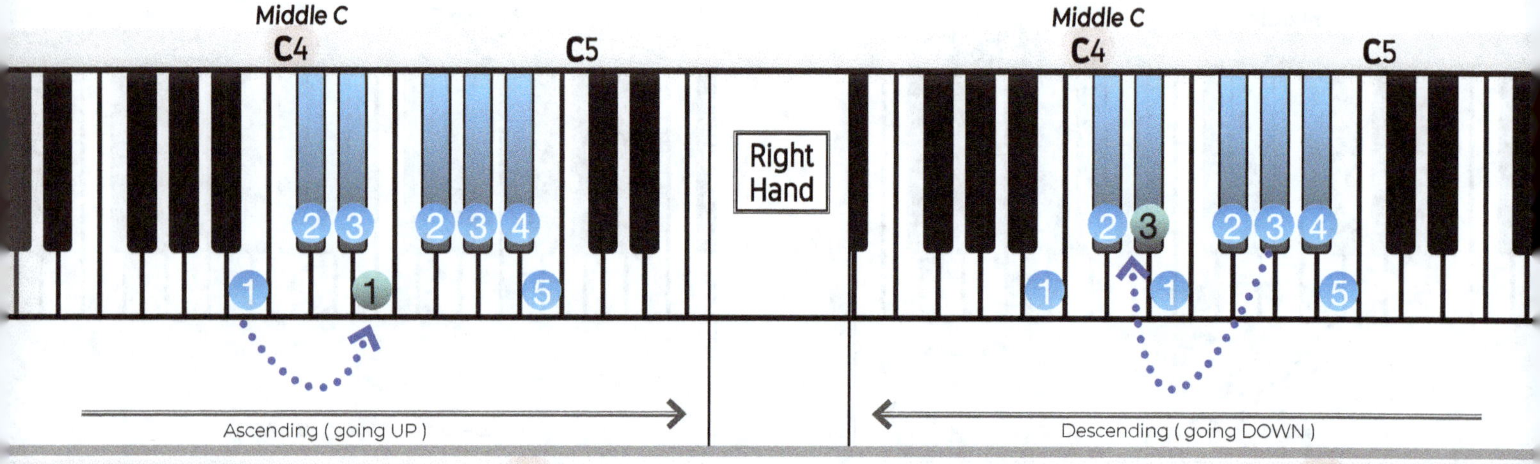

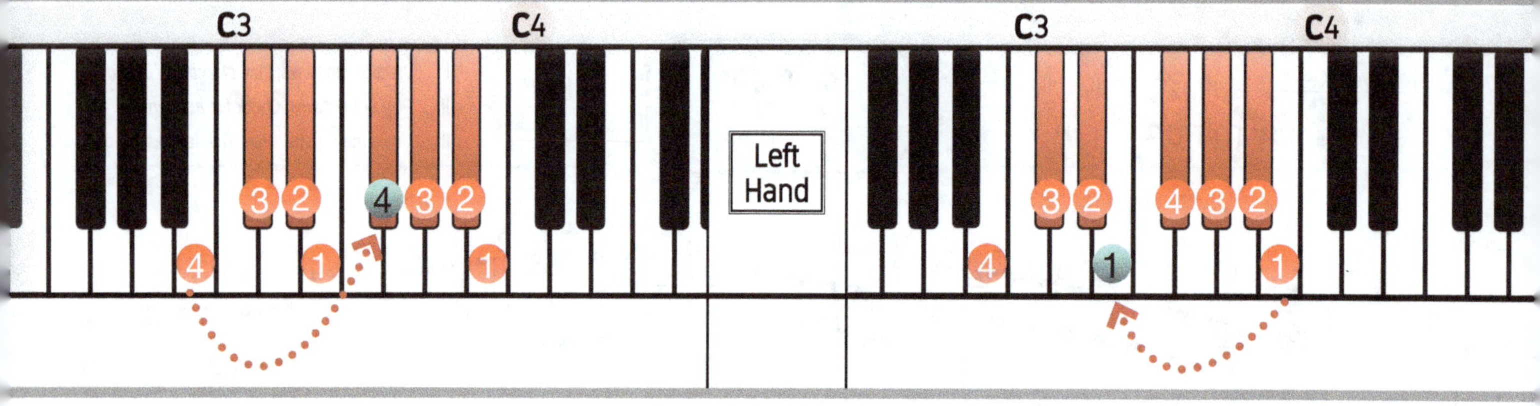

1   2   3   1   2   3   4   5   4   3   2   1   3   2   1

4   3   2   1   4   3   2   1   2   3   4   1   2   3   4

Middle C
C4   C5
Right Hand
2 3   2 3 4
1   1   5
Ascending (going UP)

Middle C
C4   C5
2 3   2 3 4
1   1   5
Descending (going DOWN)

C3   C4
Left Hand
3 2   4 3 2
4   1   1
4   1   1

C3   C4
3 2   4 3 2
4   1   1

Basic Chord:
B major chord (B, D#, F#)
---> B is the root note

The root note
of the B major
scale is B

B major
Chords &
Inversions

Inversion: (different note at the bottom of the chord)
1st Inversion   ---> D#   as bottom note
2nd Inversion   ---> F#   as bottom note

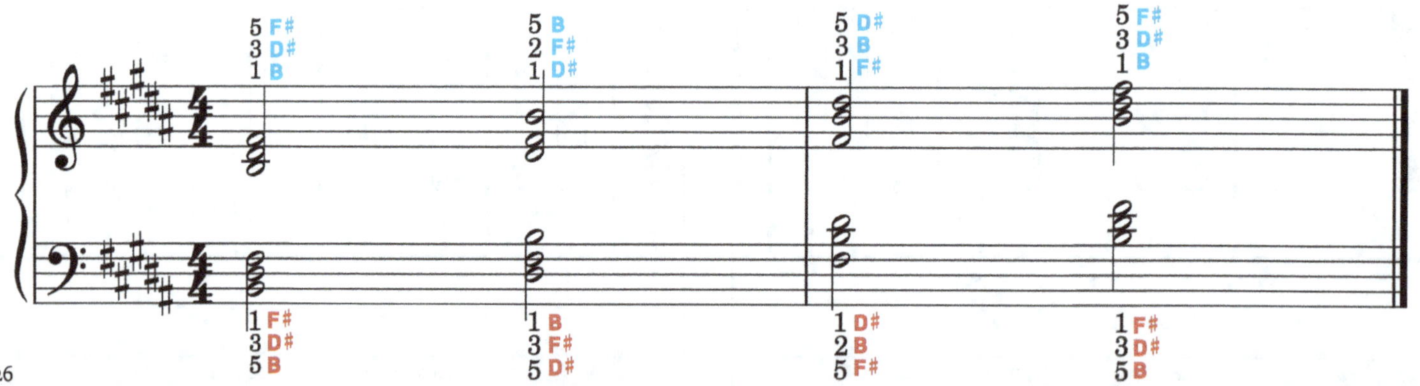

5 F#   5 B   5 D#   5 F#
3 D#   2 F#   3 B   3 D#
1 B   1 D#   1 F#   1 B

1 F#   1 B   1 D#   1 F#
3 D#   3 F#   2 B   3 D#
5 B   5 D#   5 F#   5 B

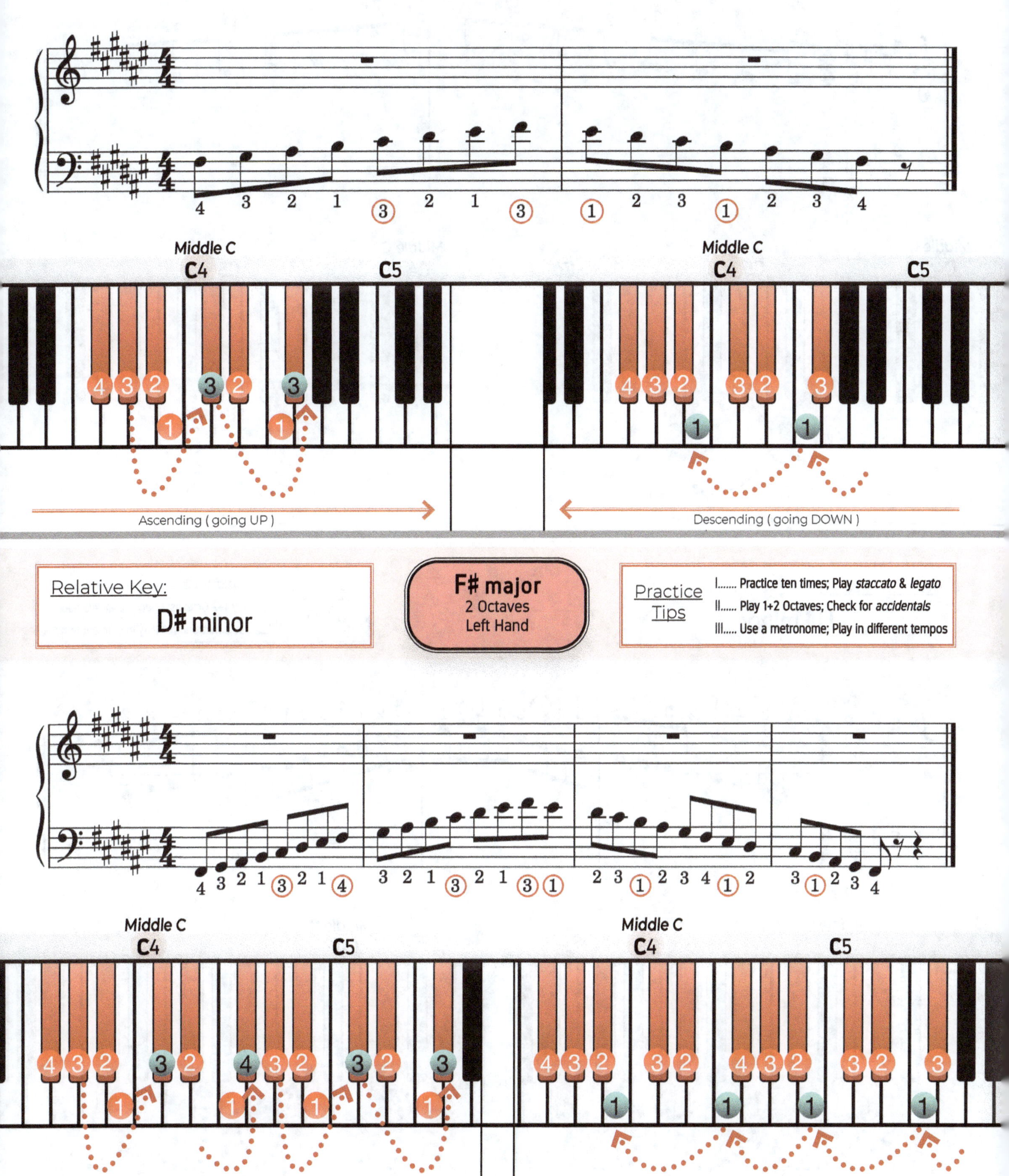

Notes of the Scale:
F#, G#, A#, B, C#, D#, E#

F# major
1 Octave
Left Hand

Key Signature:
Six Sharps (F#, C#, G#, D#, A#, E#)

Middle C
C4
C5
Middle C
C4
C5

Ascending (going UP)
Descending (going DOWN)

Relative Key:
D# minor

F# major
2 Octaves
Left Hand

Practice Tips
I....... Practice ten times; Play staccato & legato
II...... Play 1+2 Octaves; Check for accidentals
III..... Use a metronome; Play in different tempos

Middle C
C4
C5
Middle C
C4
C5

Ascending (going UP)
Descending (going DOWN)

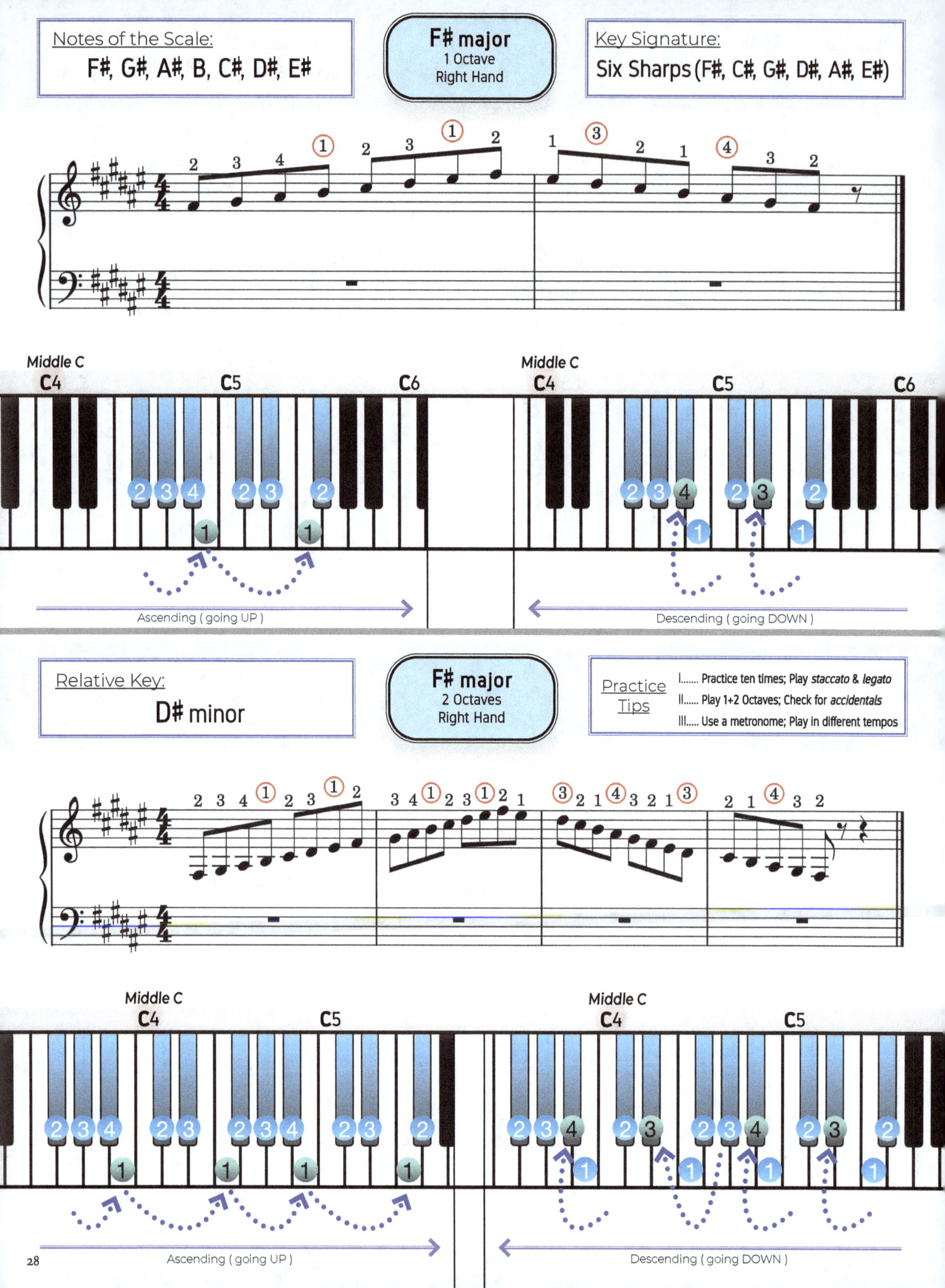

Notes of the Scale:
F#, G#, A#, B, C#, D#, E#

F# major
1 Octave
Right Hand

Key Signature:
Six Sharps (F#, C#, G#, D#, A#, E#)

Middle C
C4   C5   C6
Middle C
C4   C5   C6

Ascending (going UP)
Descending (going DOWN)

Relative Key:
D# minor

F# major
2 Octaves
Right Hand

Practice Tips
I....... Practice ten times; Play staccato & legato
II...... Play 1+2 Octaves; Check for accidentals
III..... Use a metronome; Play in different tempos

Middle C
C4   C5
Middle C
C4   C5

Ascending (going UP)
Descending (going DOWN)

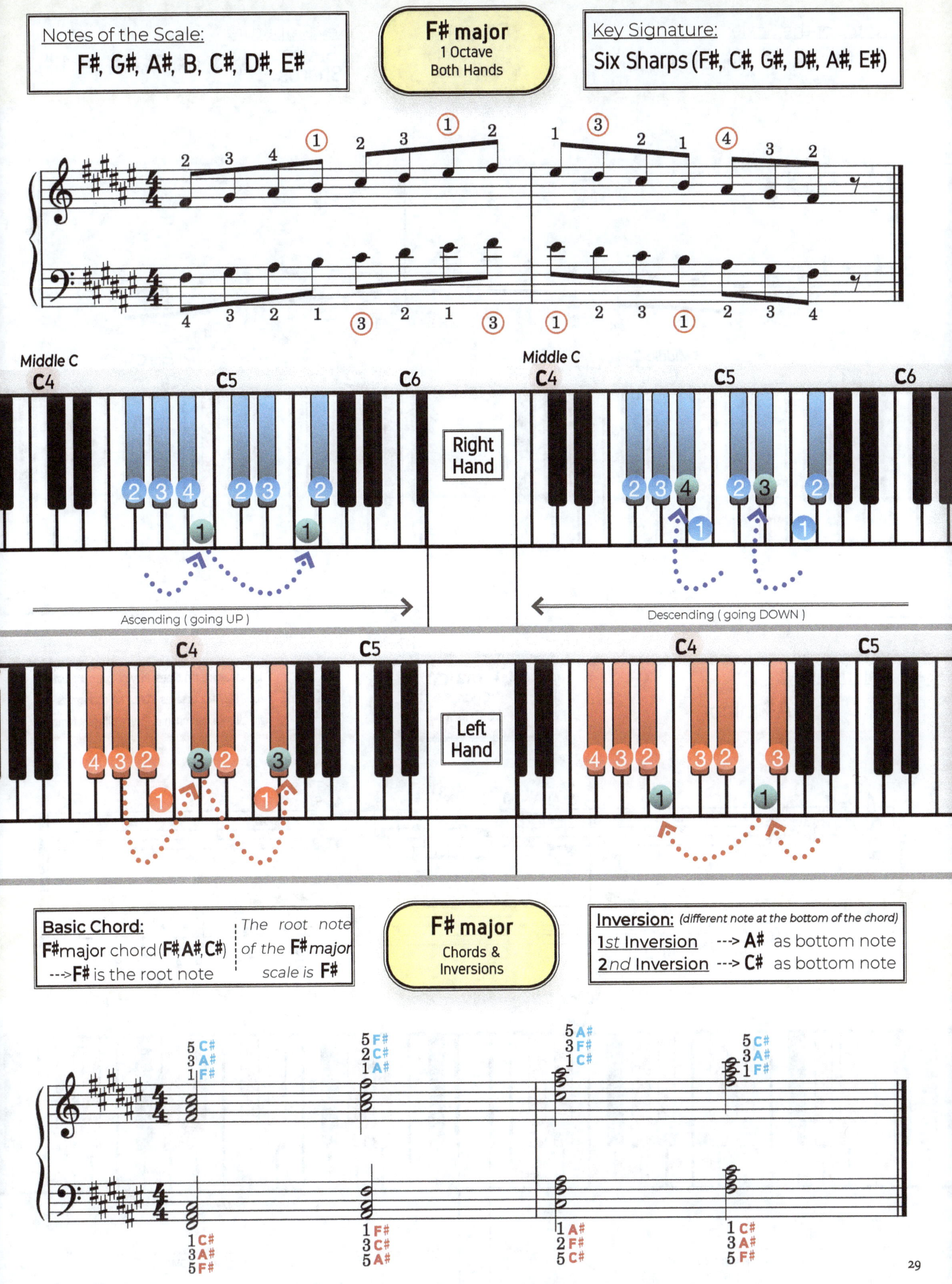

Notes of the Scale:
F#, G#, A#, B, C#, D#, E#

F# major
1 Octave
Both Hands

Key Signature:
Six Sharps (F#, C#, G#, D#, A#, E#)

Middle C
C4
C5
C6
Right Hand
2 3 4 2 3 2
1 1
Ascending (going UP)

Middle C
C4
C5
C6
2 3 4 2 3 2
1 1
Descending (going DOWN)

C4
C5
Left Hand
4 3 2 3 2 3
1 1

C4
C5
4 3 2 3 2 3
1 1

Basic Chord:
F# major chord (F#, A#, C#)
---> F# is the root note

The root note of the F# major scale is F#

F# major
Chords &
Inversions

Inversion: (different note at the bottom of the chord)
1st Inversion ---> A# as bottom note
2nd Inversion ---> C# as bottom note

5 C#
3 A#
1 F#

5 F#
2 C#
1 A#

5 A#
3 F#
1 C#

5 C#
3 A#
1 F#

1 C#
3 A#
5 F#

1 F#
3 C#
5 A#

1 A#
2 F#
5 C#

1 C#
3 A#
5 F#

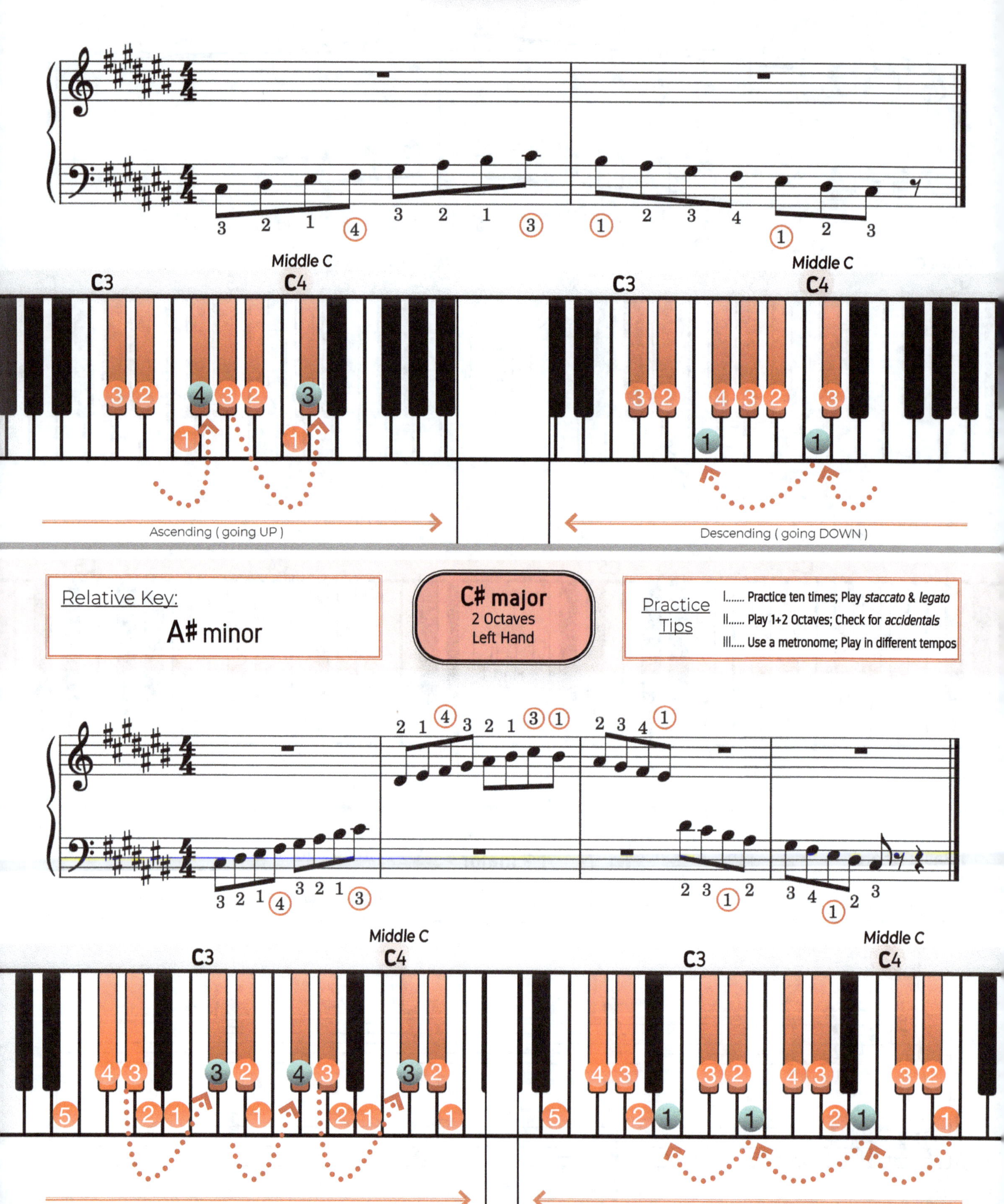

Notes of the Scale:
C#, D#, E#, F#, G#, A#, B#
C# major
1 Octave
Left Hand
Key Signature:
Seven Sharps (F#, C#, G#, D#, A#, E#, B#)
Middle C
C3
C4
3 2 1 4 3 2 1 3
1 2 3 4 1 2 3
Middle C
C3
C4
3 2 4 3 2 3
1 1
Ascending (going UP)
Descending (going DOWN)
Relative Key:
A# minor
C# major
2 Octaves
Left Hand
Practice Tips
I....... Practice ten times; Play staccato & legato
II...... Play 1+2 Octaves; Check for accidentals
III..... Use a metronome; Play in different tempos
2 1 4 3 2 1 3 1
2 3 4 1
3 2 1 4 3 2 1 3
2 3 1 2
3 4 2 3
Middle C
C3
C4
4 3 3 2 4 3 3 2
5 2 1 1 2 1 1
Middle C
C3
C4
4 3 3 2 4 3 3 2
5 2 1 1 2 1 1
Ascending (going UP)
Descending (going DOWN)

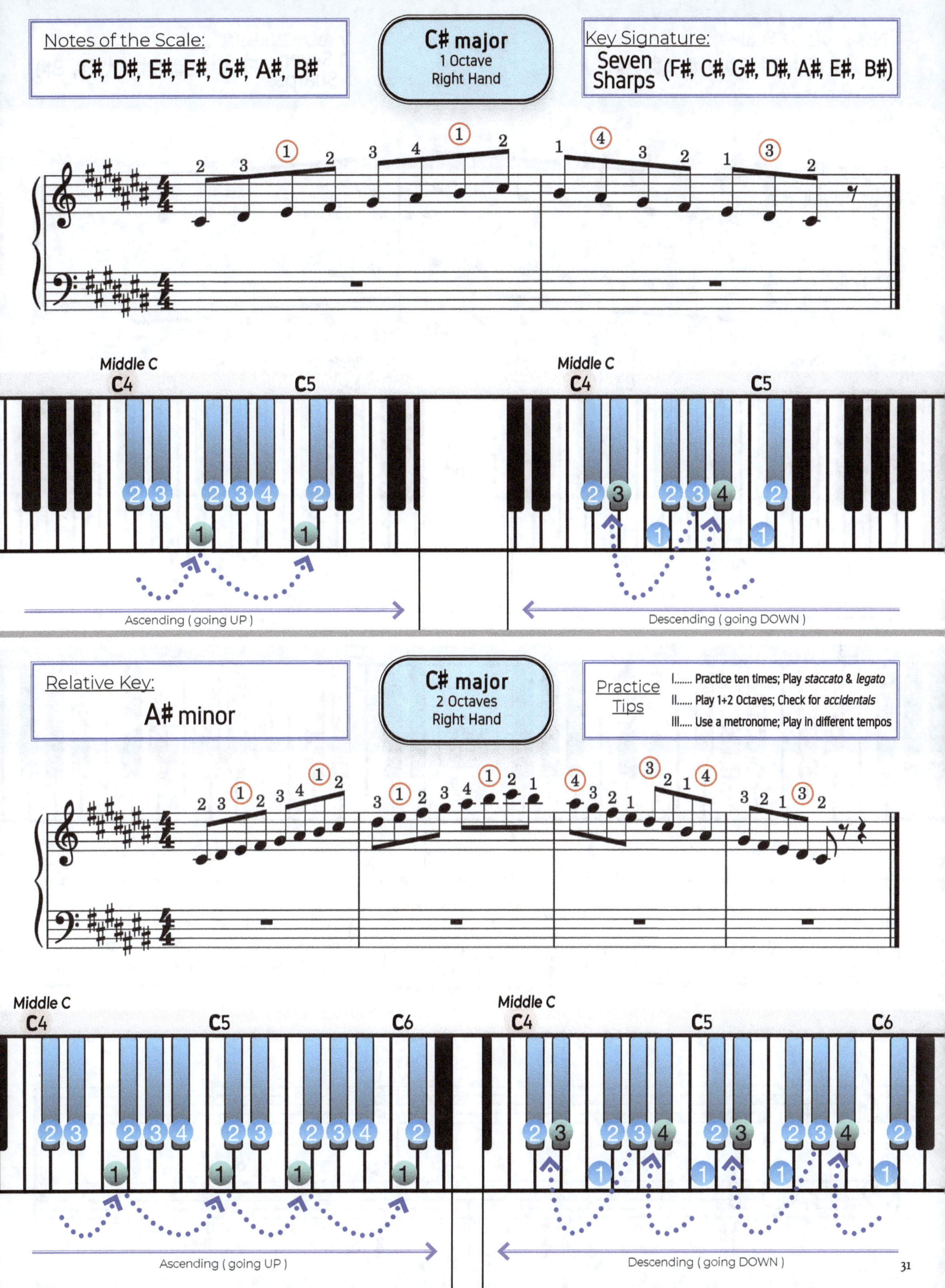

Notes of the Scale:
C#, D#, E#, F#, G#, A#, B#
C# major
1 Octave
Right Hand
Key Signature:
Seven Sharps (F#, C#, G#, D#, A#, E#, B#)
Middle C
C4
C5
Ascending (going UP)
Middle C
C4
C5
Descending (going DOWN)
Relative Key:
A# minor
C# major
2 Octaves
Right Hand
Practice Tips
I...... Practice ten times; Play staccato & legato
II...... Play 1+2 Octaves; Check for accidentals
III..... Use a metronome; Play in different tempos
Middle C
C4
C5
C6
Ascending (going UP)
Middle C
C4
C5
C6
Descending (going DOWN)
31

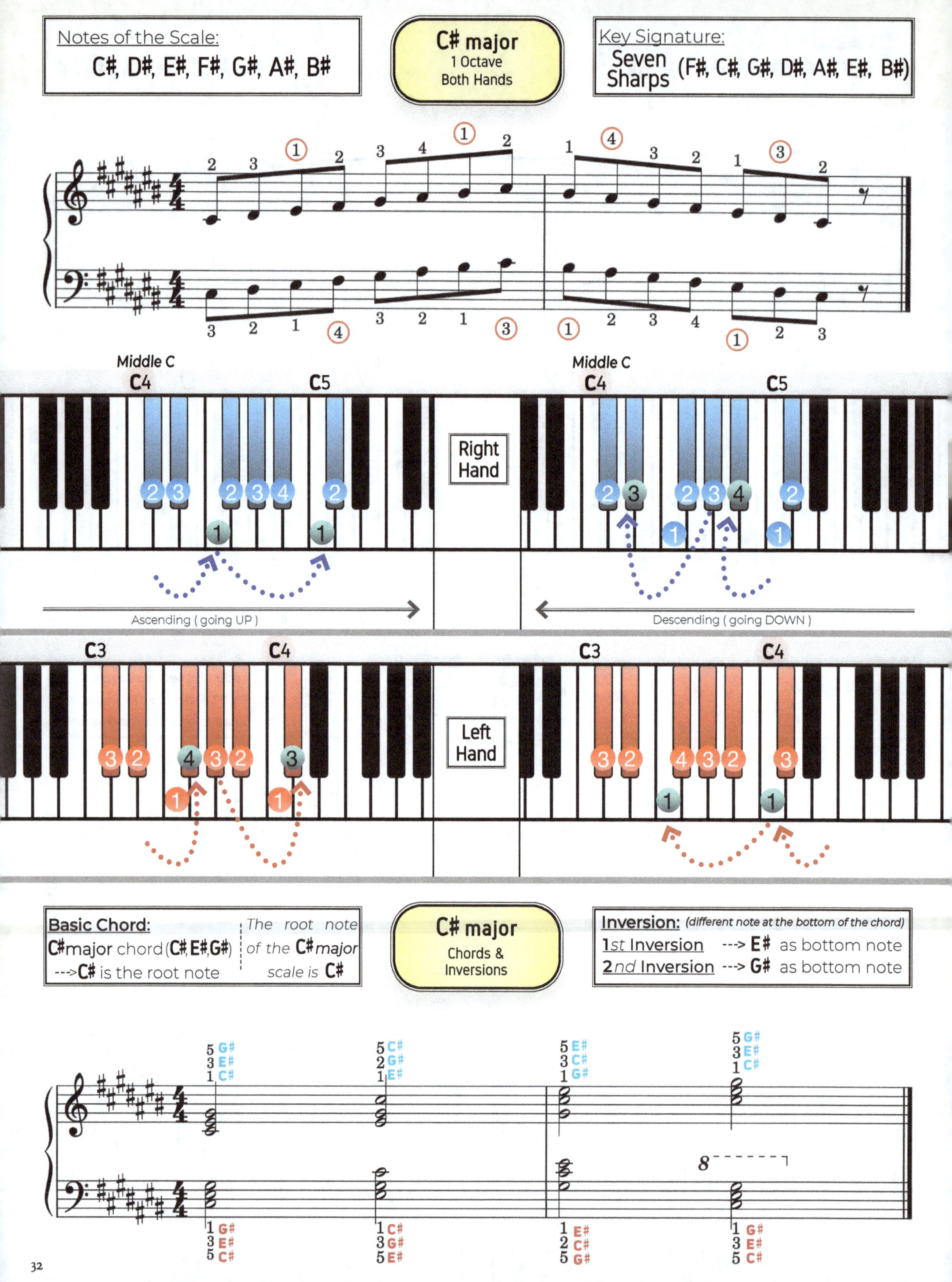

Notes of the Scale:
C#, D#, E#, F#, G#, A#, B#

C# major
1 Octave
Both Hands

Key Signature:
Seven Sharps (F#, C#, G#, D#, A#, E#, B#)

Middle C
C4
C5

Right Hand

Ascending (going UP)
Descending (going DOWN)

C3
C4

Left Hand

Basic Chord:
C# major chord (C#, E#, G#)
---> C# is the root note

The root note of the C# major scale is C#

C# major
Chords & Inversions

Inversion: (different note at the bottom of the chord)
1st Inversion ---> E# as bottom note
2nd Inversion ---> G# as bottom note

5 G#
3 E#
1 C#

5 C#
2 G#
1 E#

5 E#
3 C#
1 G#

5 G#
3 E#
1 C#

8

1 G#
3 E#
5 C#

1 C#
3 G#
5 E#

1 E#
2 C#
5 G#

1 G#
3 E#
5 C#

Major Scales

Moving **COUNTER - CLOCKWISE**

F major (1 flat) ---> C♭ major (7 flats)

KEY SIGNATURE

(Number of flats, Increase ♭ +1)
(Number of sharps, Decrease # -1)

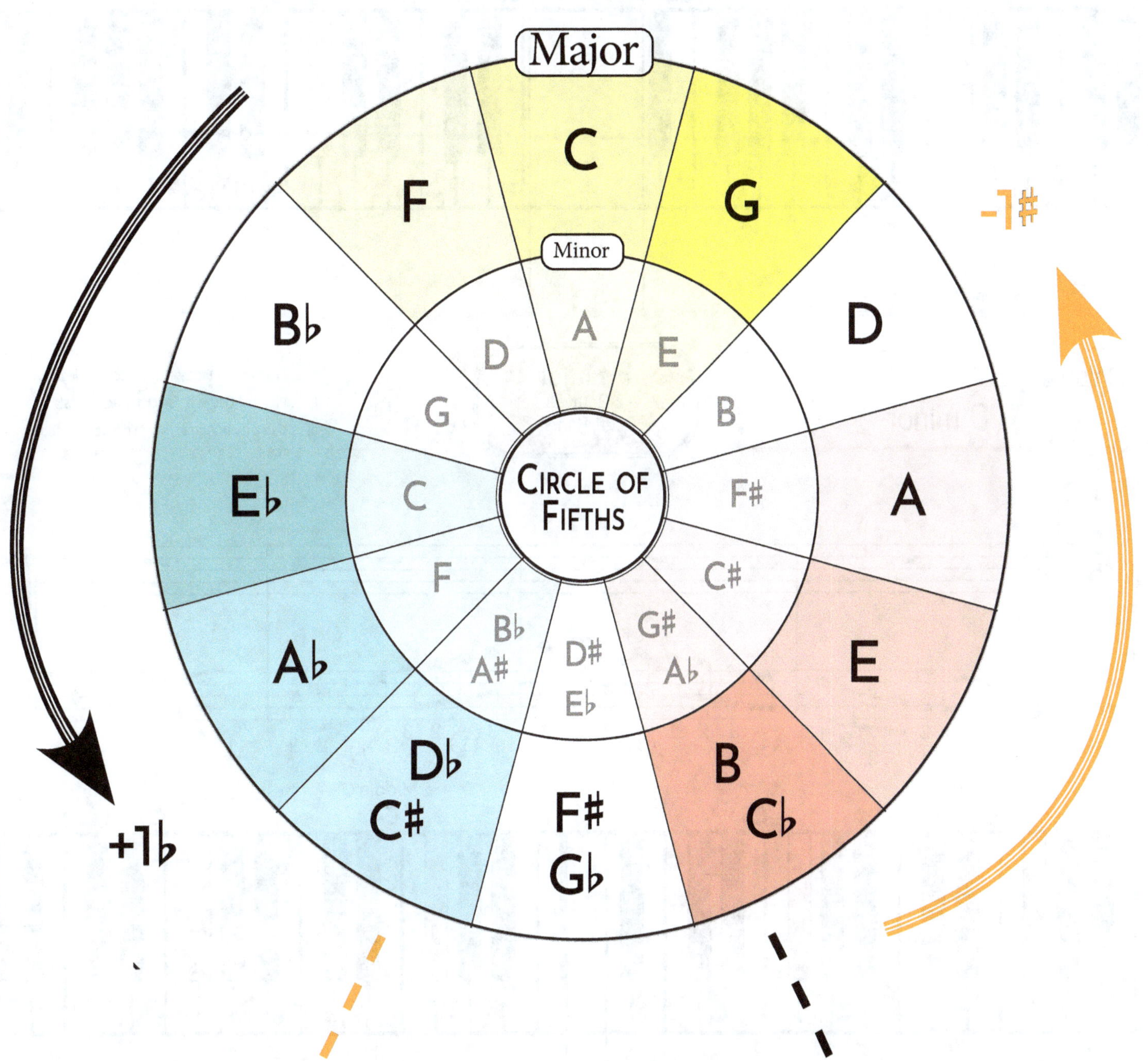

Notes of the Scale:
F, G, A, B♭, C, D, E

F major
1 Octave
Left Hand

Key Signature:
One Flat (B♭)

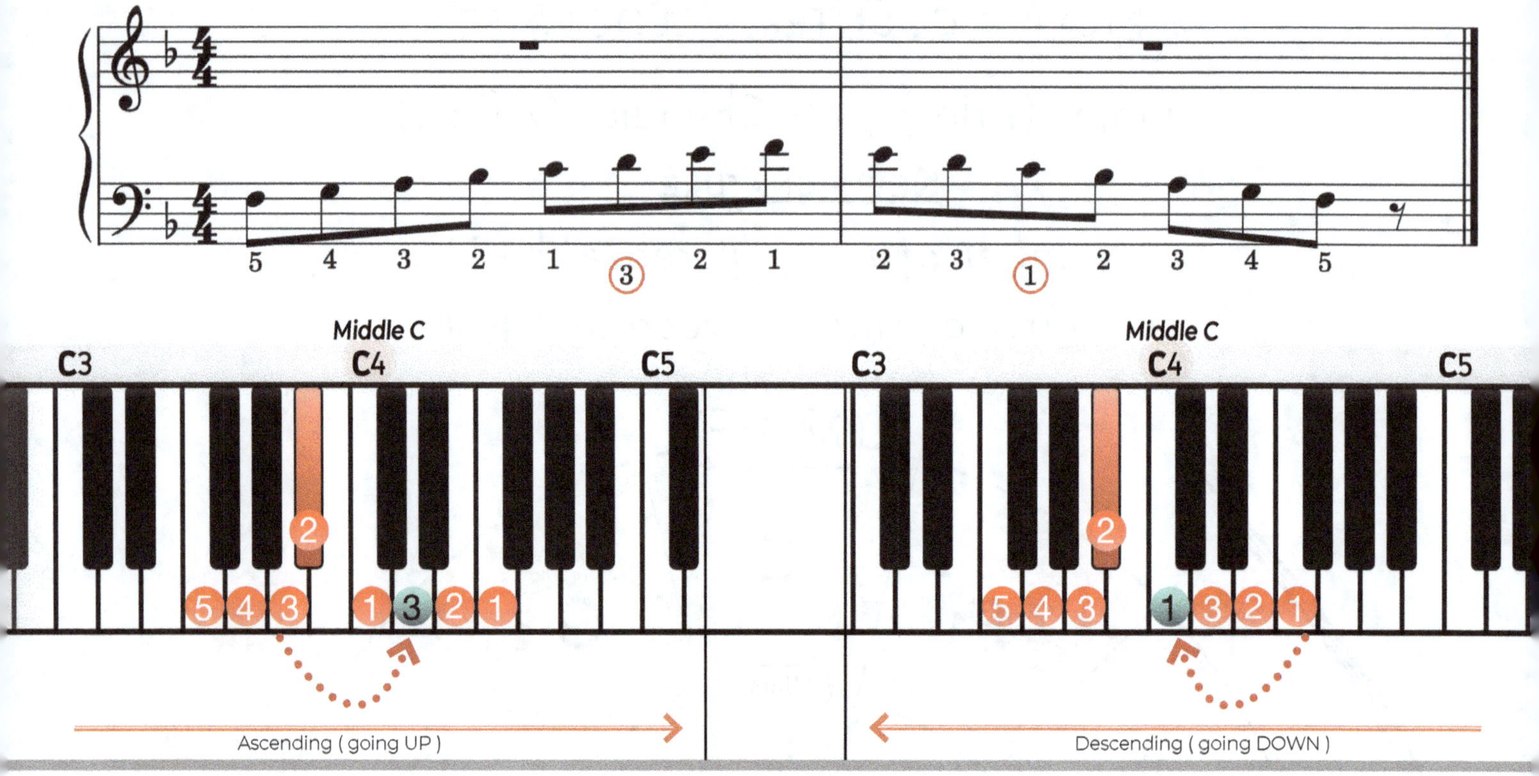

Middle C
C3
C4
C5
5 4 3 2 1 3 2 1
2
5 4 3 1 3 2 1
Ascending (going UP)

Middle C
C3
C4
C5
2 3 1 2 3 4 5
2
5 4 3 1 3 2 1
Descending (going DOWN)

Relative Key:
D minor

F major
2 Octaves
Left Hand

Practice Tips
I....... Practice ten times; Play staccato & legato
II...... Play 1+2 Octaves; Check for accidentals
III..... Use a metronome; Play in different tempos

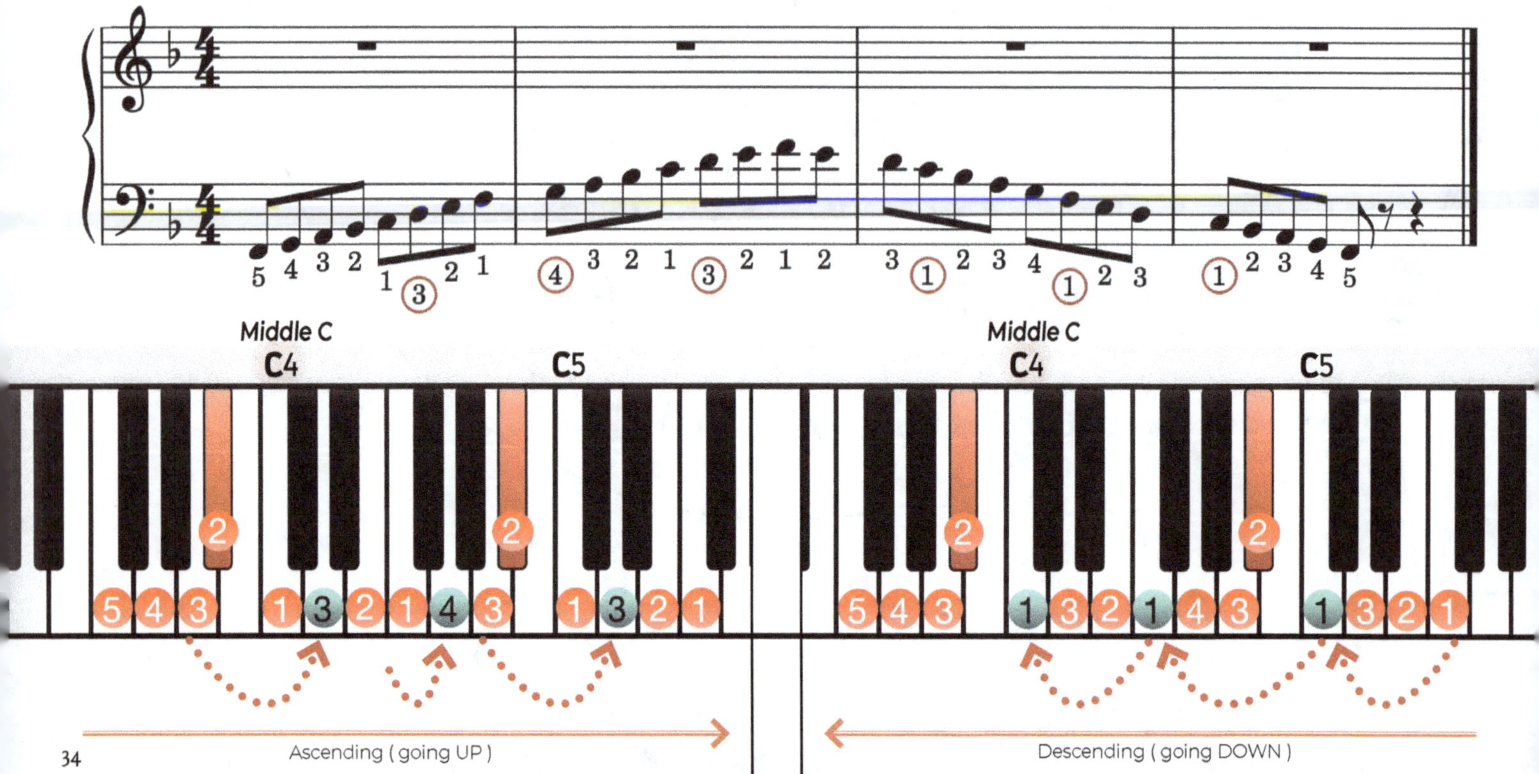

5 4 3 2 1 2 1 3
4 3 2 1 3 2 1 2
3 1 2 3 4 1 2 3
1 2 3 4 5

Middle C
C4
C5
5 4 3 1 3 2 1 4 3 1 3 2 1
2 2
Ascending (going UP)

Middle C
C4
C5
5 4 3 1 3 2 1 4 3 1 3 2 1
2 2
Descending (going DOWN)

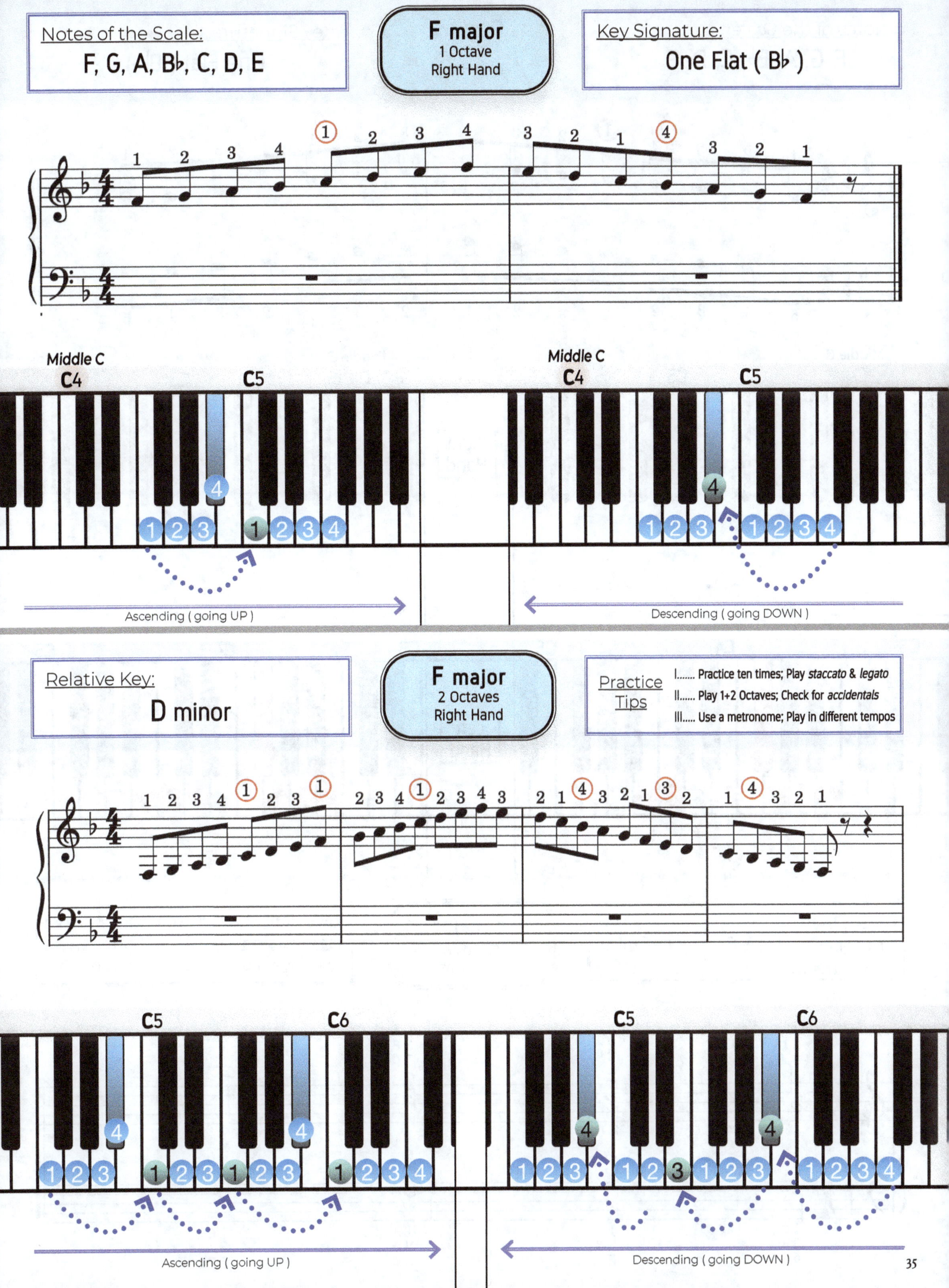

Notes of the Scale:
F, G, A, B♭, C, D, E
F major
1 Octave
Right Hand
Key Signature:
One Flat (B♭)
Middle C
C4
C5
4
1 2 3 1 2 3 4
Ascending (going UP)
Middle C
C4
C5
4
1 2 3 1 2 3 4
Descending (going DOWN)
Relative Key:
D minor
F major
2 Octaves
Right Hand
Practice Tips
I....... Practice ten times; Play staccato & legato
II...... Play 1+2 Octaves; Check for accidentals
III..... Use a metronome; Play in different tempos
C5
C6
4
4
1 2 3 1 2 3 1 2 3 1 2 3 4
Ascending (going UP)
C5
C6
4
4
1 2 3 1 2 3 1 2 3 1 2 3 4
Descending (going DOWN)

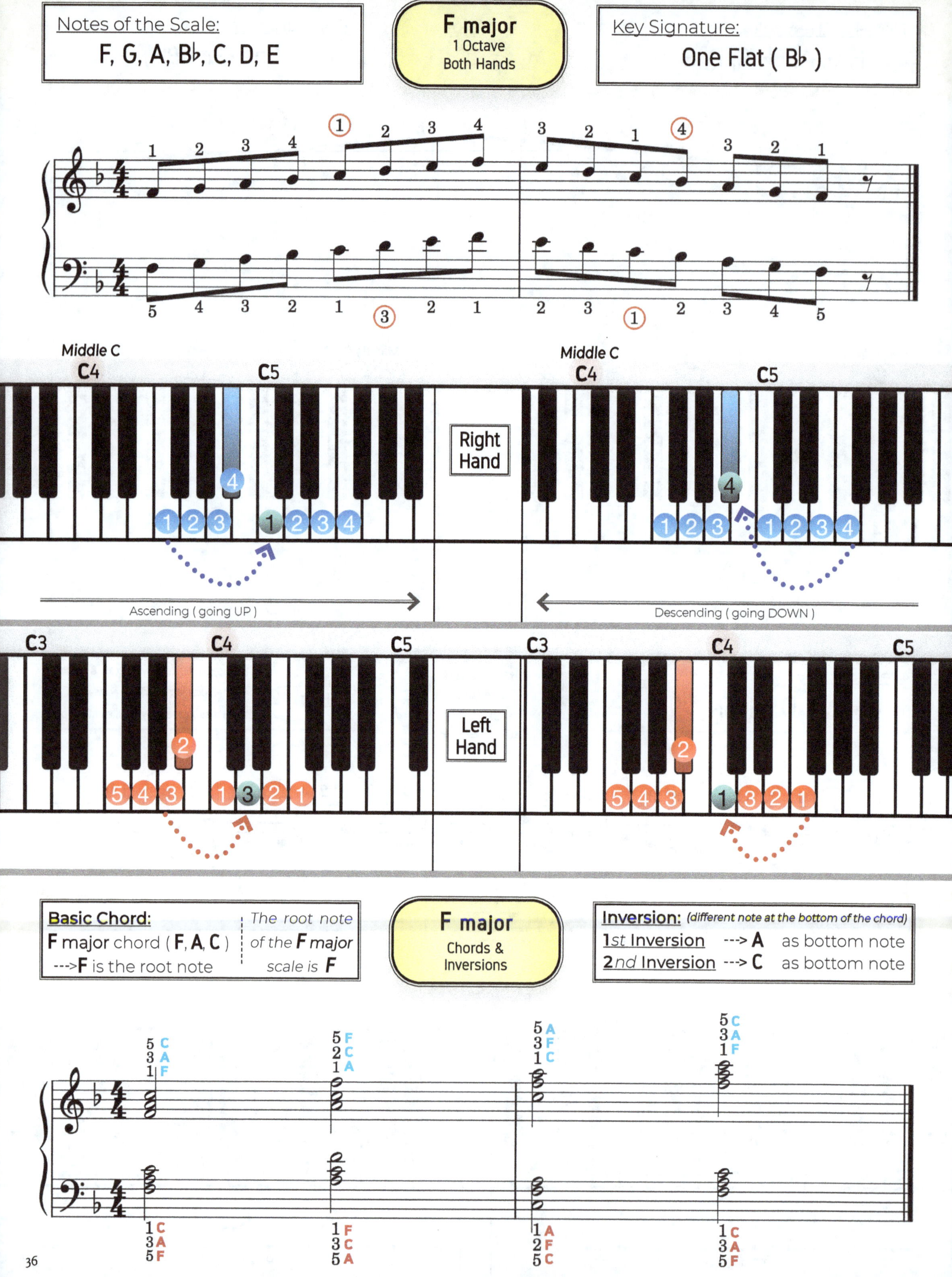

Notes of the Scale:
F, G, A, B♭, C, D, E
F major
1 Octave
Both Hands
Key Signature:
One Flat (B♭)
Middle C
C4
C5
Right Hand
Ascending (going UP)
Descending (going DOWN)
C3
C4
C5
Left Hand
Basic Chord:
F major chord (F, A, C)
--->F is the root note
The root note of the F major scale is F
F major
Chords & Inversions
Inversion: (different note at the bottom of the chord)
1st Inversion ---> A as bottom note
2nd Inversion ---> C as bottom note

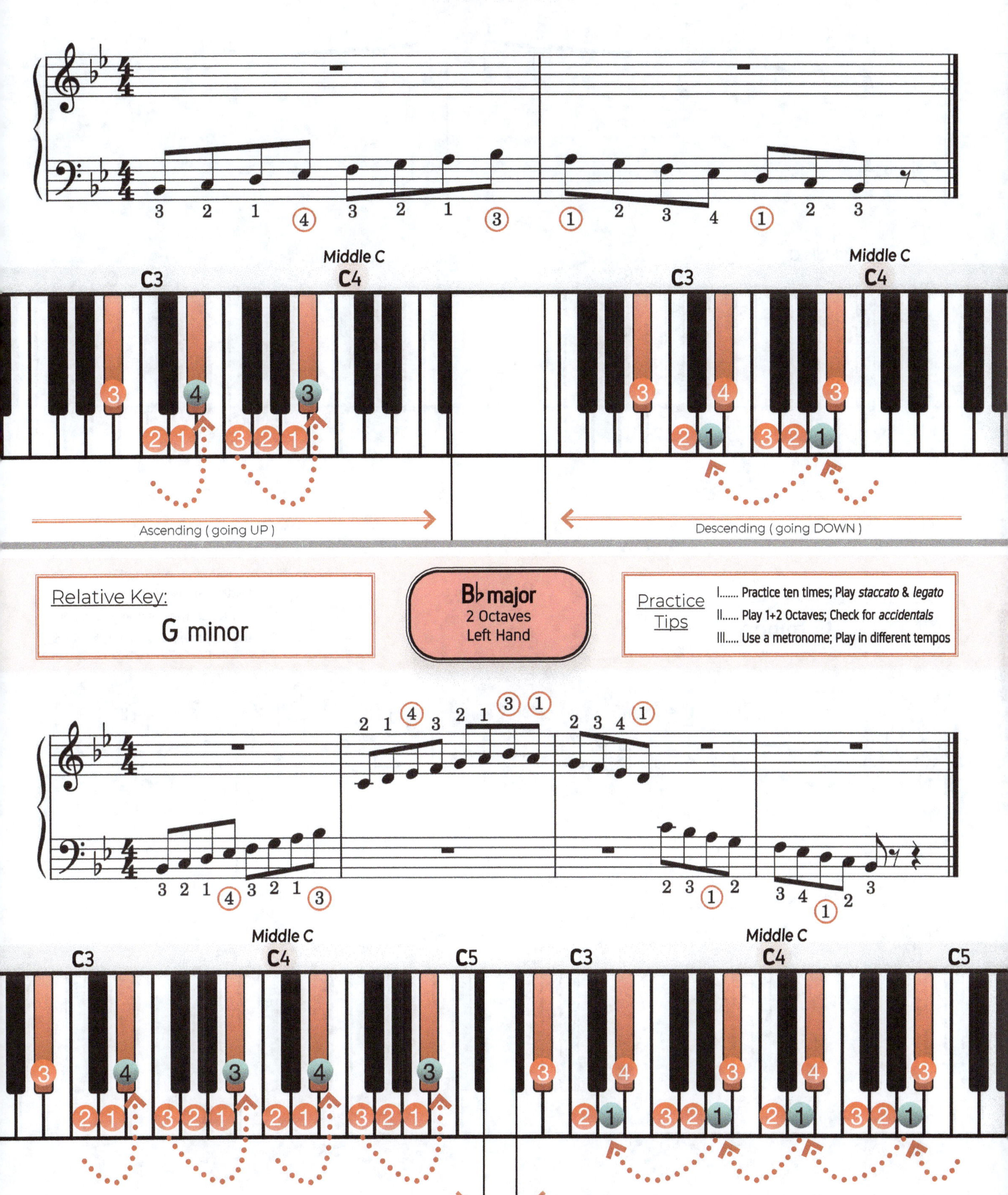

Notes of the Scale:
B♭, C, D, E♭, F, G, A
B♭ major
1 Octave
Left Hand
Key Signature:
Two Flats (B♭, E♭)
Middle C
C3
C4
3 2 1 4 3 2 1 3
1 2 3 4 1 2 3
C3
Middle C
C4
3 4 3
2 1 3 2 1
Ascending (going UP)
Descending (going DOWN)
Relative Key:
G minor
B♭ major
2 Octaves
Left Hand
Practice Tips
I....... Practice ten times; Play staccato & legato
II....... Play 1+2 Octaves; Check for accidentals
III..... Use a metronome; Play in different tempos
2 1 4 3 2 1 3 1
2 3 4 1
3 2 1 4 3 2 1 3
2 3 1 2
3 4 1 2
Middle C
C3
C4
C5
3 4 3 4 3
2 1 3 2 1 2 1 3 2 1
C3
Middle C
C4
C5
3 4 3 4 3
2 1 3 2 1 2 1 3 2 1
Ascending (going UP)
Descending (going DOWN)

Notes of the Scale:
Bb, C, D, Eb, F, G, A

Bb major
1 Octave
Right Hand

Key Signature:
Two Flats (Bb, Eb)

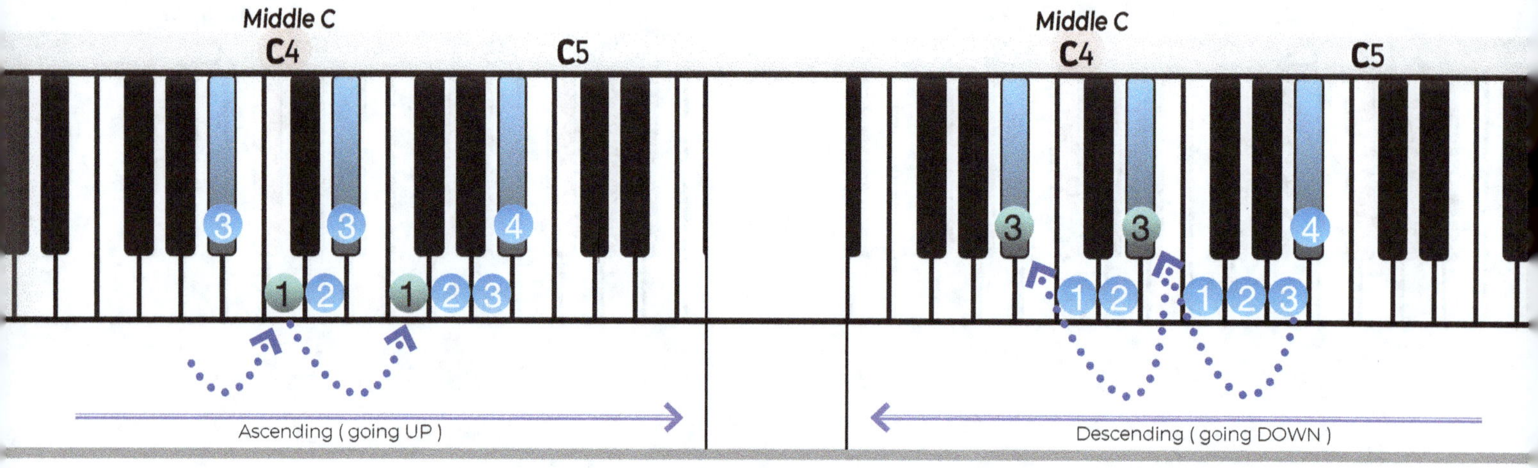

Middle C
C4
C5

Middle C
C4
C5

3   3   4
1   2   1   2   3

3   3   4
1   2   1   2   3

Ascending (going UP)
Descending (going DOWN)

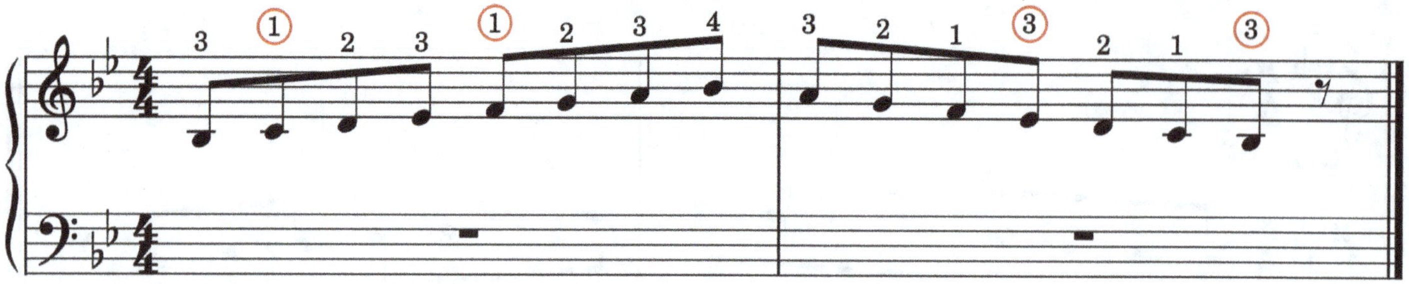

Relative Key:
G minor

Bb major
2 Octaves
Right Hand

Practice Tips

I....... Practice ten times; Play staccato & legato
II...... Play 1+2 Octaves; Check for accidentals
III..... Use a metronome; Play in different tempos

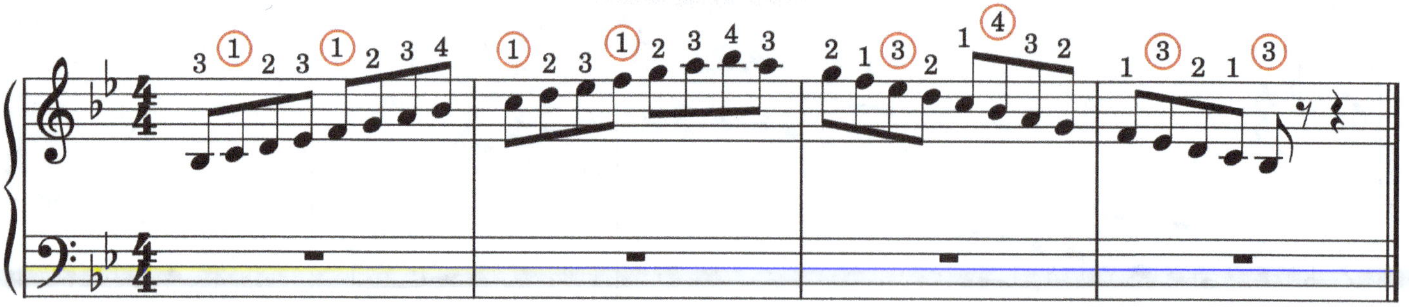

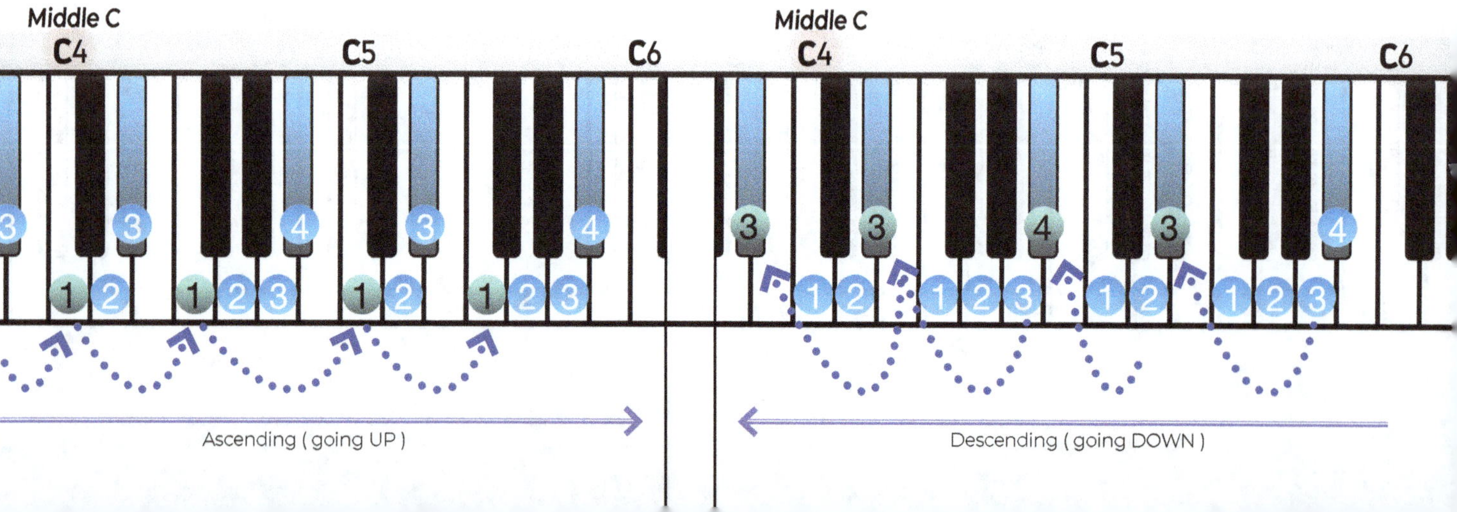

Middle C
C4
C5
C6

Middle C
C4
C5
C6

3   3   4   3   4
1   2   1   2   3   1   2   1   2   3

3   3   4   3   4
1   2   1   2   3   1   2   1   2   3

Ascending (going UP)
Descending (going DOWN)

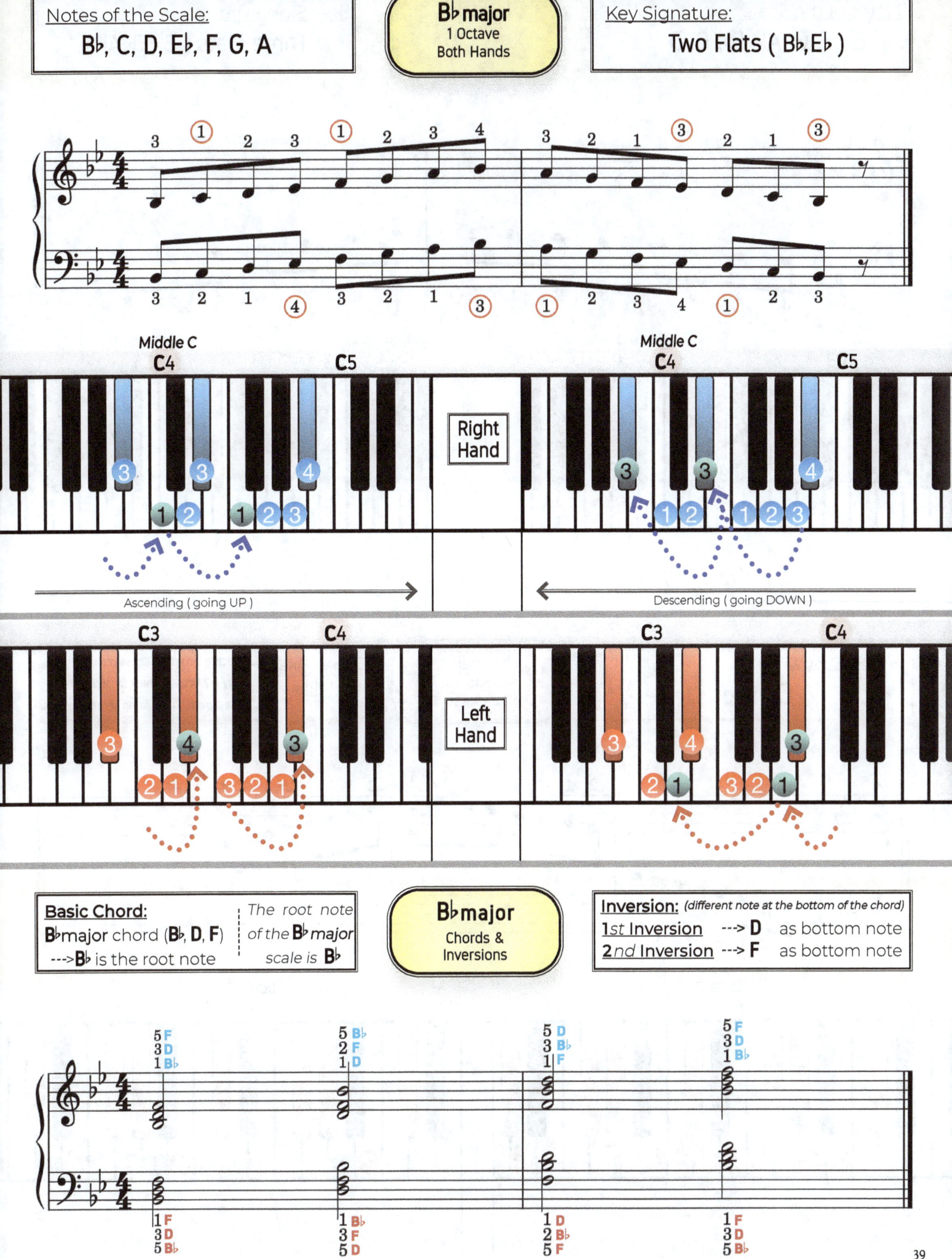

Notes of the Scale:
Bb, C, D, Eb, F, G, A

Bb major
1 Octave
Both Hands

Key Signature:
Two Flats (Bb, Eb)

Middle C
C4
C5
Right Hand
Ascending (going UP)

Middle C
C4
C5
Descending (going DOWN)

C3
C4
Left Hand

C3
C4

Basic Chord:
Bb major chord (Bb, D, F)
---> Bb is the root note
The root note of the Bb major scale is Bb

Bb major
Chords & Inversions

Inversion: (different note at the bottom of the chord)
1st Inversion ---> D as bottom note
2nd Inversion ---> F as bottom note

5 F
3 D
1 Bb

5 Bb
2 F
1 D

5 D
3 Bb
1 F

5 F
3 D
1 Bb

1 F
3 D
5 Bb

1 Bb
3 F
5 D

1 D
2 Bb
5 F

1 F
3 D
5 Bb

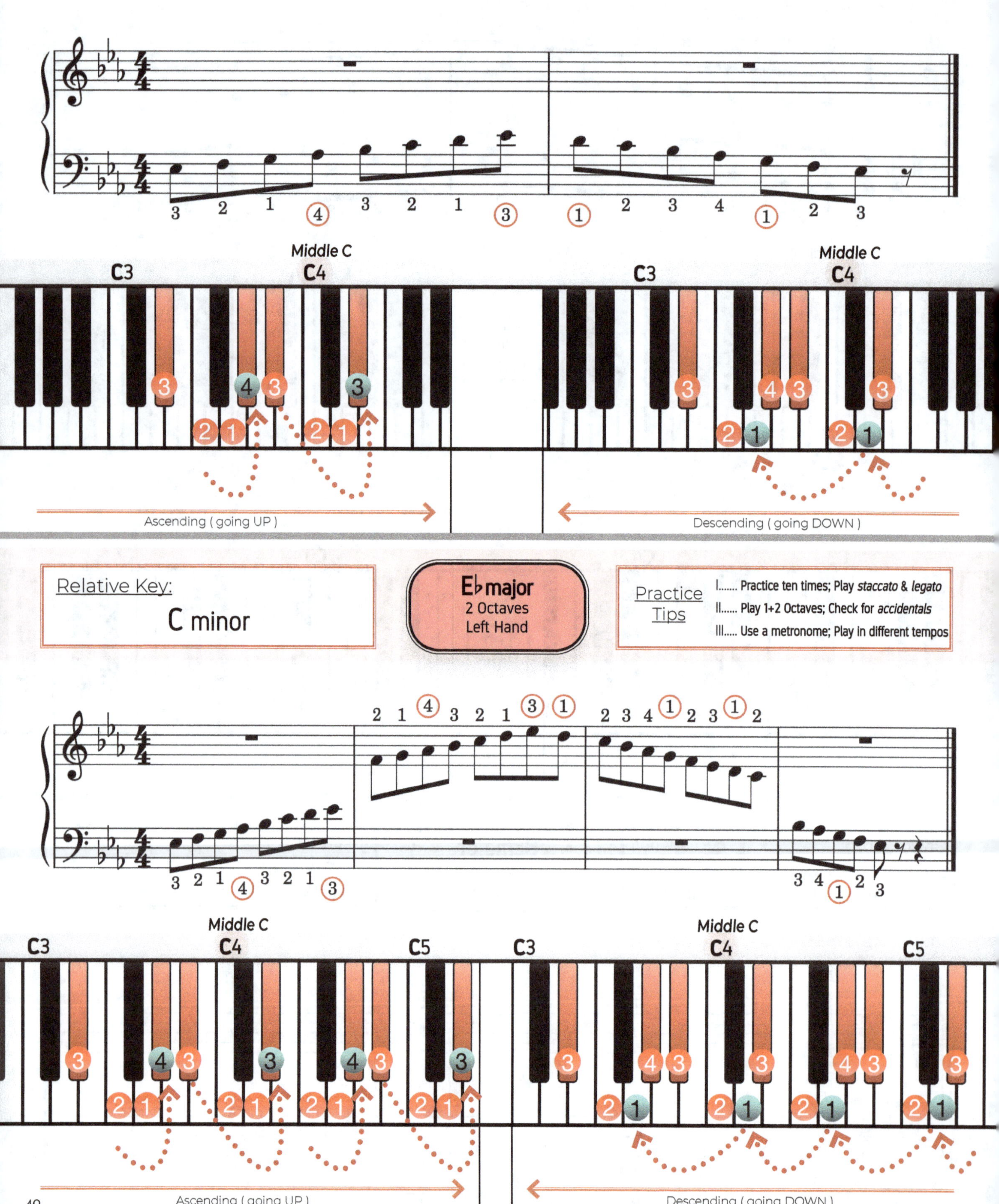

Notes of the Scale:
E♭, F, G, A♭, B♭, C, D
E♭ major
1 Octave
Left Hand
Key Signature:
Three Flats (B♭, E♭, A♭)
Middle C
C4
C3
C3
Middle C
C4
Ascending (going UP)
Descending (going DOWN)
Relative Key:
C minor
E♭ major
2 Octaves
Left Hand
Practice Tips
I....... Practice ten times; Play staccato & legato
II...... Play 1+2 Octaves; Check for accidentals
III..... Use a metronome; Play in different tempos
Middle C
C4
C3
C5
C3
Middle C
C4
C5
Ascending (going UP)
Descending (going DOWN)
40

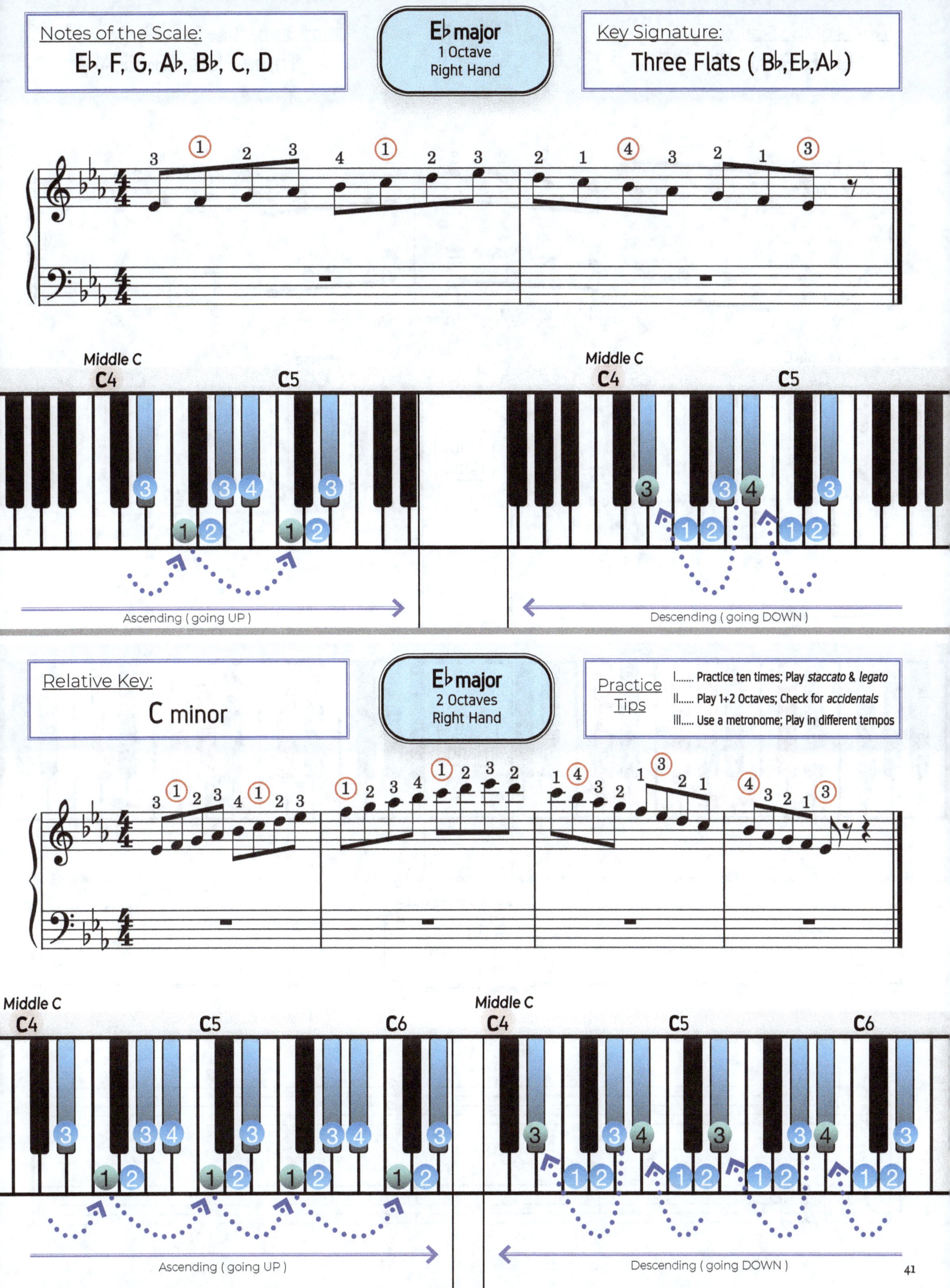

Notes of the Scale:
Eb, F, G, Ab, Bb, C, D

Eb major
1 Octave
Right Hand

Key Signature:
Three Flats (Bb, Eb, Ab)

Middle C
C4
C5
3 1 2 3 4 1 2 3 2 1 4 3 2 1 3
1 2 1 2
Ascending (going UP)
Descending (going DOWN)

Relative Key:
C minor

Eb major
2 Octaves
Right Hand

Practice Tips
I....... Practice ten times; Play staccato & legato
II...... Play 1+2 Octaves; Check for accidentals
III..... Use a metronome; Play in different tempos

Middle C
C4
C5
C6
Ascending (going UP)
Descending (going DOWN)

Notes of the Scale:
E♭, F, G, A♭, B♭, C, D

E♭ major
1 Octave
Both Hands

Key Signature:
Three Flats (B♭, E♭, A♭)

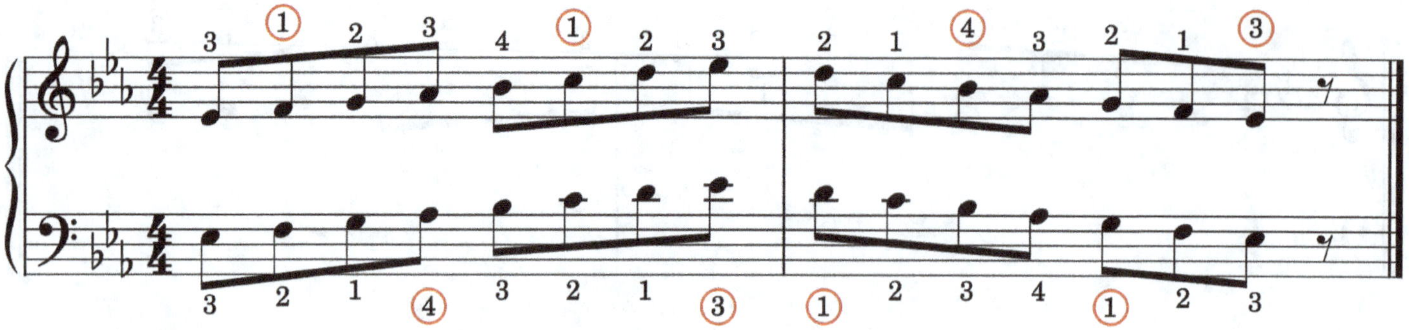

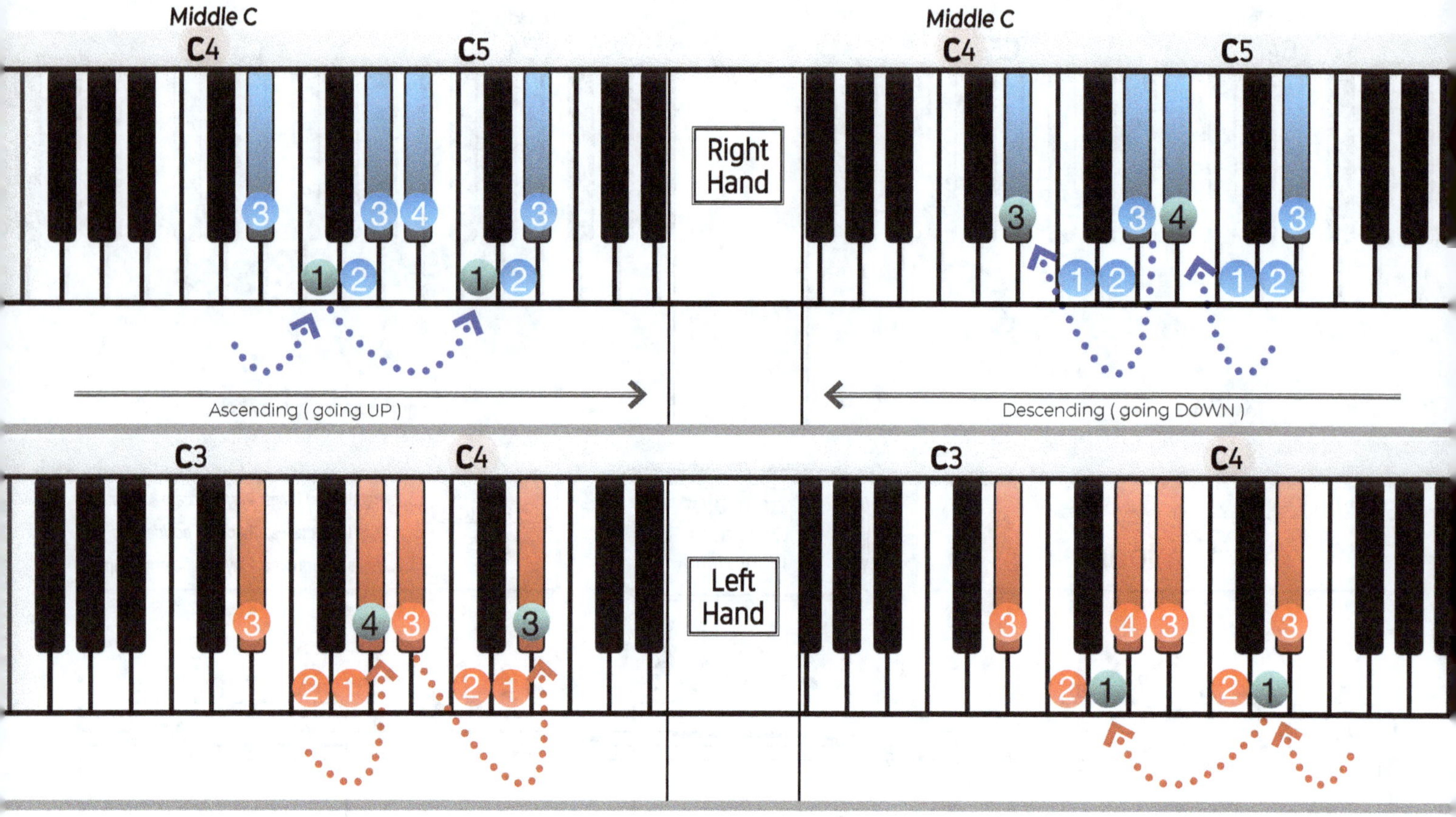

Middle C
C4
C5
Right Hand
Ascending (going UP)
Descending (going DOWN)

C3
C4
Left Hand

Basic Chord:
E♭ major chord (E♭, G, B♭)
---> E♭ is the root note

The root note of the E♭ major scale is E♭

E♭ major
Chords & Inversions

Inversion: (different note at the bottom of the chord)
1st Inversion ---> G as bottom note
2nd Inversion ---> B♭ as bottom note

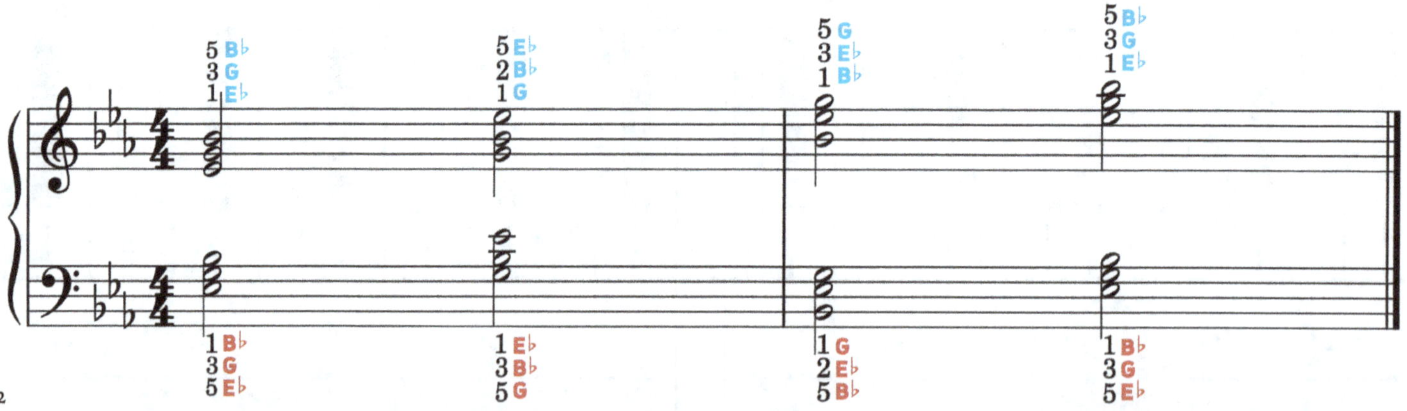

5 B♭
3 G
1 E♭

5 E♭
2 B♭
1 G

5 G
3 E♭
1 B♭

5 B♭
3 G
1 E♭

1 B♭
3 G
5 E♭

1 E♭
3 B♭
5 G

1 G
2 E♭
5 B♭

1 B♭
3 G
5 E♭

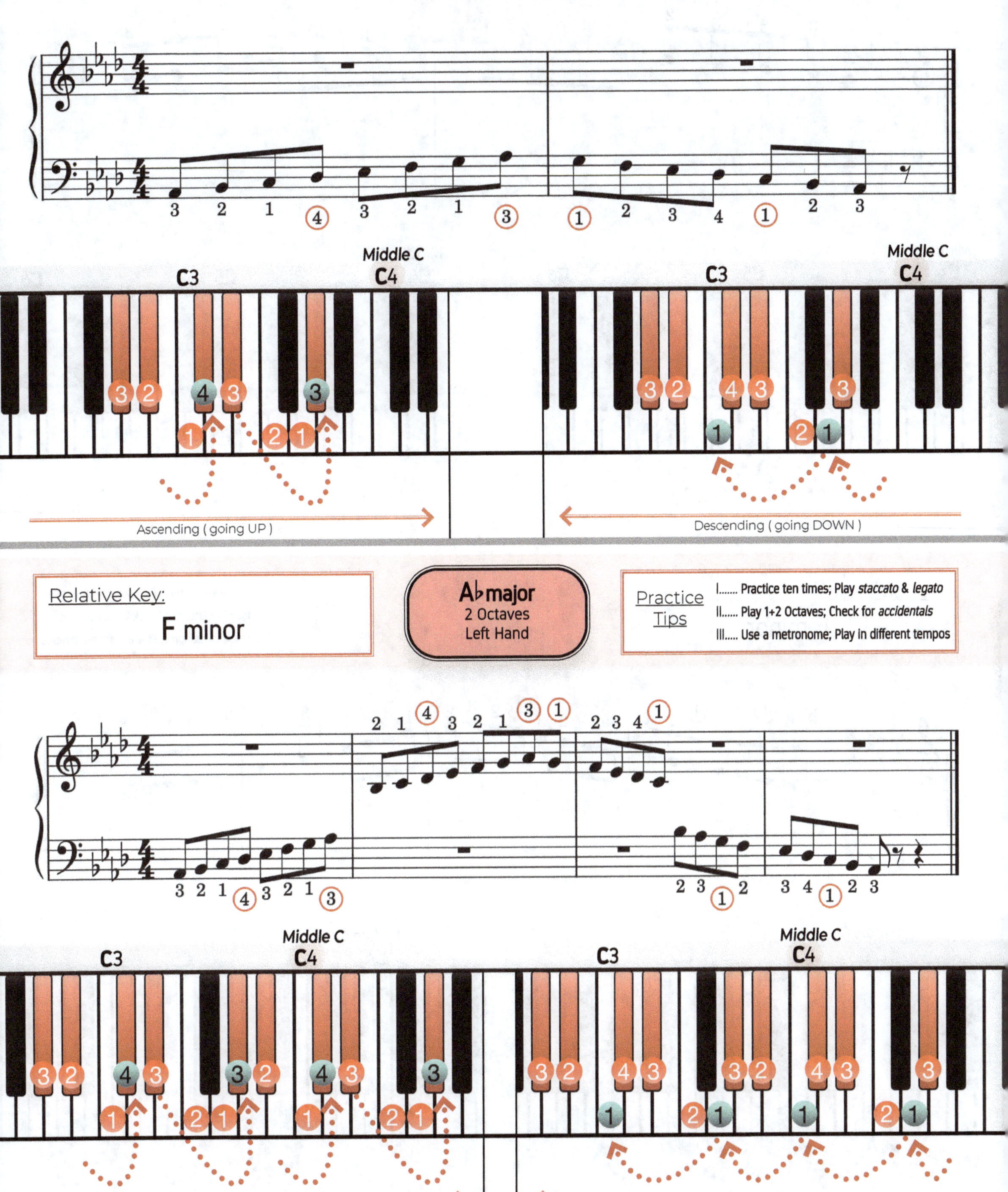

Notes of the Scale:
Ab, Bb, C, Db, Eb, F, G

Ab major
1 Octave
Left Hand

Key Signature:
Four Flats (Bb, Eb, Ab, Db)

Middle C
C3
C4

3 2 1 4 3 2 1 3 1 2 3 4 1 2 3

Ascending (going UP)
Descending (going DOWN)

Relative Key:
F minor

Ab major
2 Octaves
Left Hand

Practice Tips
I....... Practice ten times; Play staccato & legato
II...... Play 1+2 Octaves; Check for accidentals
III..... Use a metronome; Play in different tempos

Middle C
C3
C4

Ascending (going UP)
Descending (going DOWN)

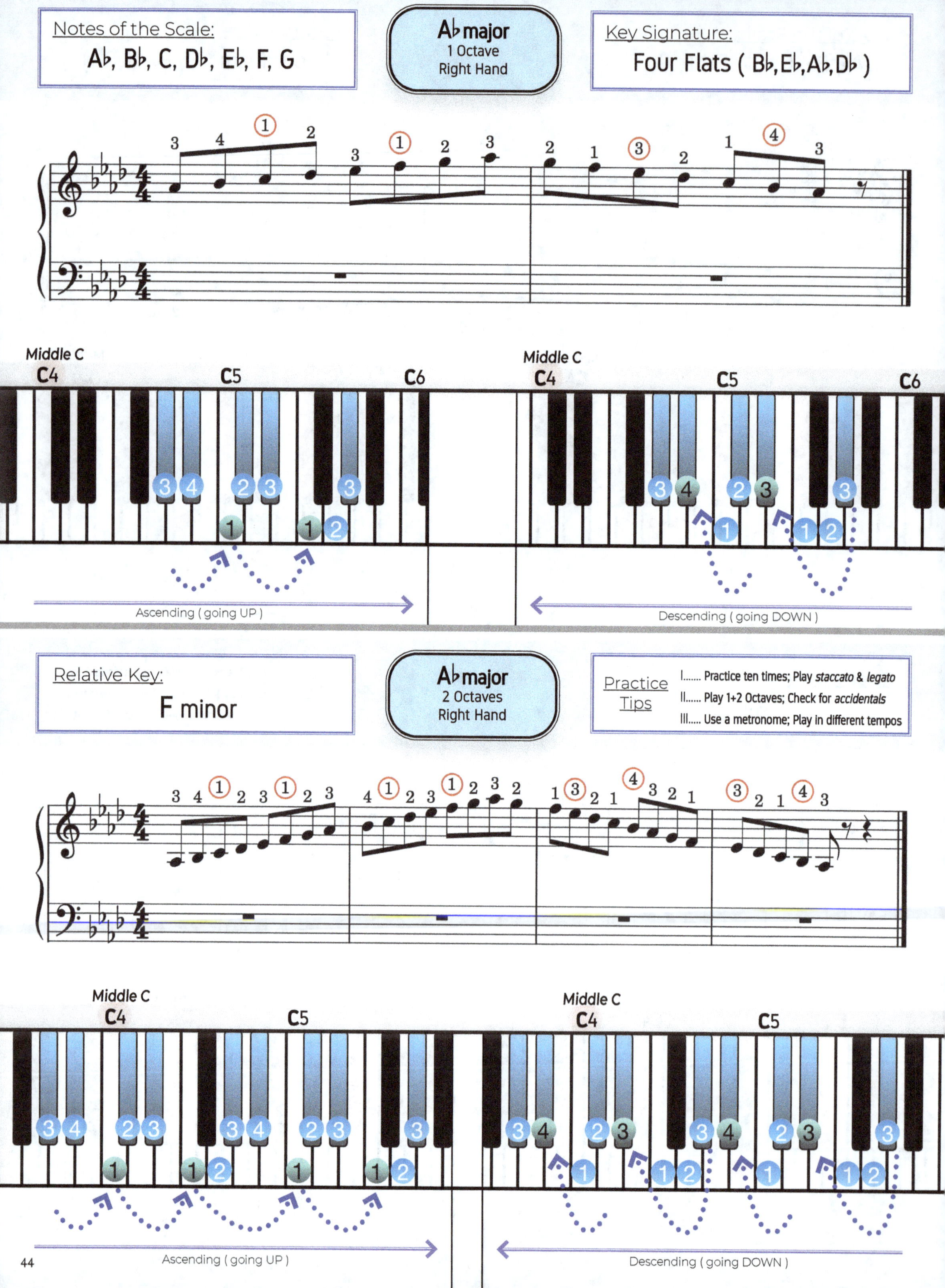

Notes of the Scale:
Ab, Bb, C, Db, Eb, F, G

Ab major
1 Octave
Right Hand

Key Signature:
Four Flats (Bb, Eb, Ab, Db)

Middle C
C4
C5
C6

Middle C
C4
C5
C6

Ascending (going UP)
Descending (going DOWN)

Relative Key:
F minor

Ab major
2 Octaves
Right Hand

Practice Tips
I....... Practice ten times; Play staccato & legato
II...... Play 1+2 Octaves; Check for accidentals
III..... Use a metronome; Play in different tempos

Middle C
C4
C5

Middle C
C4
C5

Ascending (going UP)
Descending (going DOWN)

44

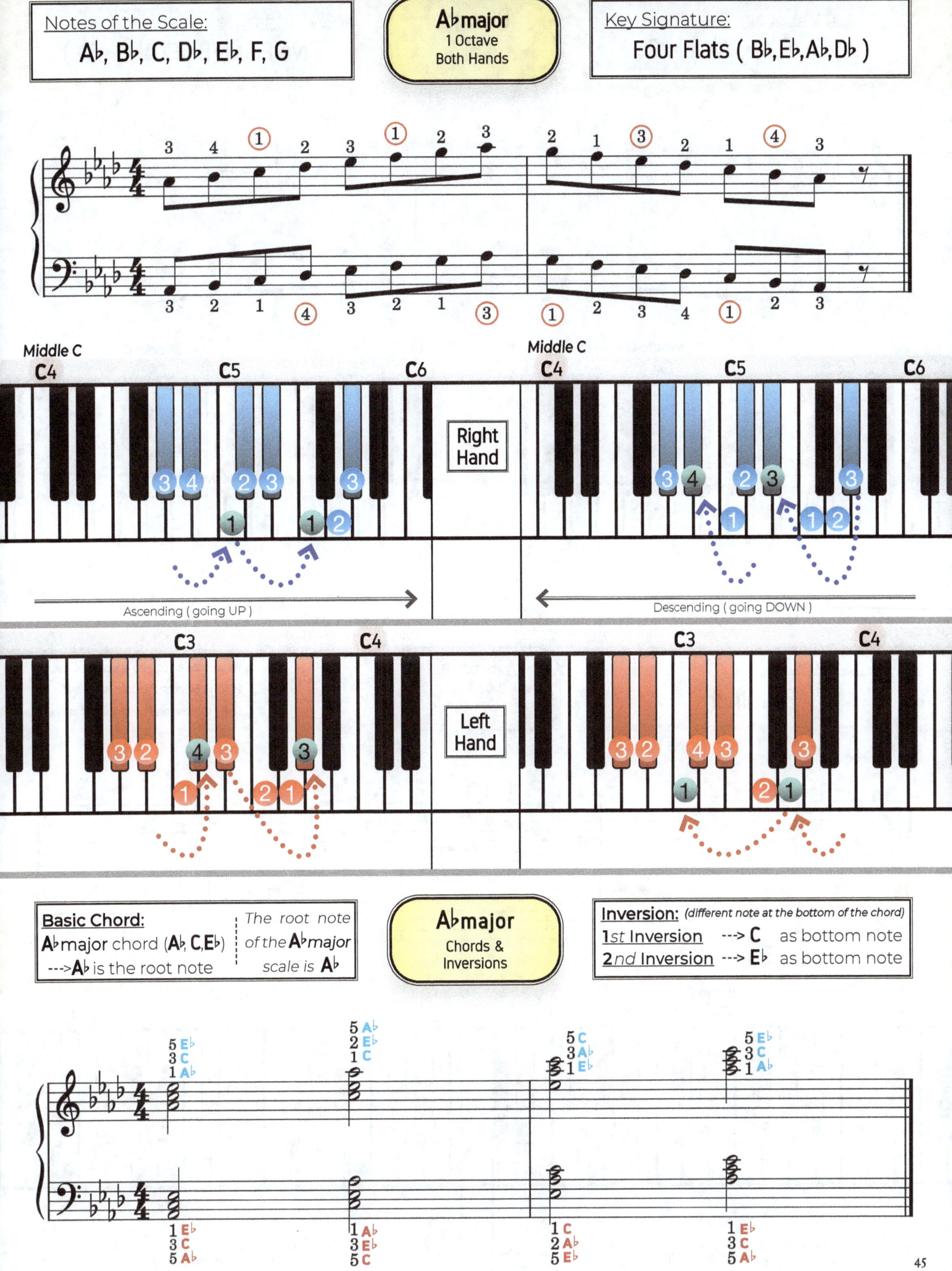

Notes of the Scale:
Ab, Bb, C, Db, Eb, F, G

Ab major
1 Octave
Both Hands

Key Signature:
Four Flats (Bb, Eb, Ab, Db)

Middle C
C4
C5
C6
Right Hand
Ascending (going UP)

Middle C
C4
C5
C6
Descending (going DOWN)

C3
C4
Left Hand

C3
C4

Basic Chord:
Ab major chord (Ab, C, Eb)
---> Ab is the root note

The root note of the Ab major scale is Ab

Ab major
Chords &
Inversions

Inversion: (different note at the bottom of the chord)
1st Inversion ---> C as bottom note
2nd Inversion ---> Eb as bottom note

5 Eb
3 C
1 Ab

5 Ab
2 Eb
1 C

5 C
3 Ab
1 Eb

5 Eb
3 C
1 Ab

1 Eb
3 C
5 Ab

1 Ab
3 E
5 C

1 C
2 Ab
5 Eb

1 Eb
3 C
5 Ab

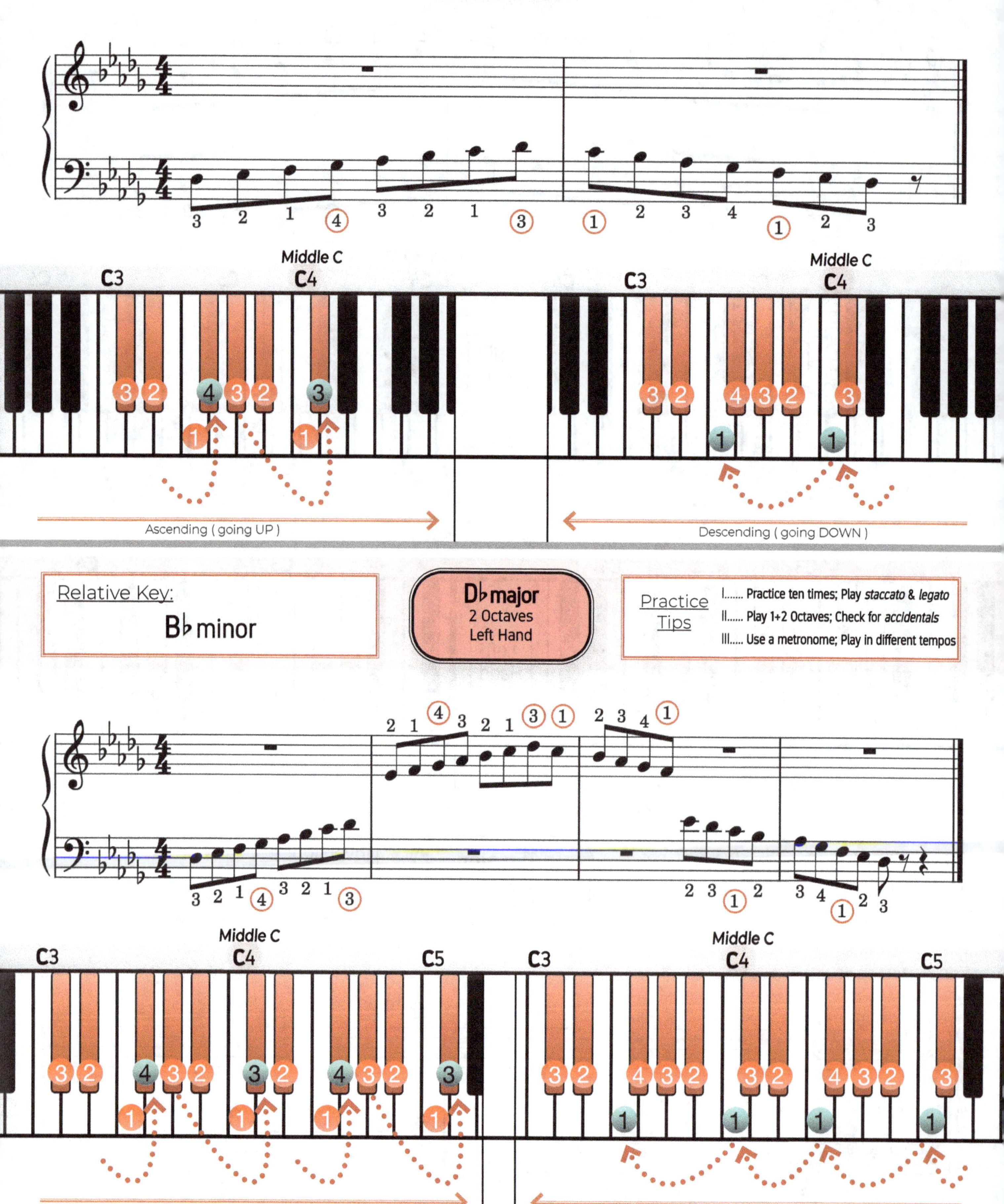

Notes of the Scale:
Db, Eb, F, Gb, Ab, Bb, C

Db major
1 Octave
Left Hand

Key Signature:
Five Flats (Bb, Eb, Ab, Db, Gb)

C3
Middle C
C4
C3
Middle C
C4

3 2 1 4 3 2 1 3
1 2 3 4 1 2 3
3 2 4 3 2 3
1 1
3 2 4 3 2 3
1 1

Ascending (going UP)
Descending (going DOWN)

Relative Key:
Bb minor

Db major
2 Octaves
Left Hand

Practice Tips
I....... Practice ten times; Play staccato & legato
II...... Play 1+2 Octaves; Check for accidentals
III..... Use a metronome; Play in different tempos

2 1 4 3 2 1 3 1 2 3 4 1
3 2 1 4 3 2 1 3
2 3 1 2 3 4 1 2 3

Middle C
C3 C4 C5
Middle C
C3 C4 C5

3 2 4 3 2 3 2 4 3 2 3
1 1 1 1
3 2 4 3 2 3 2 4 3 2 3
1 1 1 1

Ascending (going UP)
Descending (going DOWN)

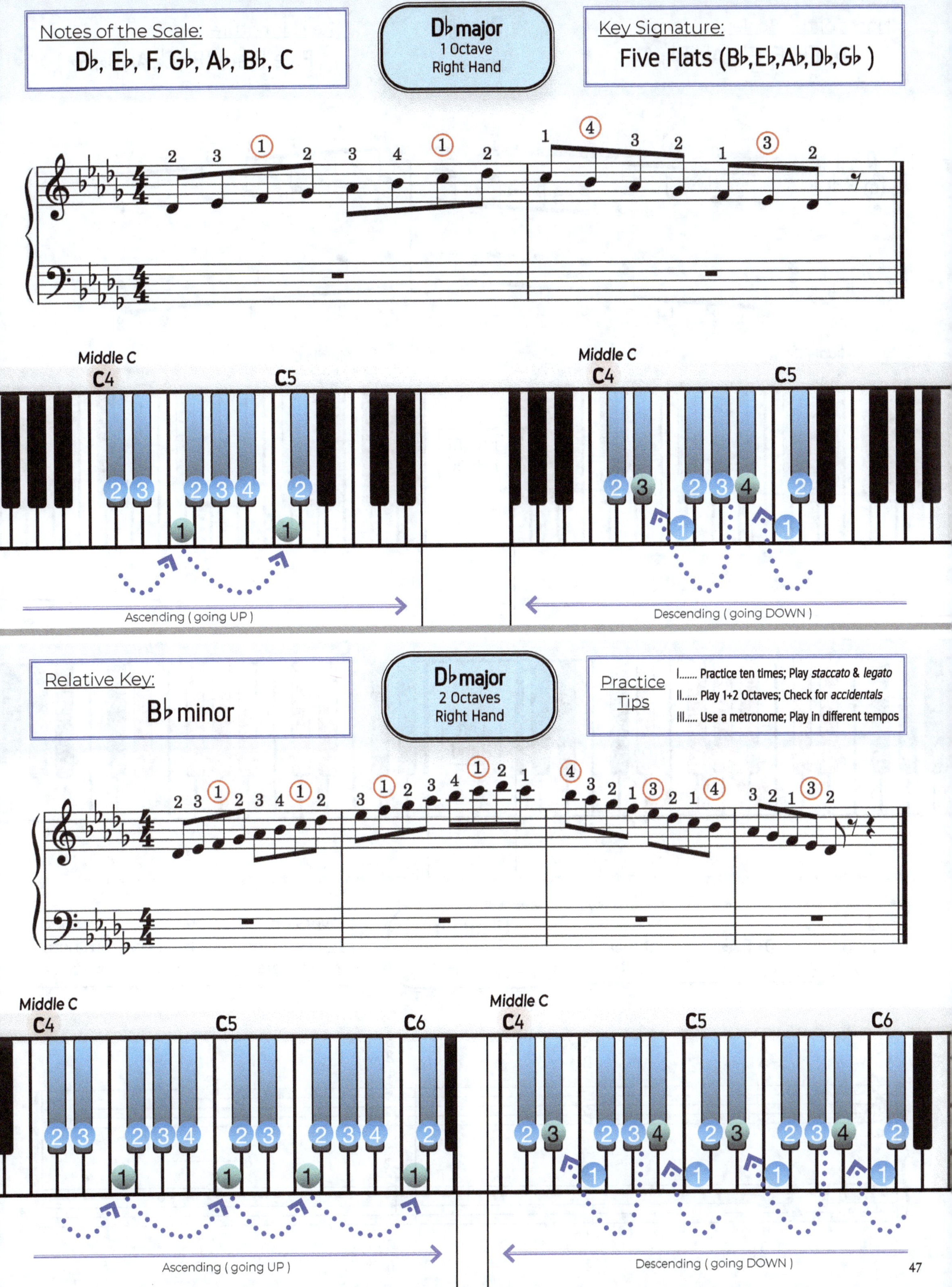

Notes of the Scale:
Db, Eb, F, Gb, Ab, Bb, C
Db major
1 Octave
Right Hand
Key Signature:
Five Flats (Bb, Eb, Ab, Db, Gb)
Middle C
C4
C5
Ascending (going UP)
Descending (going DOWN)
Relative Key:
Bb minor
Db major
2 Octaves
Right Hand
Practice Tips
I....... Practice ten times; Play staccato & legato
II...... Play 1+2 Octaves; Check for accidentals
III..... Use a metronome; Play in different tempos
Middle C
C4
C5
C6
Ascending (going UP)
Descending (going DOWN)

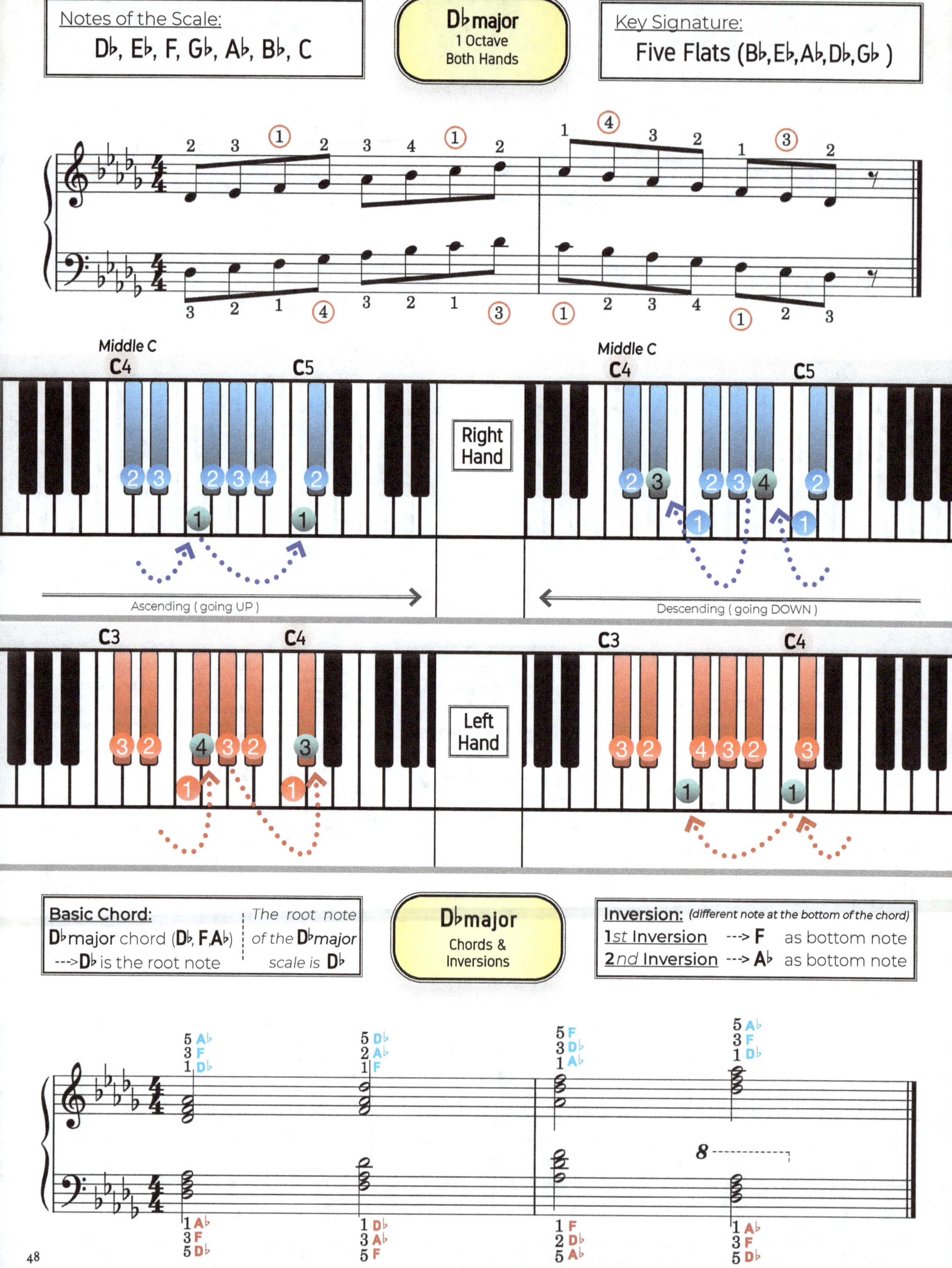

Notes of the Scale:
Db, Eb, F, Gb, Ab, Bb, C
Db major
1 Octave
Both Hands
Key Signature:
Five Flats (Bb, Eb, Ab, Db, Gb)
Middle C
C4
C5
Right Hand
Ascending (going UP)
Descending (going DOWN)
Middle C
C4
C5
C3
C4
Left Hand
C3
C4
Basic Chord:
Db major chord (Db, F, Ab)
---> Db is the root note
The root note of the Db major scale is Db
Db major
Chords & Inversions
Inversion: (different note at the bottom of the chord)
1st Inversion ---> F as bottom note
2nd Inversion ---> Ab as bottom note
5 Ab
3 F
1 Db
5 Db
2 Ab
1 F
5 F
3 Db
1 Ab
5 Ab
3 F
1 Db
8
1 Ab
3 F
5 Db
1 Db
3 Ab
5 F
1 F
2 D
5 A
1 Ab
3 F
5 Db

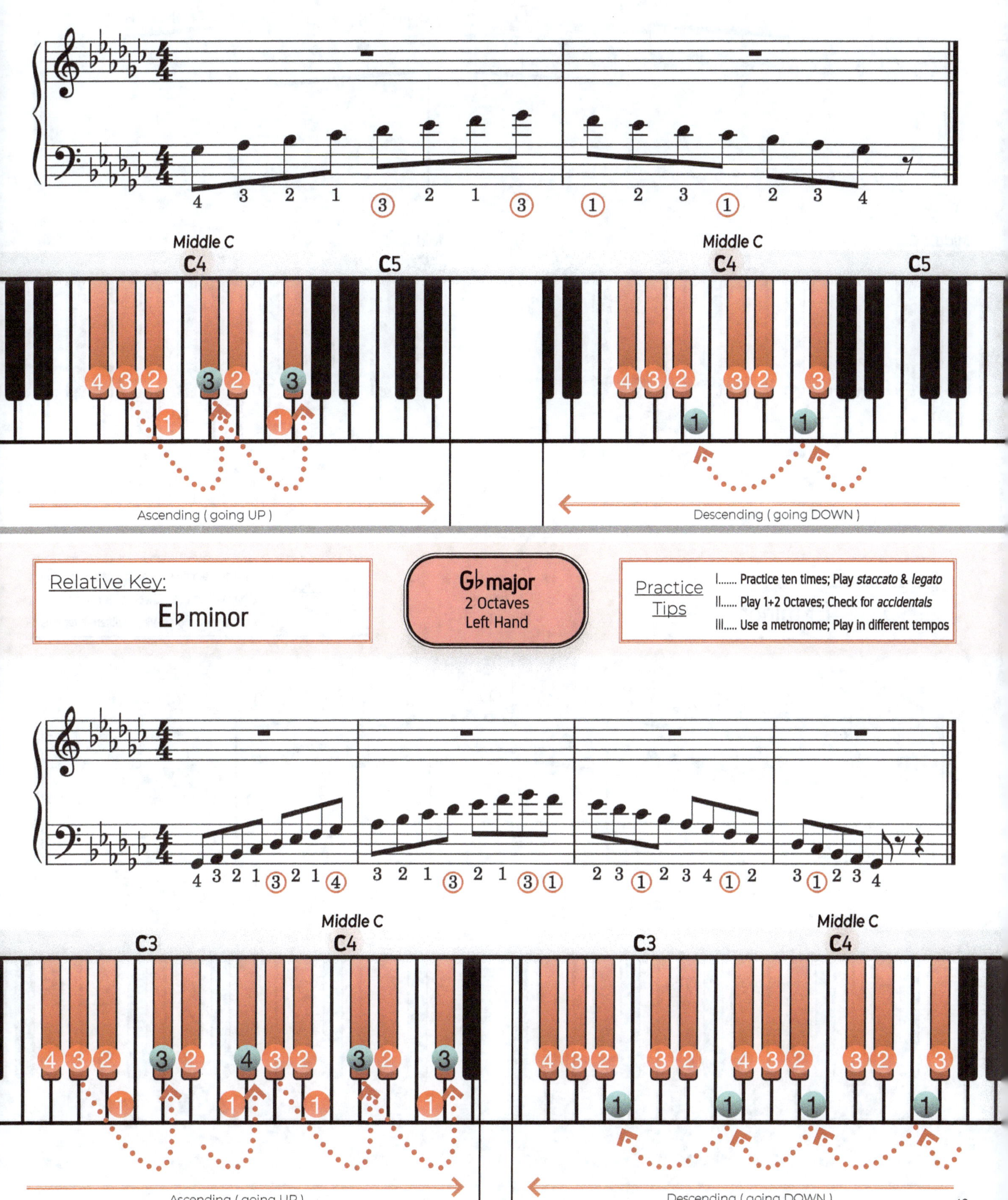

Notes of the Scale:
Gb, Ab, Bb, Cb, Db, Eb, F

Gb major
1 Octave
Left Hand

Key Signature:
Six Flats (Bb,Eb,Ab,Db,Gb,Cb)

Middle C
C4
C5
Middle C
C4
C5

4 3 2 3 2 3
1 1
Ascending (going UP)

4 3 2 3 2 3
1 1
Descending (going DOWN)

Relative Key:
Eb minor

Gb major
2 Octaves
Left Hand

Practice Tips
I....... Practice ten times; Play staccato & legato
II...... Play 1+2 Octaves; Check for accidentals
III..... Use a metronome; Play in different tempos

Middle C
C3
C4

Middle C
C3
C4

4 3 2 3 2 4 3 2 3 2 3
1 1 1 1
Ascending (going UP)

4 3 2 3 2 4 3 2 3 2 3
1 1 1 1
Descending (going DOWN)

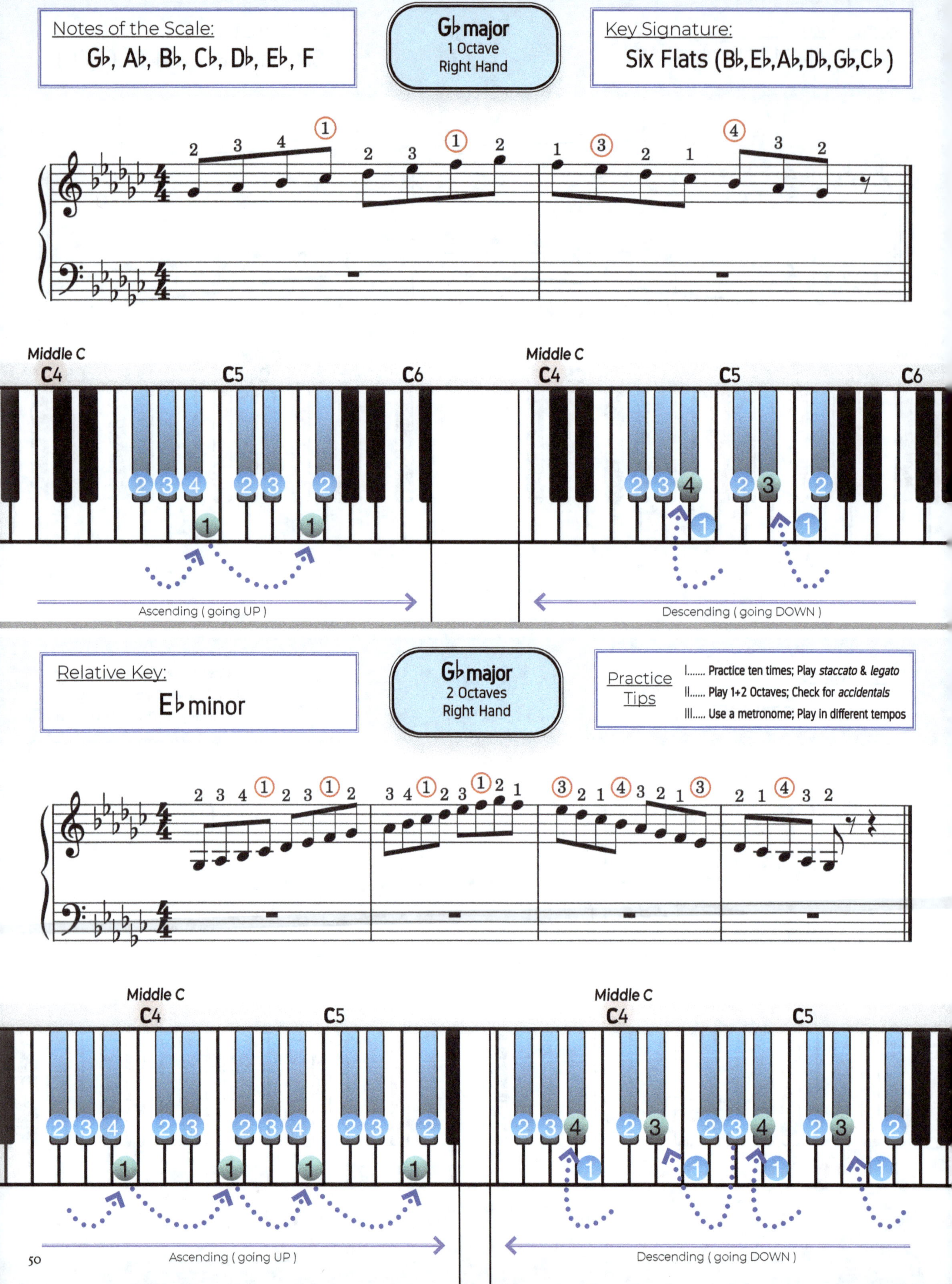

Notes of the Scale:
Gb, Ab, Bb, Cb, Db, Eb, F

Gb major
1 Octave
Right Hand

Key Signature:
Six Flats (Bb, Eb, Ab, Db, Gb, Cb)

Middle C
C4
C5
C6
2 3 4 1 2 3 1
Ascending (going UP)

Middle C
C4
C5
C6
2 3 4 2 3 2 1 1
Descending (going DOWN)

Relative Key:
Eb minor

Gb major
2 Octaves
Right Hand

Practice Tips
I........ Practice ten times; Play staccato & legato
II....... Play 1+2 Octaves; Check for accidentals
III...... Use a metronome; Play in different tempos

Middle C
C4
C5
Ascending (going UP)

Middle C
C4
C5
Descending (going DOWN)

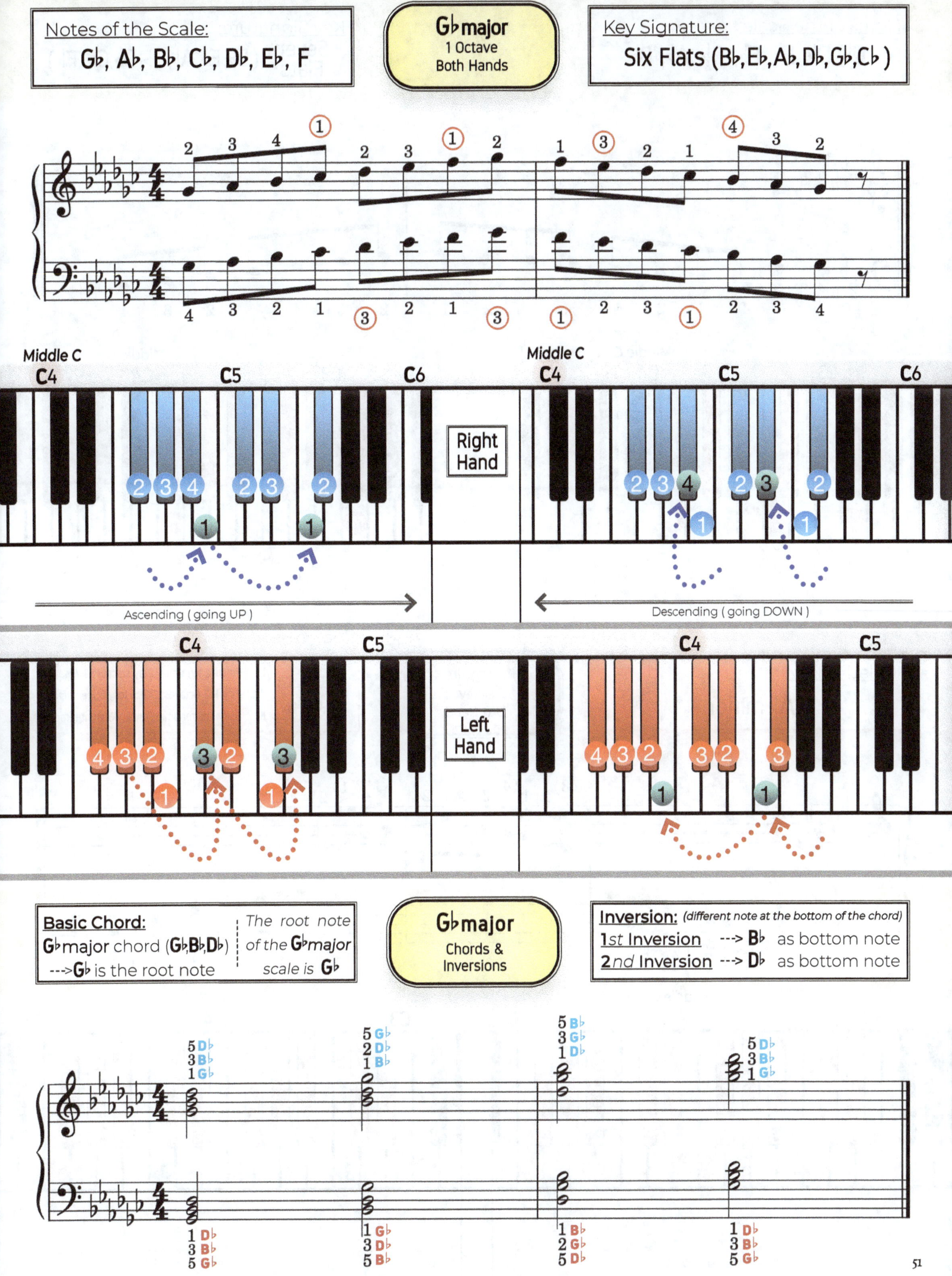

Notes of the Scale:
Gb, Ab, Bb, Cb, Db, Eb, F

Gb major
1 Octave
Both Hands

Key Signature:
Six Flats (Bb, Eb, Ab, Db, Gb, Cb)

Middle C
C4
C5
C6
Right Hand
2 3 4 2 3 2
1 1
Ascending (going UP)

Middle C
C4
C5
C6
2 3 4 2 3 2
1 1
Descending (going DOWN)

C4
C5
Left Hand
4 3 2 3 2 3
1 1
4 3 2 3 2 3
1 1

Basic Chord:
Gb major chord (Gb, Bb, Db)
--->Gb is the root note

The root note of the Gb major scale is Gb

Gb major
Chords &
Inversions

Inversion: (different note at the bottom of the chord)
1st Inversion ---> Bb as bottom note
2nd Inversion ---> Db as bottom note

5 Db
3 Bb
1 Gb

5 Gb
2 Db
1 Bb

5 Bb
3 Gb
1 Db

5 Db
3 Bb
1 Gb

1 Db
3 Bb
5 Gb

1 Gb
3 Db
5 Bb

1 Bb
2 Gb
5 Db

1 Db
3 Bb
5 Gb

Notes of the Scale:
Cb, Db, Eb, Fb, Gb, Ab, Bb

Cb major
1 Octave
Left Hand

Key Signature:
Seven Flats (Bb, Eb, Ab, Db, Gb, Cb ,Fb)

Middle C
C4
C3

4 3 2 1 4 3 2 1 2 3 4 1 2 3 4
3 2 4 3 2 3 2 4 3 2
4 1 1 1 4 1 1

Ascending (going UP)
Descending (going DOWN)

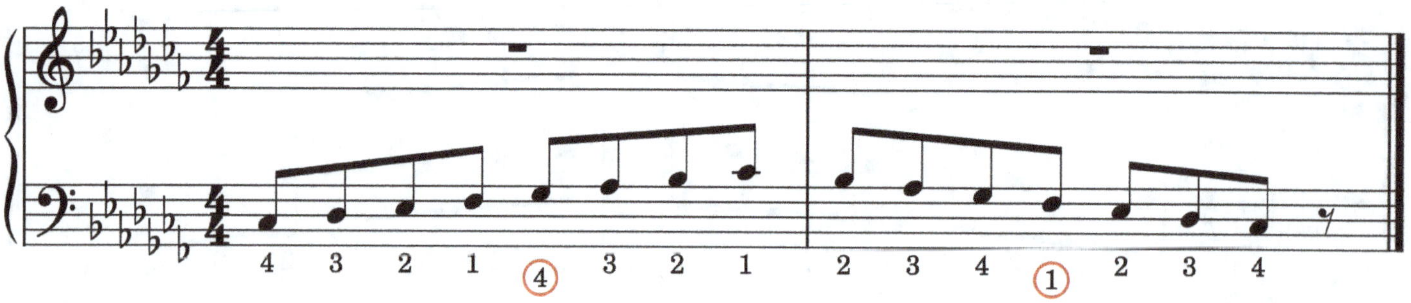

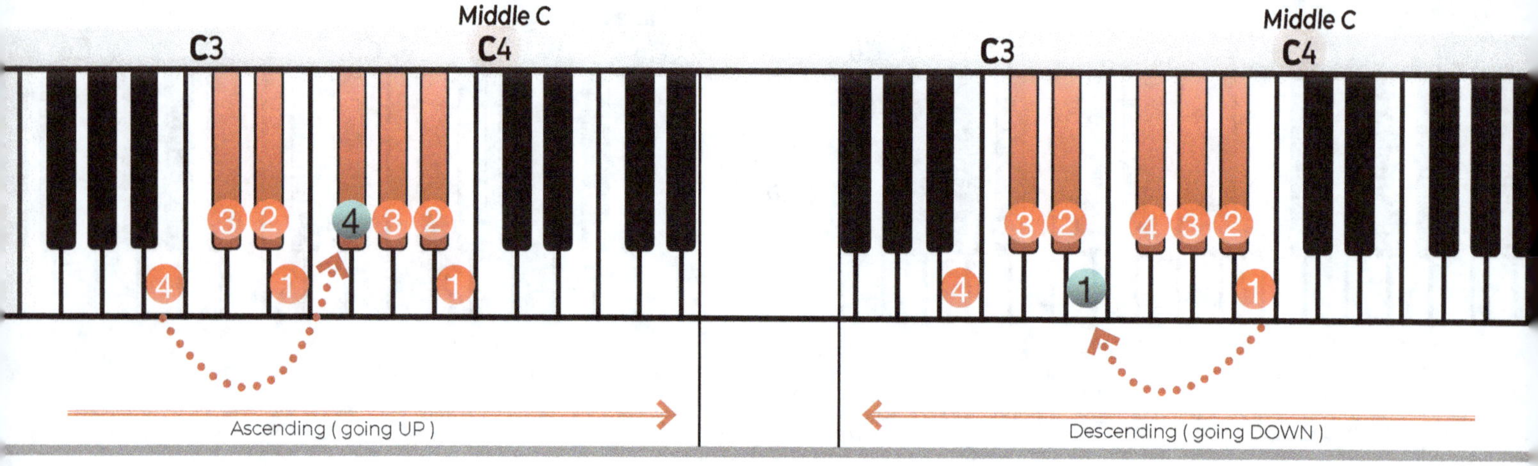

Relative Key:
Ab minor

Cb major
2 Octaves
Left Hand

Practice Tips
I....... Practice ten times; Play staccato & legato
II...... Play 1+2 Octaves; Check for accidentals
III..... Use a metronome; Play in different tempos

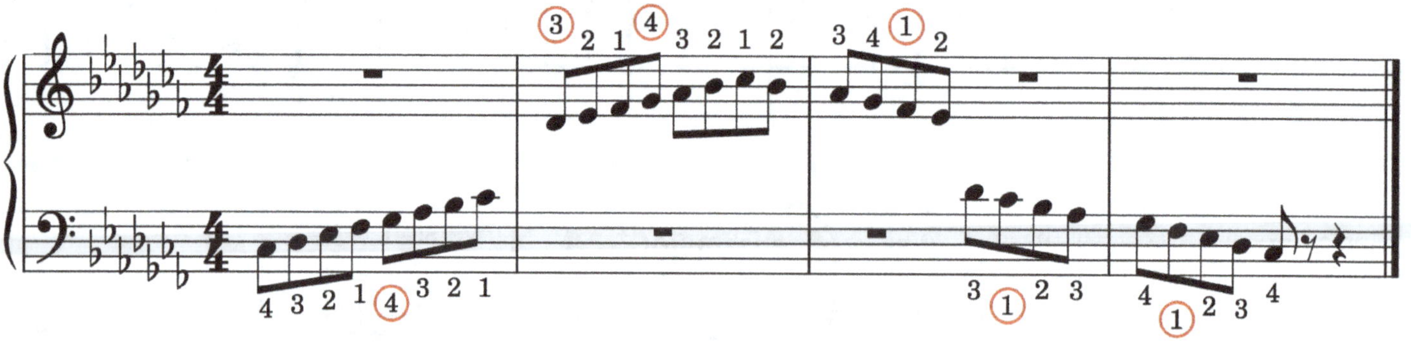

3 2 1 4 3 2 1 2 3 4 1 2
4 3 2 1 4 3 2 1 3 1 2 3 4 1 2 3 4

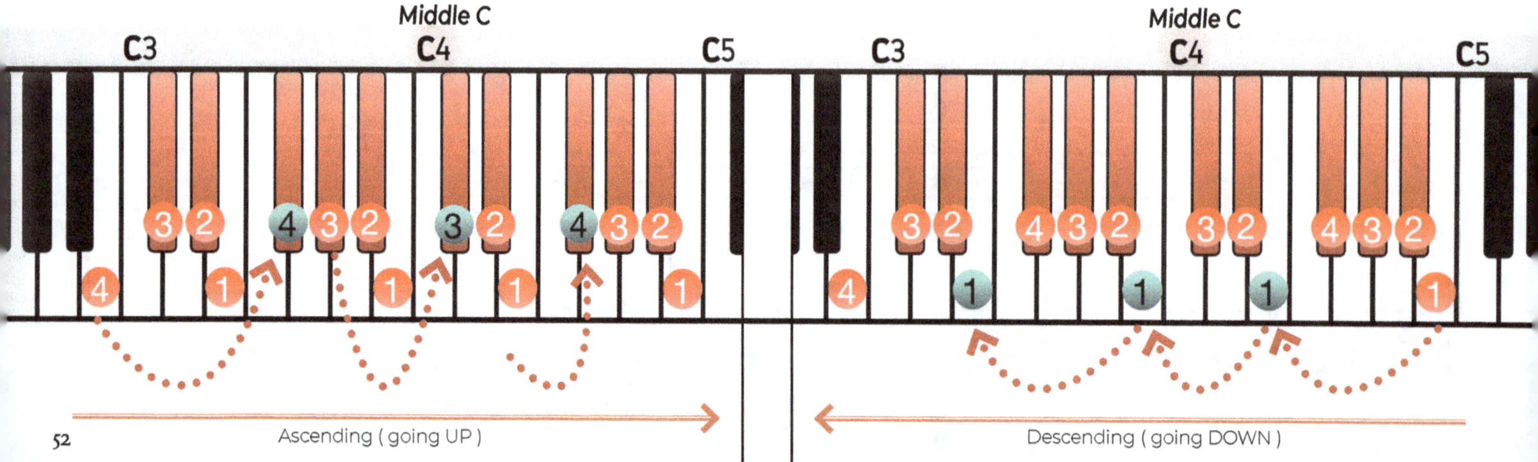

Middle C
C4
C3 C5
Middle C
C4
C3 C5

3 2 4 3 2 3 2 4 3 2 3 2 4 3 2 3 2 4 3 2
4 1 1 1 4 1 1 4 1 1 1 1

Ascending (going UP)
Descending (going DOWN)

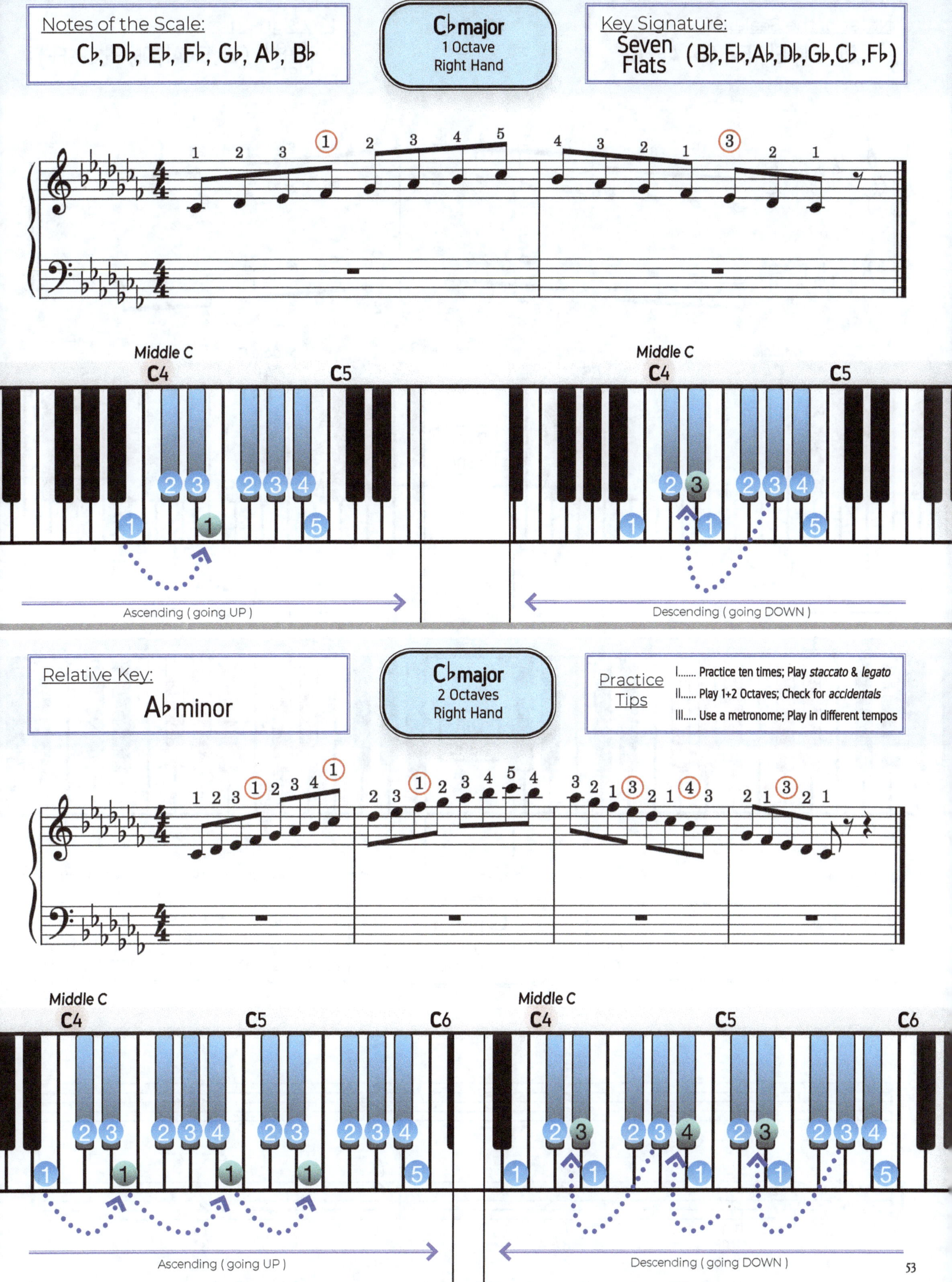

Notes of the Scale:
Cb, Db, Eb, Fb, Gb, Ab, Bb
Cb major
1 Octave
Right Hand
Key Signature:
Seven Flats (Bb, Eb, Ab, Db, Gb, Cb, Fb)
Middle C
C4
C5
Ascending (going UP)
Descending (going DOWN)
Relative Key:
Ab minor
Cb major
2 Octaves
Right Hand
Practice Tips
I....... Practice ten times; Play staccato & legato
II...... Play 1+2 Octaves; Check for accidentals
III..... Use a metronome; Play in different tempos
Middle C
C4
C5
C6
Ascending (going UP)
Descending (going DOWN)
53

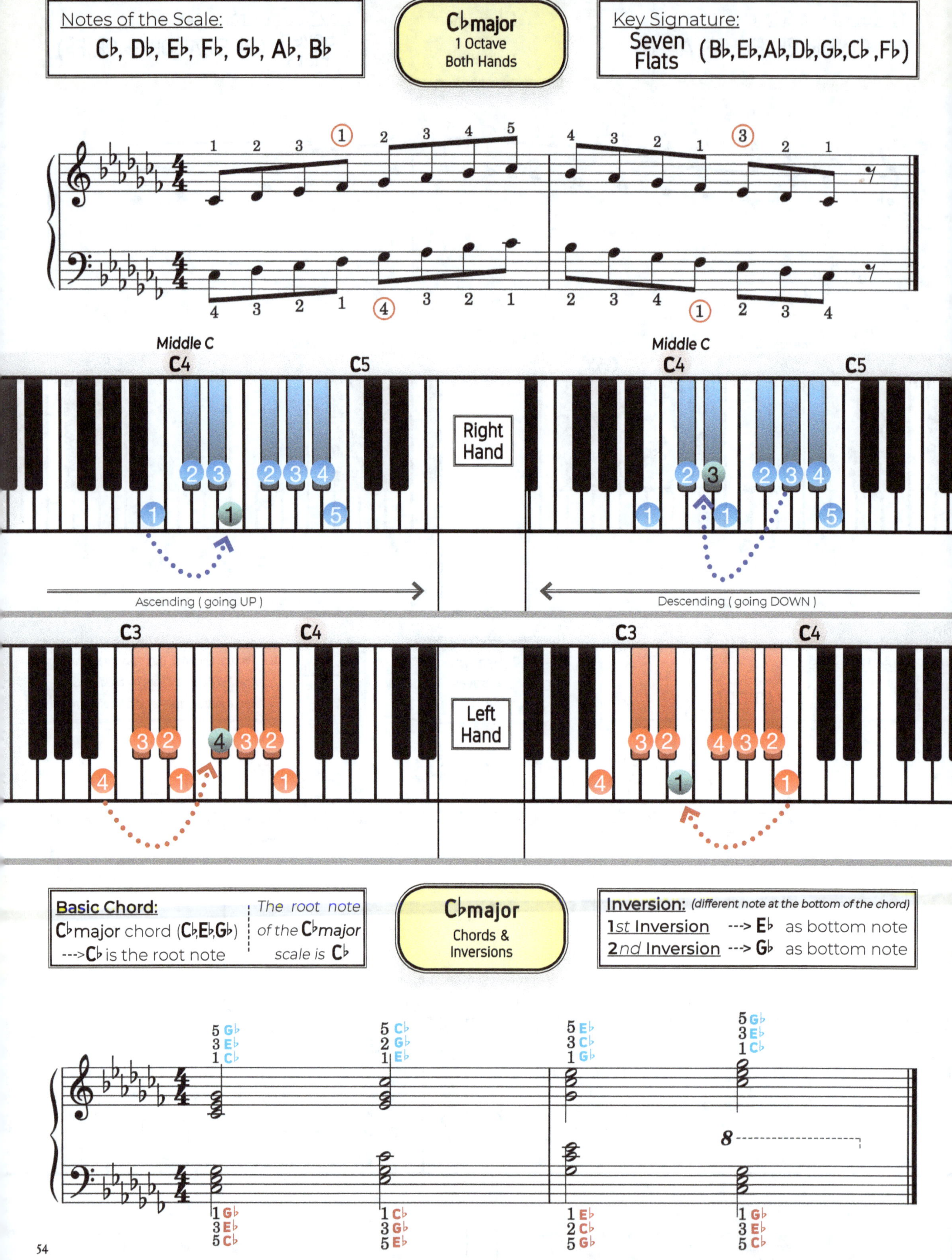

Notes of the Scale:
Cb, Db, Eb, Fb, Gb, Ab, Bb

Cb major
1 Octave
Both Hands

Key Signature:
Seven Flats (Bb, Eb, Ab, Db, Gb, Cb, Fb)

Middle C
C4
C5
Right Hand
Ascending (going UP)
Descending (going DOWN)
Middle C
C4
C5

C3
C4
Left Hand
C3
C4

Basic Chord:
Cb major chord (Cb, Eb, Gb)
---> Cb is the root note
The root note of the Cb major scale is Cb

Cb major
Chords & Inversions

Inversion: (different note at the bottom of the chord)
1st Inversion ---> Eb as bottom note
2nd Inversion ---> Gb as bottom note

5 Gb
3 Eb
1 Cb

5 Cb
2 Gb
1 Eb

5 Eb
3 Cb
1 Gb

5 Gb
3 Eb
1 Cb

1 Gb
3 Eb
5 Cb

1 Cb
3 Gb
5 Eb

1 Eb
2 Cb
5 Gb

1 Gb
3 Eb
5 Cb

MINOR SCALES

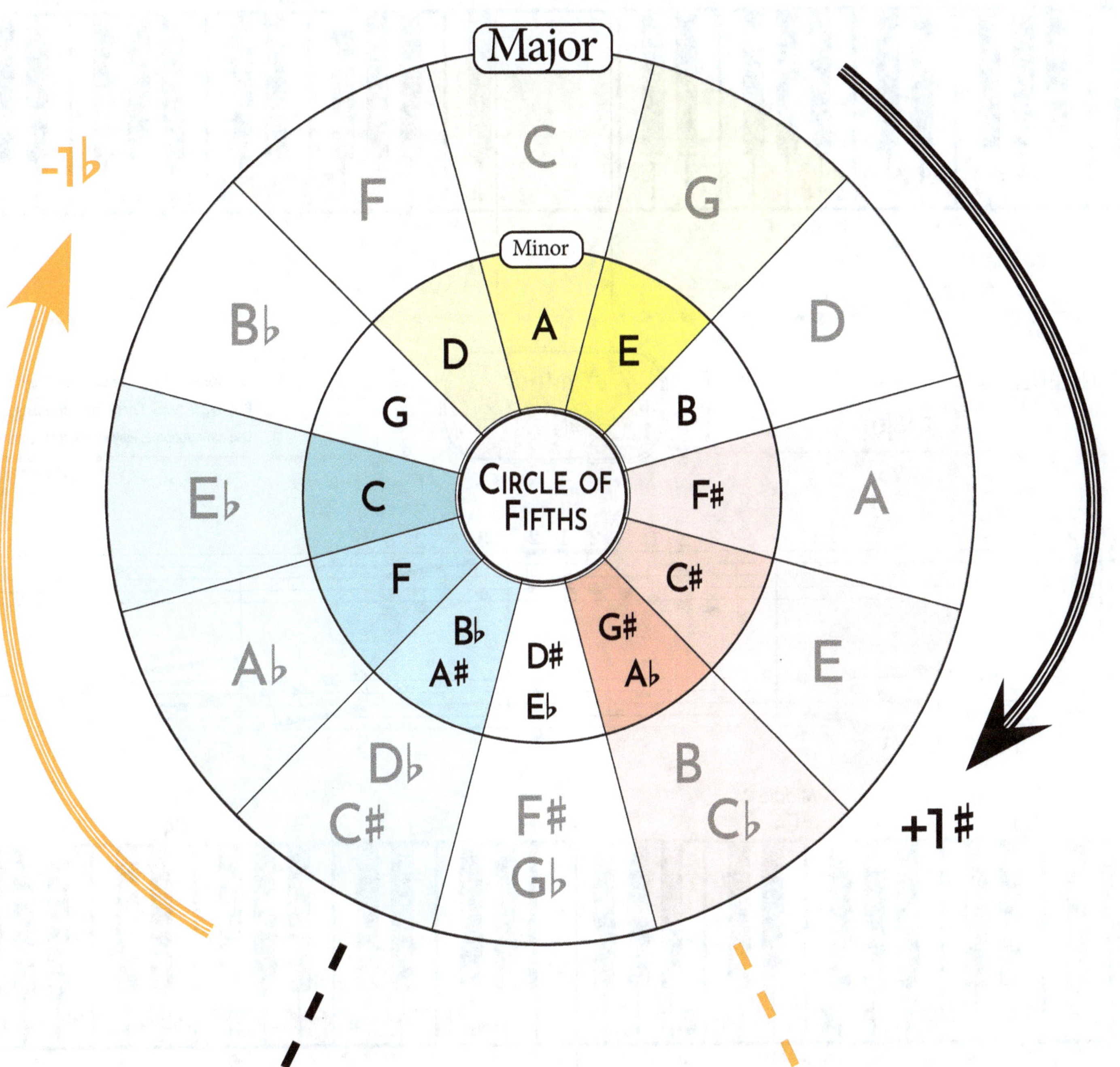

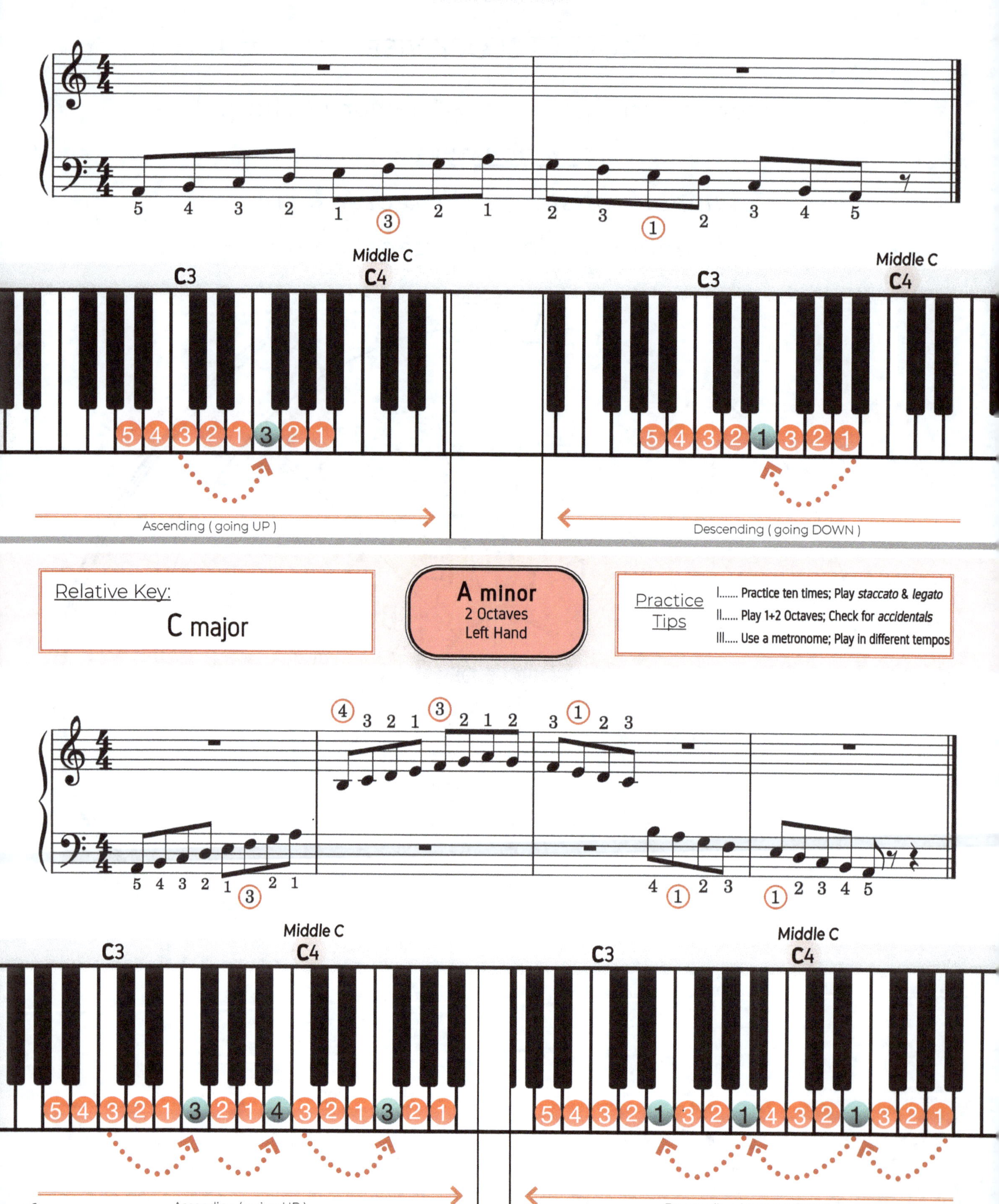

Notes of the Scale:
A, B, C, D, E, F, G

A minor
1 Octave
Left Hand

Key Signature:
No Flats / No Sharps

C3
Middle C
C4
Middle C
C4

5 4 3 2 1 3 2 1
5 4 3 2 1 3 2 1

Ascending (going UP)
Descending (going DOWN)

Relative Key:
C major

A minor
2 Octaves
Left Hand

Practice Tips
I....... Practice ten times; Play staccato & legato
II..... Play 1+2 Octaves; Check for accidentals
III..... Use a metronome; Play in different tempos

4 3 2 1 3 2 1 2 3 1 2 3
5 4 3 2 1 3 2 1
4 1 2 3 1 2 3 4 5

C3
Middle C
C4
C3
Middle C
C4

5 4 3 2 1 3 2 1 4 3 2 1 3 2 1
5 4 3 2 1 3 2 1 4 3 2 1 3 2 1

Ascending (going UP)
Descending (going DOWN)

Notes of the Scale:
A, B, C, D, E, F, G

A minor
1 Octave
Right Hand

Key Signature:
No Flats / No Sharps

1 2 3 1 2 3 4 5
4 3 2 1 3 2 1

Middle C
C4
C5
1 2 3 1 2 3 4 5
Ascending (going UP)
Middle C
C4
C5
1 2 3 1 2 3 4 5
Descending (going DOWN)

Relative Key:
C major

A minor
2 Octaves
Right Hand

Practice Tips
I....... Practice ten times; Play staccato & legato
II...... Play 1+2 Octaves; Check for accidentals
III..... Use a metronome; Play in different tempos

1 2 3 1 2 3 4 1 2 3 1 2 3 4 5 4
3 2 1 3 2 1 4 3 2 1 3 2 1

Middle C
C4
C5
1 2 3 1 2 3 4 1 2 3 1 2 3 4 5
Ascending (going UP)
Middle C
C4
C5
1 2 3 1 2 3 4 1 2 3 1 2 3 4 5
Descending (going DOWN)

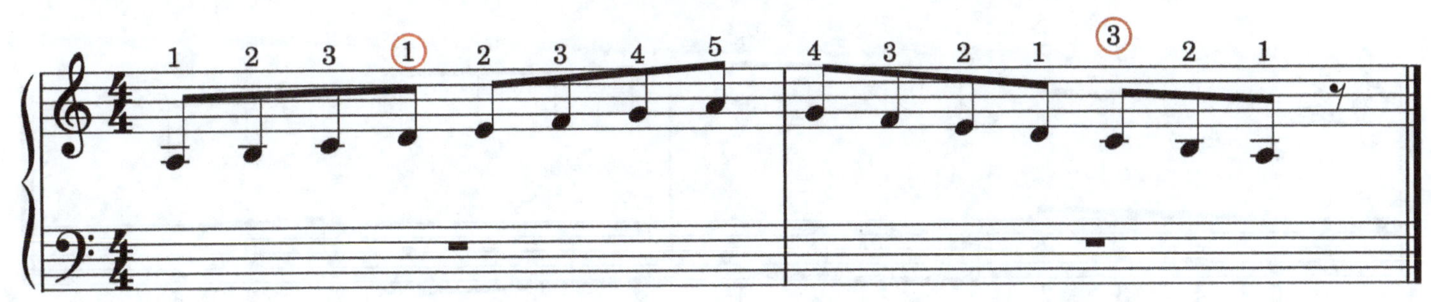

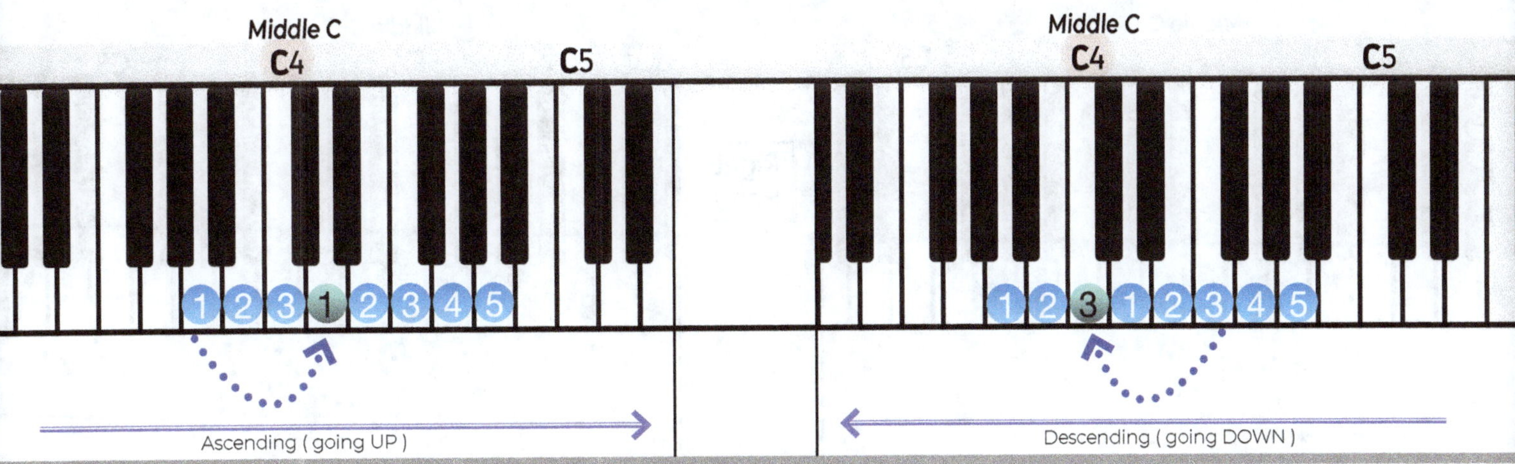

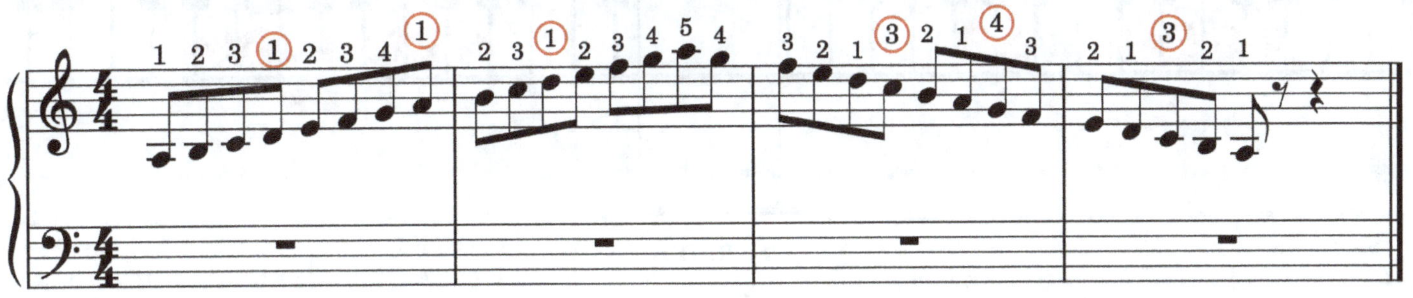

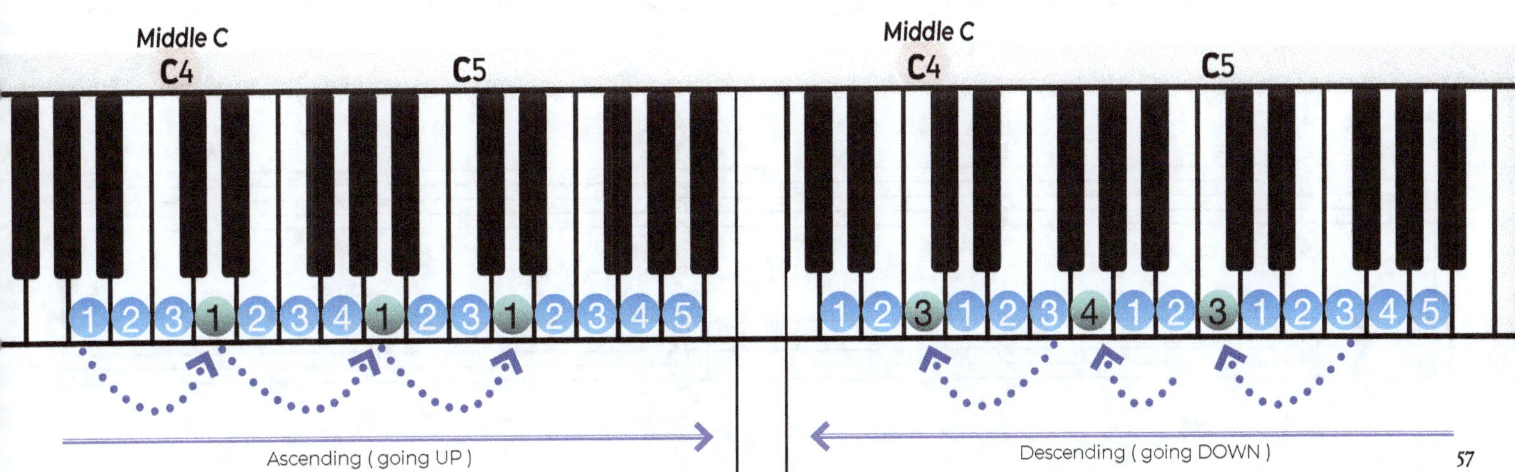

57

Notes of the Scale:
A, B, C, D, E, F, G

A minor
1 Octave
Both Hands

Key Signature:
No Flats / No Sharps

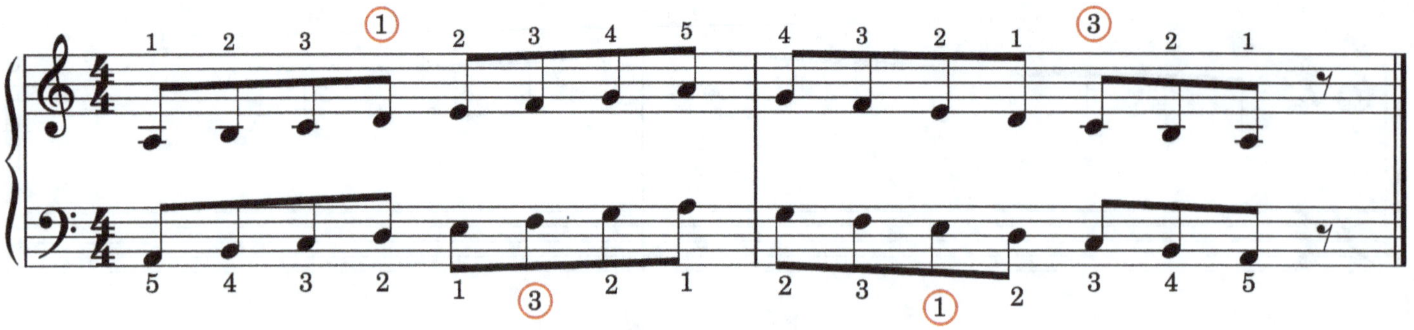

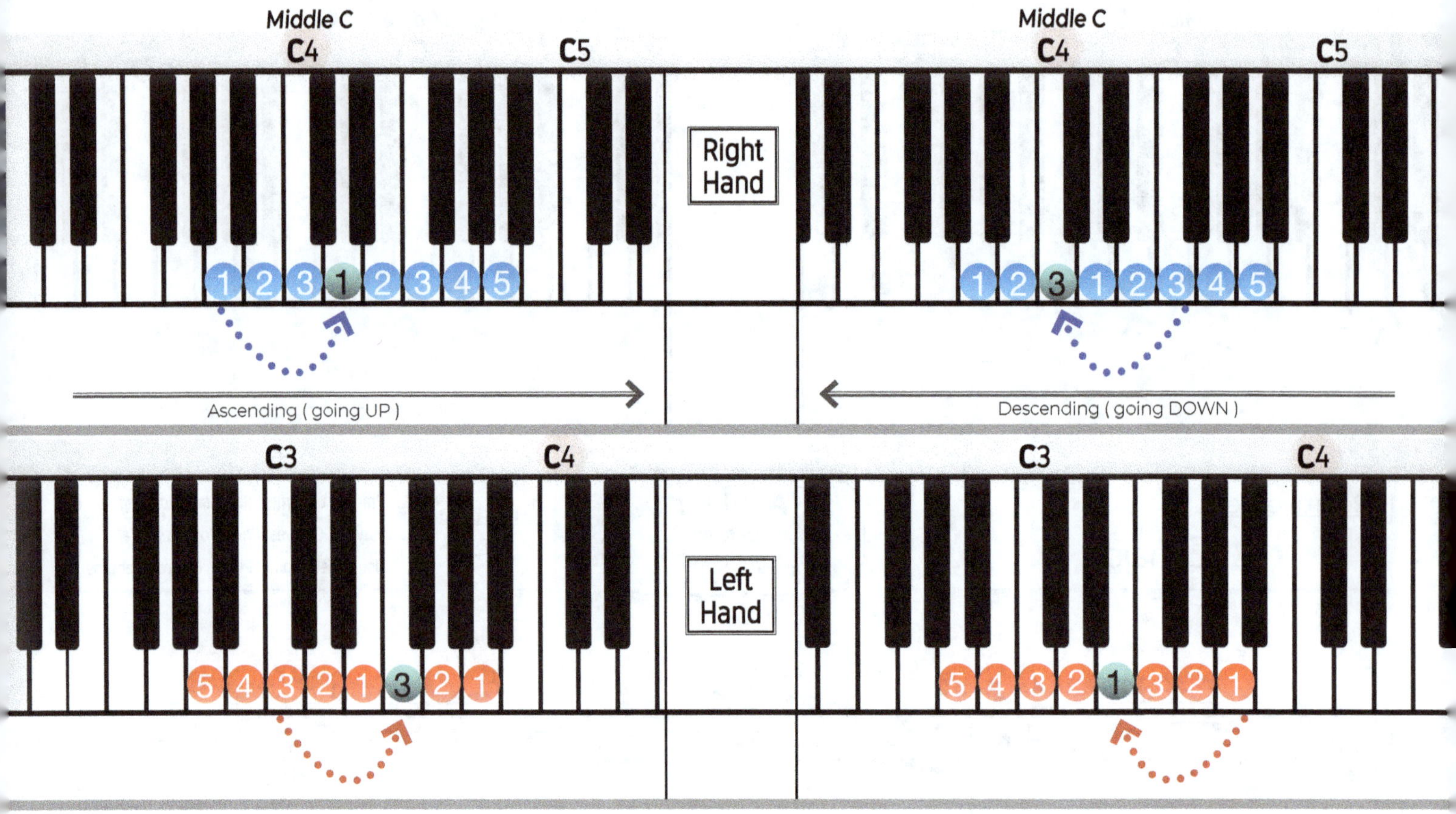

Middle C
C4   C5

Right
Hand

Ascending (going UP)

Descending (going DOWN)

Middle C
C4   C5

C3   C4

Left
Hand

C3   C4

Basic Chord:
A minor chord (A, C, E)
--->A is the root note

The root note
of the A minor
scale is A

A minor
Chords &
Inversions

Inversion: (different note at the bottom of the chord)
1st Inversion ---> C as bottom note
2nd Inversion ---> E as bottom note

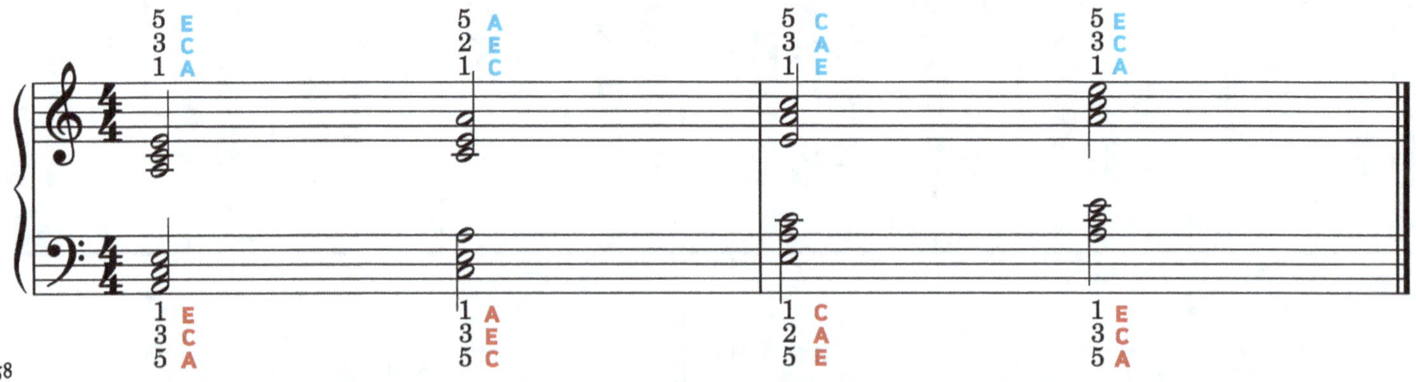

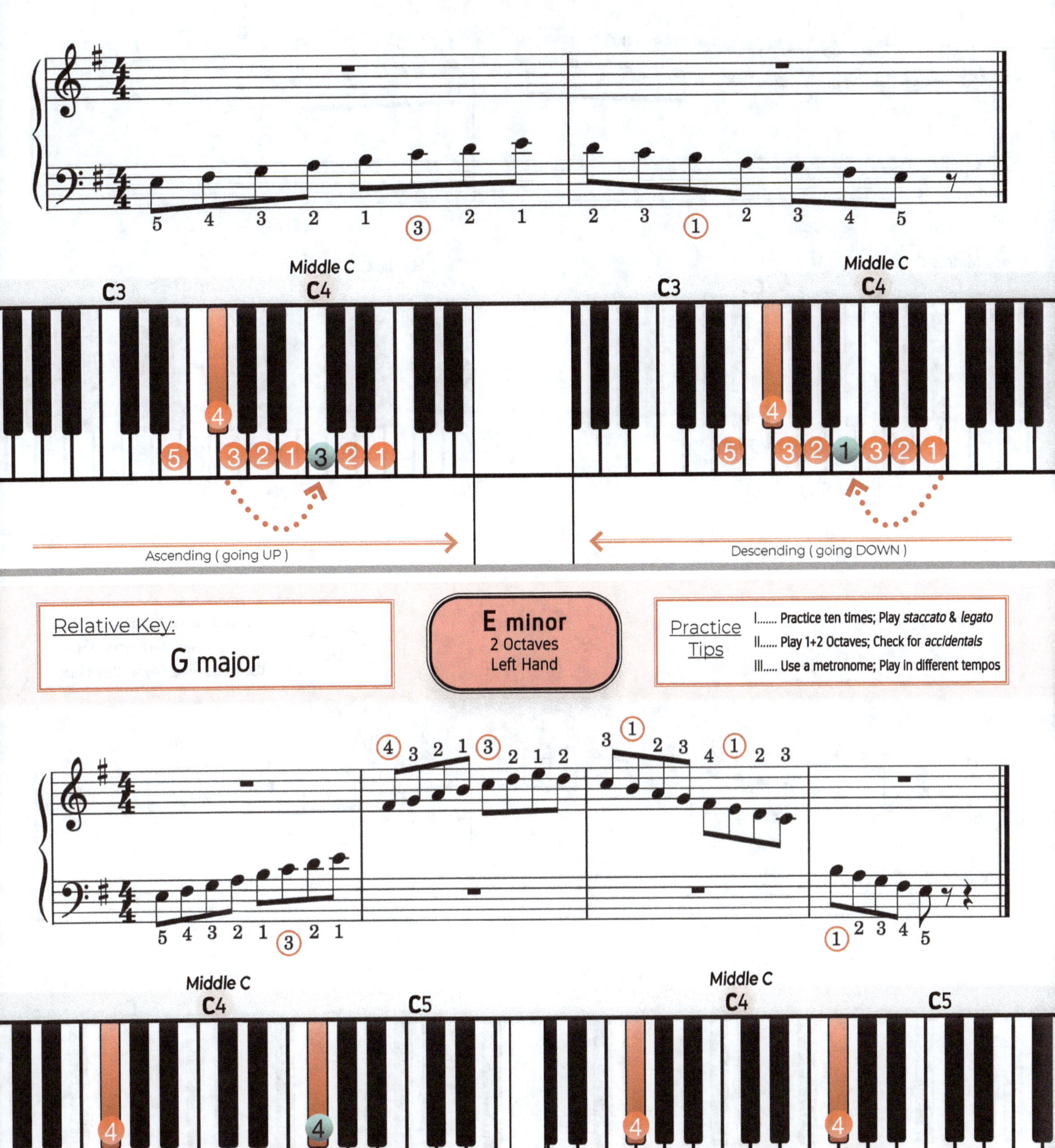

Notes of the Scale:
E, F#, G, A, B, C, D
E minor
1 Octave
Left Hand
Key Signature:
One Sharp (F#)
5 4 3 2 1 3 2 1
2 3 1 2 3 4 5
C3
Middle C
C4
C3
Middle C
C4
5 3 2 1 3 2 1
4
5 3 2 1 3 2 1
4
Ascending (going UP)
Descending (going DOWN)
Relative Key:
G major
E minor
2 Octaves
Left Hand
Practice Tips
I....... Practice ten times; Play staccato & legato
II...... Play 1+2 Octaves; Check for accidentals
III..... Use a metronome; Play in different tempos
4 3 2 1 3 2 1 2
3 1 2 3 4 1 2 3
5 4 3 2 1 3 2 1
1 2 3 4 5
Middle C
C4
C5
Middle C
C4
C5
5 3 2 1 3 2 1 3 2 1 3 2 1
4
4
5 3 2 1 3 2 1 3 2 1 3 2 1
4
4
Ascending (going UP)
Descending (going DOWN)

Notes of the Scale:
E, F#, G, A, B, C, D

E minor
1 Octave
Right Hand

Key Signature:
One Sharp (F#)

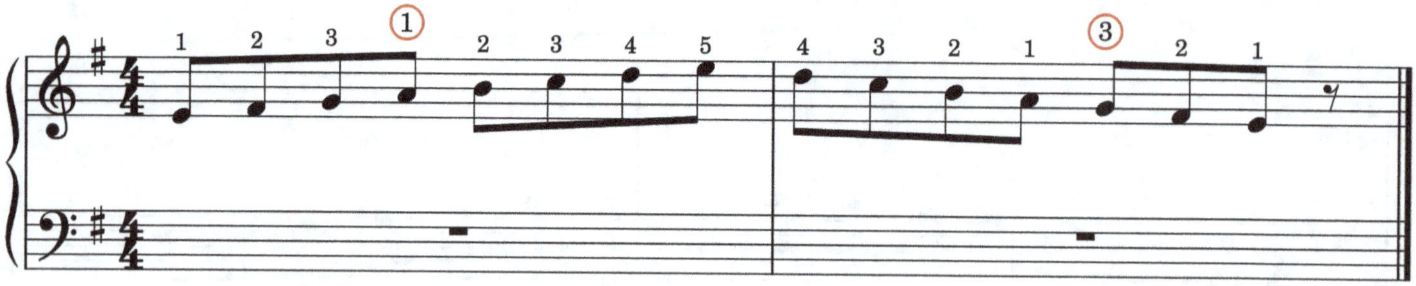

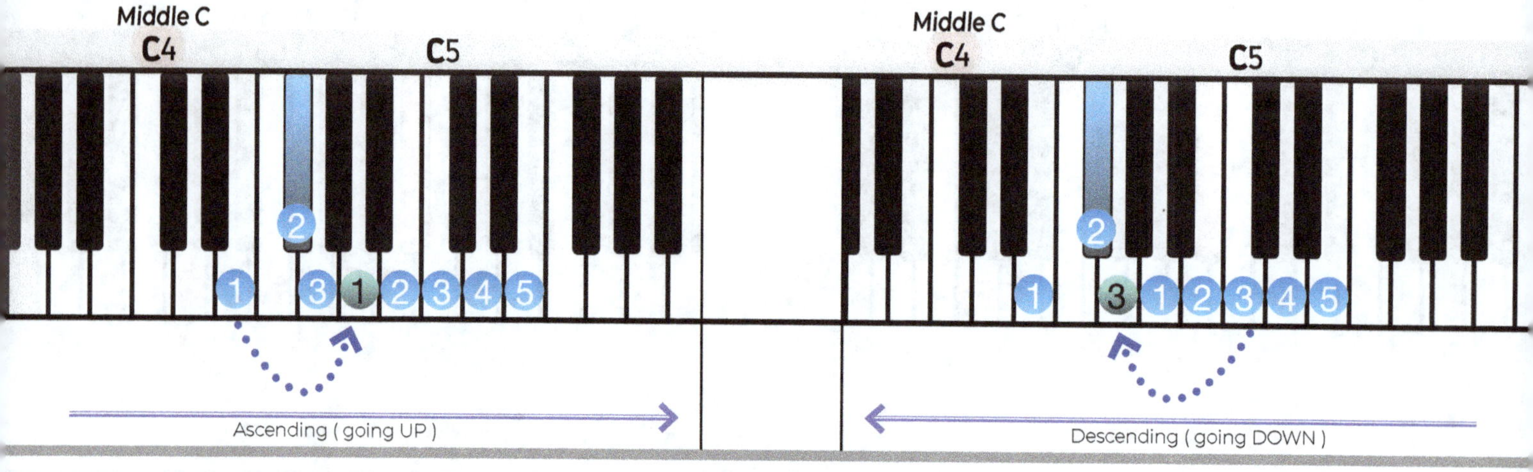

Middle C
C4
C5

2
1 3 1 2 3 4 5

Ascending (going UP)

Middle C
C4
C5

2
1 3 1 2 3 4 5

Descending (going DOWN)

Relative Key:
G major

E minor
2 Octaves
Right Hand

Practice Tips
I....... Practice ten times; Play staccato & legato
II...... Play 1+2 Octaves; Check for accidentals
III..... Use a metronome; Play in different tempos

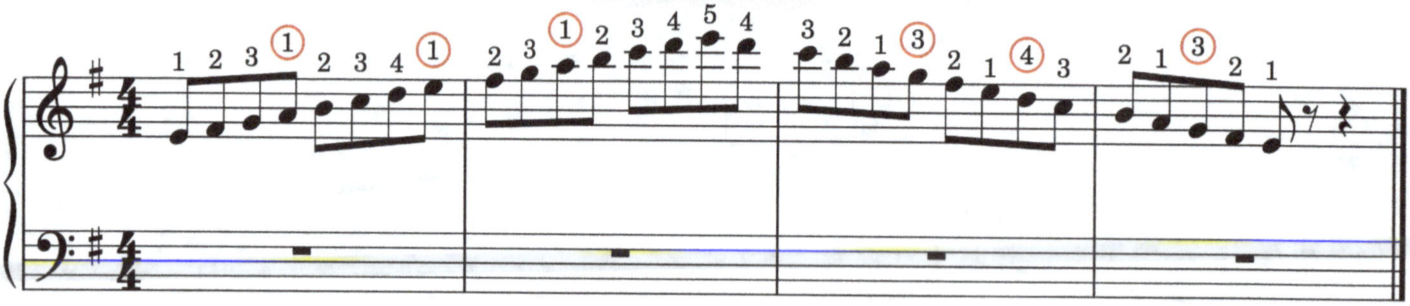

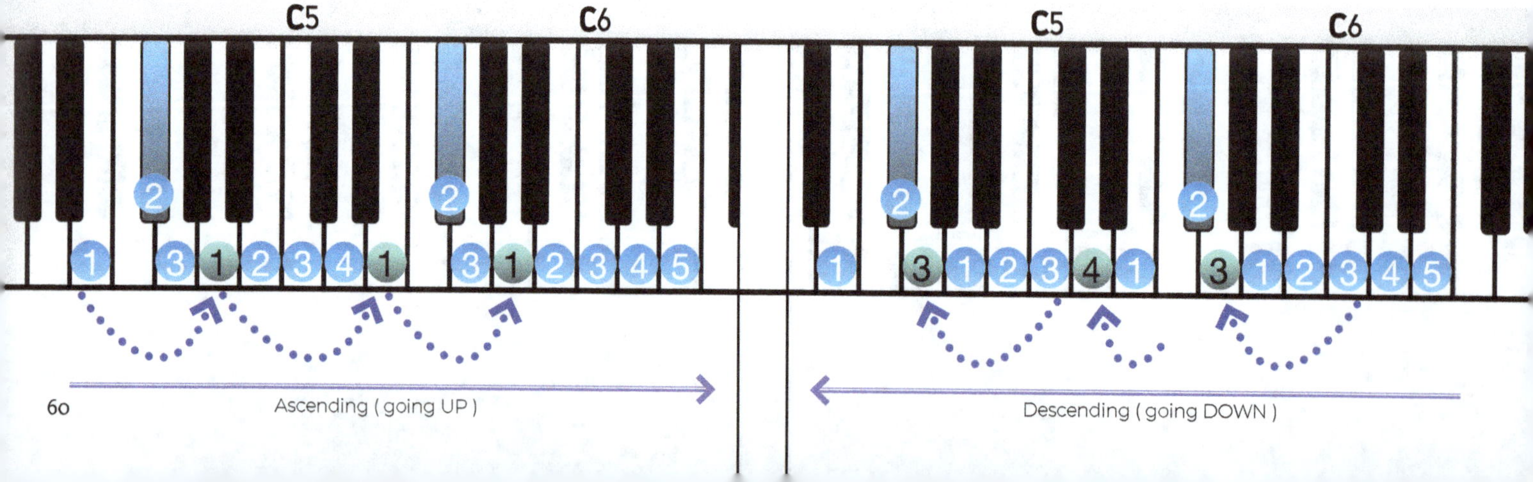

C5
C6

2
1 3 1 2 3 4 1 3 1 2 3 4 5

2

Ascending (going UP)

C5
C6

2
1 3 1 2 3 4 1 3 1 2 3 4 5

2

Descending (going DOWN)

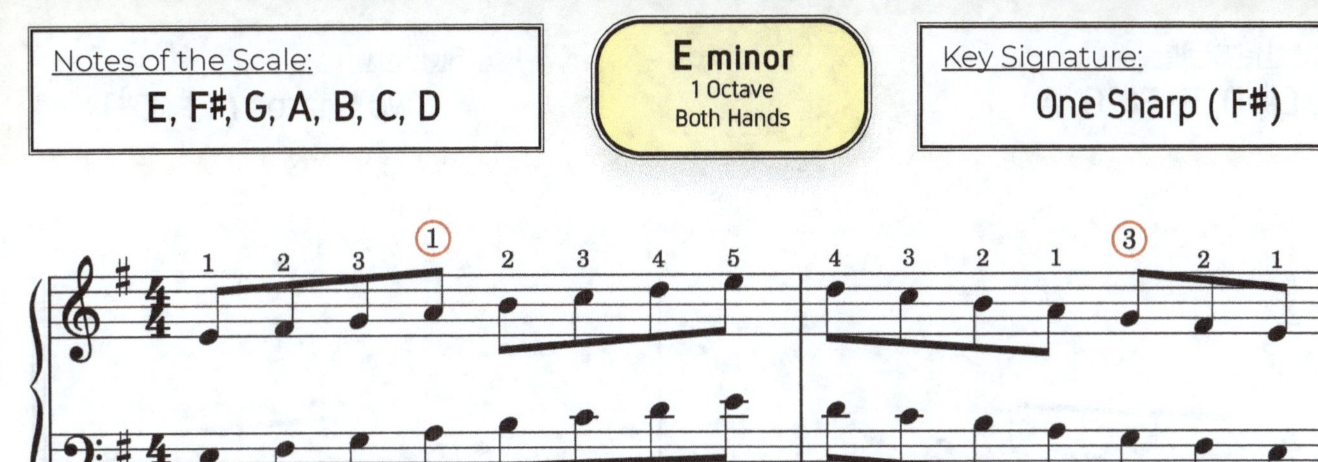

Notes of the Scale:
E, F#, G, A, B, C, D
E minor
1 Octave
Both Hands
Key Signature:
One Sharp (F#)
Middle C
C4
C5
Middle C
C4
C5

Ascending (going UP)
Descending (going DOWN)
C3
C4
C3
C4
Left
Hand

Basic Chord:
E minor chord (E, G, B)
---> E is the root note
The root note
of the E minor
scale is E
E minor
Chords &
Inversions
Inversion: (different note at the bottom of the chord)
1st Inversion ---> G as bottom note
2nd Inversion ---> B as bottom note

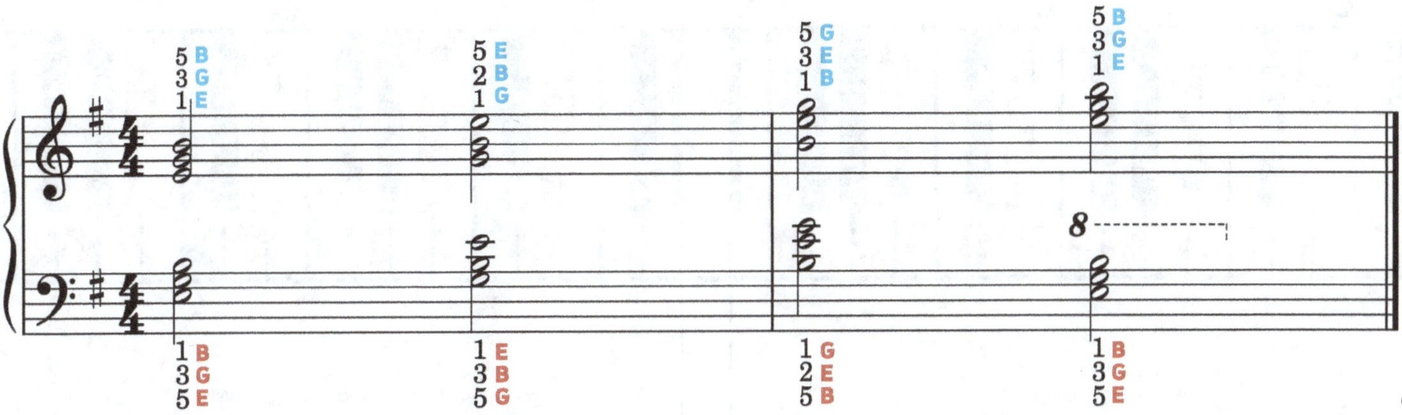

Notes of the Scale:

B, C#, D, E, F#, G, A

B minor
1 Octave
Left Hand

Key Signature:

Two Sharps (F#, C#)

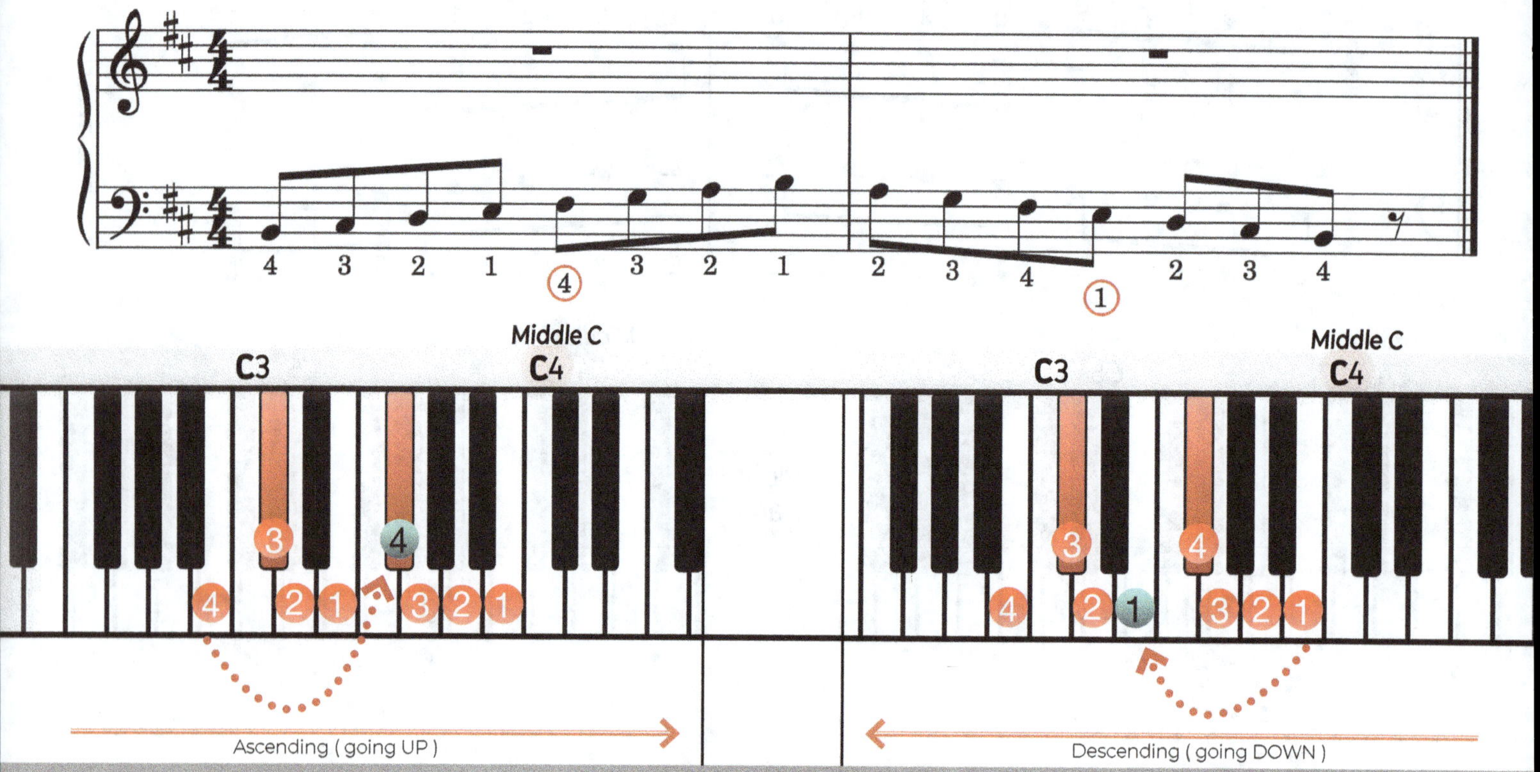

C3   Middle C
      C4

Ascending (going UP)

Descending (going DOWN)

Relative Key:

D major

B minor
2 Octaves
Left Hand

Practice Tips

I....... Practice ten times; Play *staccato* & *legato*

II...... Play 1+2 Octaves; Check for *accidentals*

III..... Use a metronome; Play in different tempos

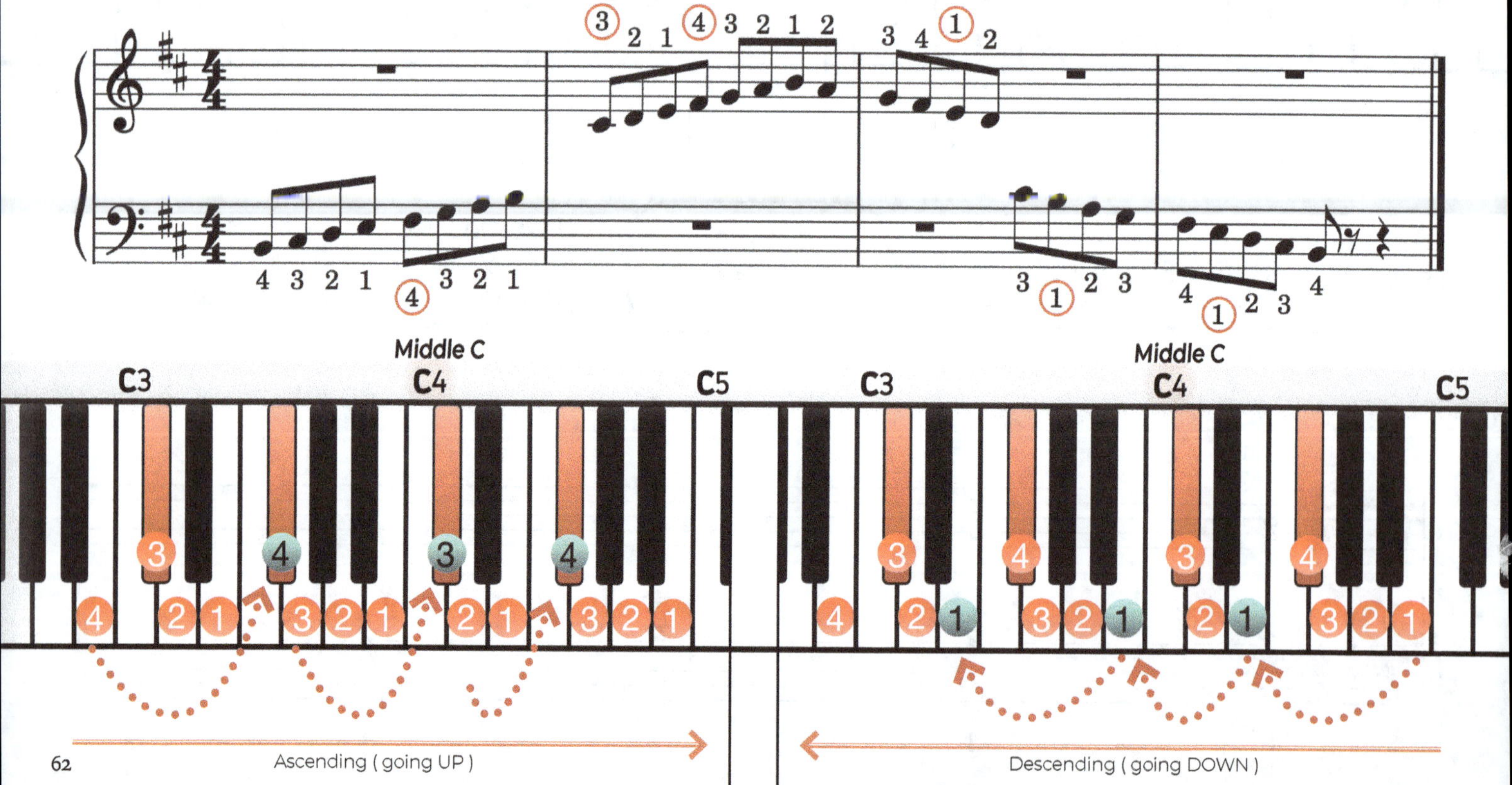

C3   Middle C   C5   C3   Middle C   C5
      C4   C4

Ascending (going UP)

Descending (going DOWN)

63

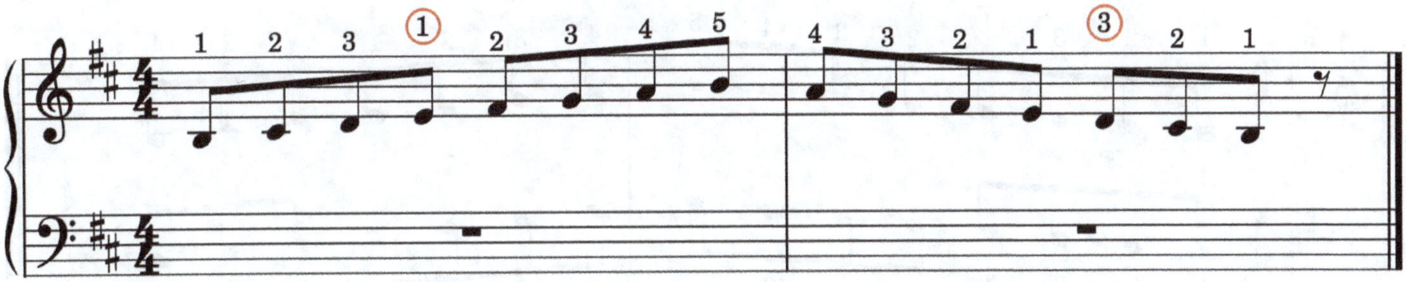

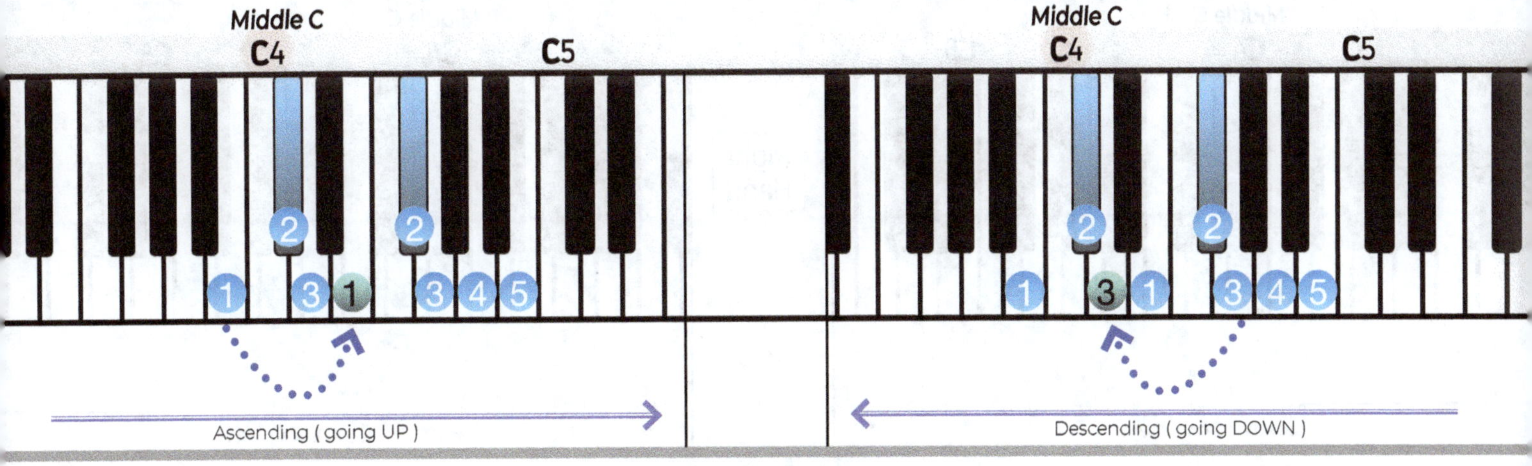

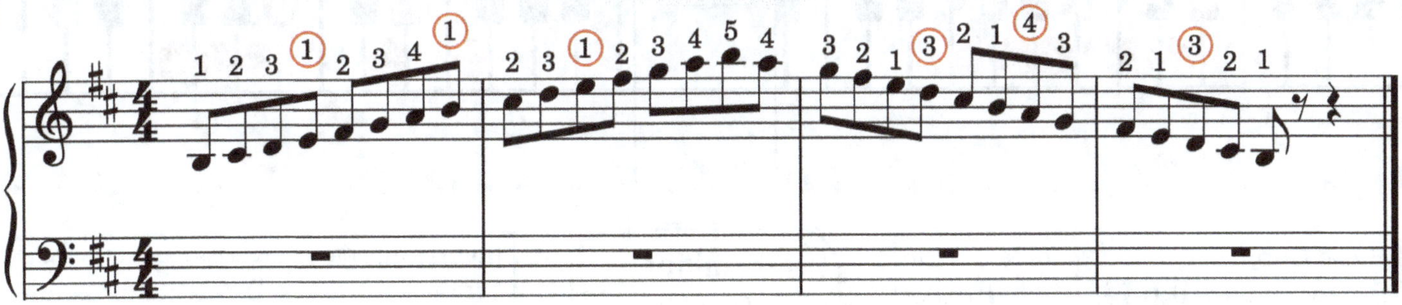

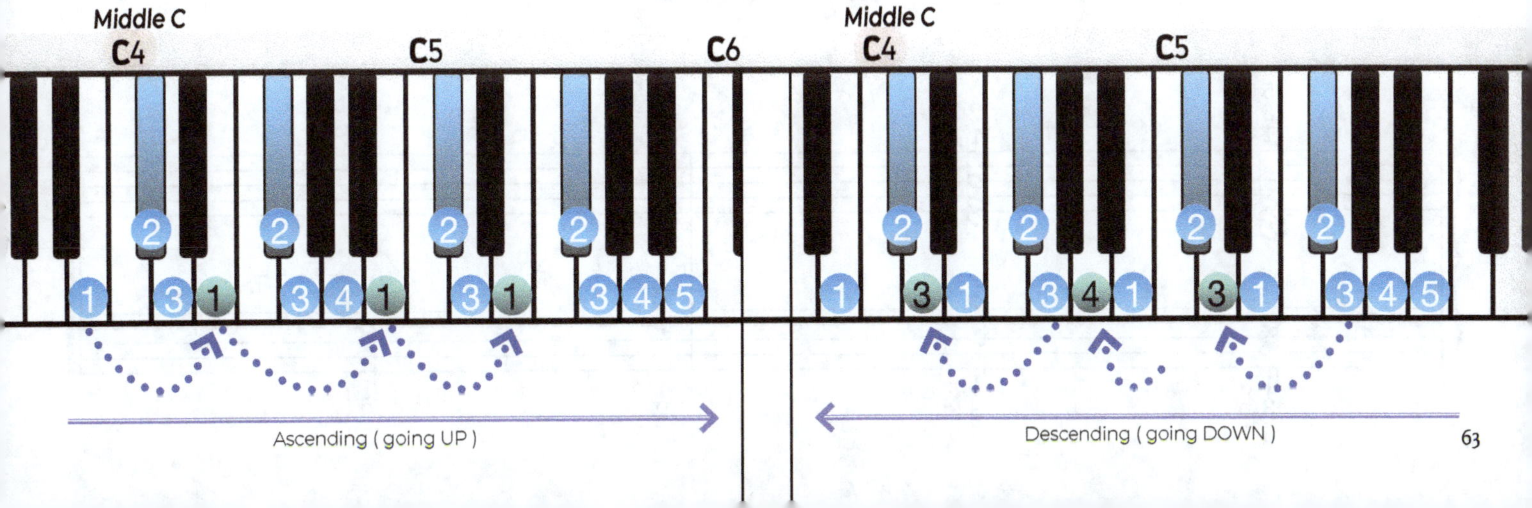

Notes of the Scale:
B, C#, D, E, F#, G, A
B minor
1 Octave
Both Hands
Key Signature:
Two Sharps (F#, C#)

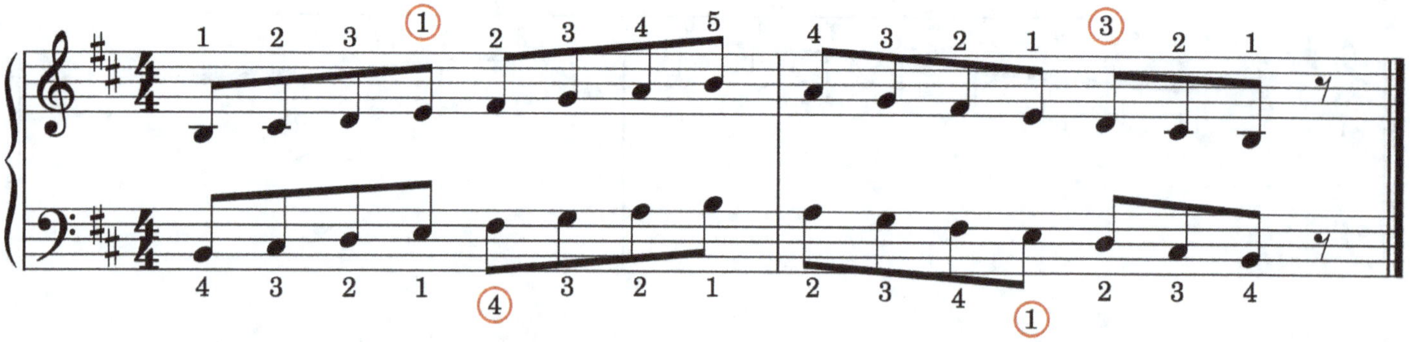

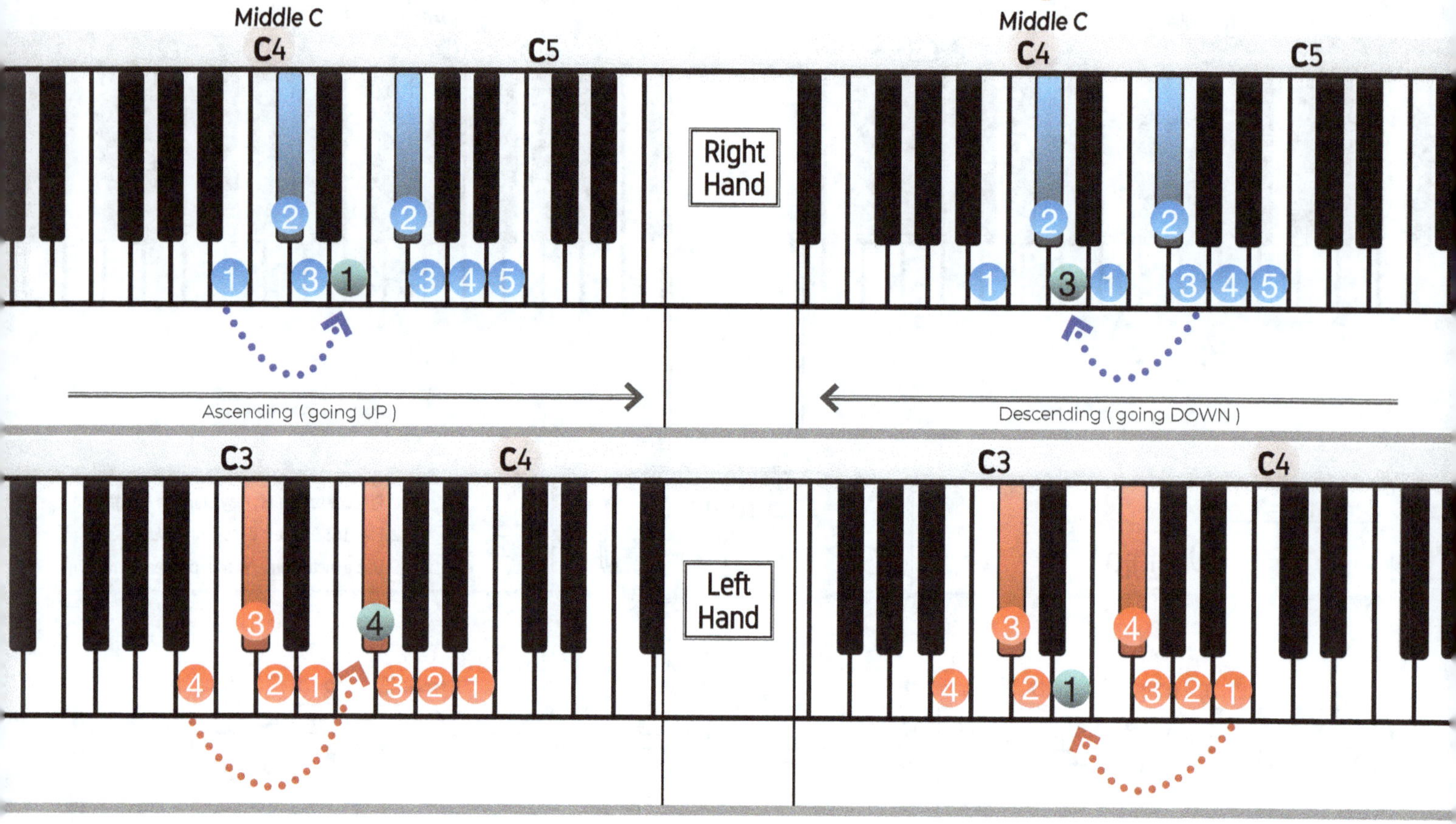

1 2 3 1 2 3 4 5
4 3 2 1 3 2 1
4 3 2 1
2 3 4 1 2 3 4

Middle C
C4
C5
Right
Hand
Middle C
C4
C5

2 2
1 3 1 3 4 5
Ascending (going UP)
2 2
1 3 1 3 4 5
Descending (going DOWN)

C3
C4
Left
Hand
C3
C4

3 4
4 2 1 3 2 1
3 4
4 2 1 3 2 1

Basic Chord:
B minor chord (B, D, F#)
--->B is the root note
The root note of the B minor scale is B
B minor
Chords & Inversions
Inversion: (different note at the bottom of the chord)
1st Inversion ---> D as bottom note
2nd Inversion ---> F# as bottom note

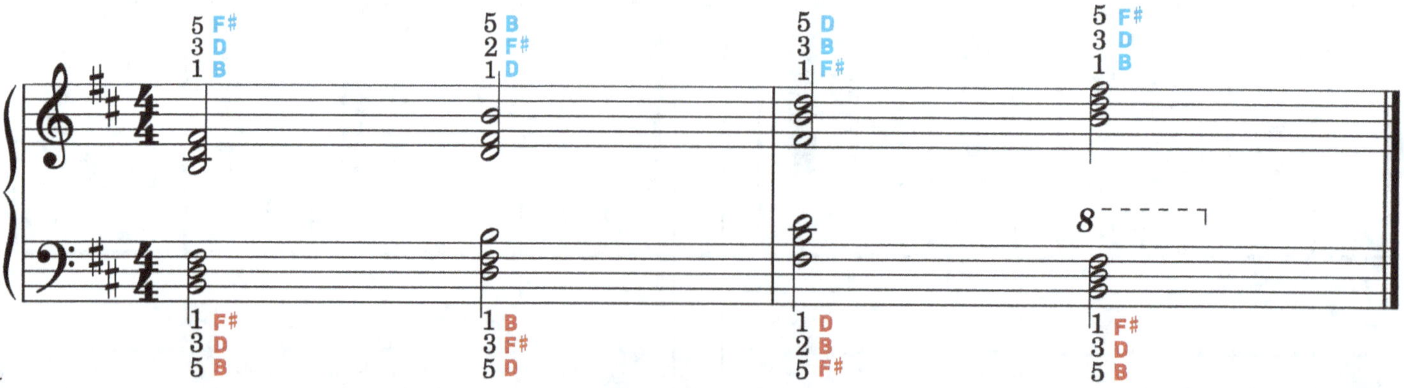

5 F#
3 D
1 B
5 B
2 F#
1 D
5 D
3 B
1 F#
5 F#
3 D
1 B

8

1 F#
3 D
5 B
1 B
3 F#
5 D
1 D
2 B
5 F#
1 F#
3 D
5 B

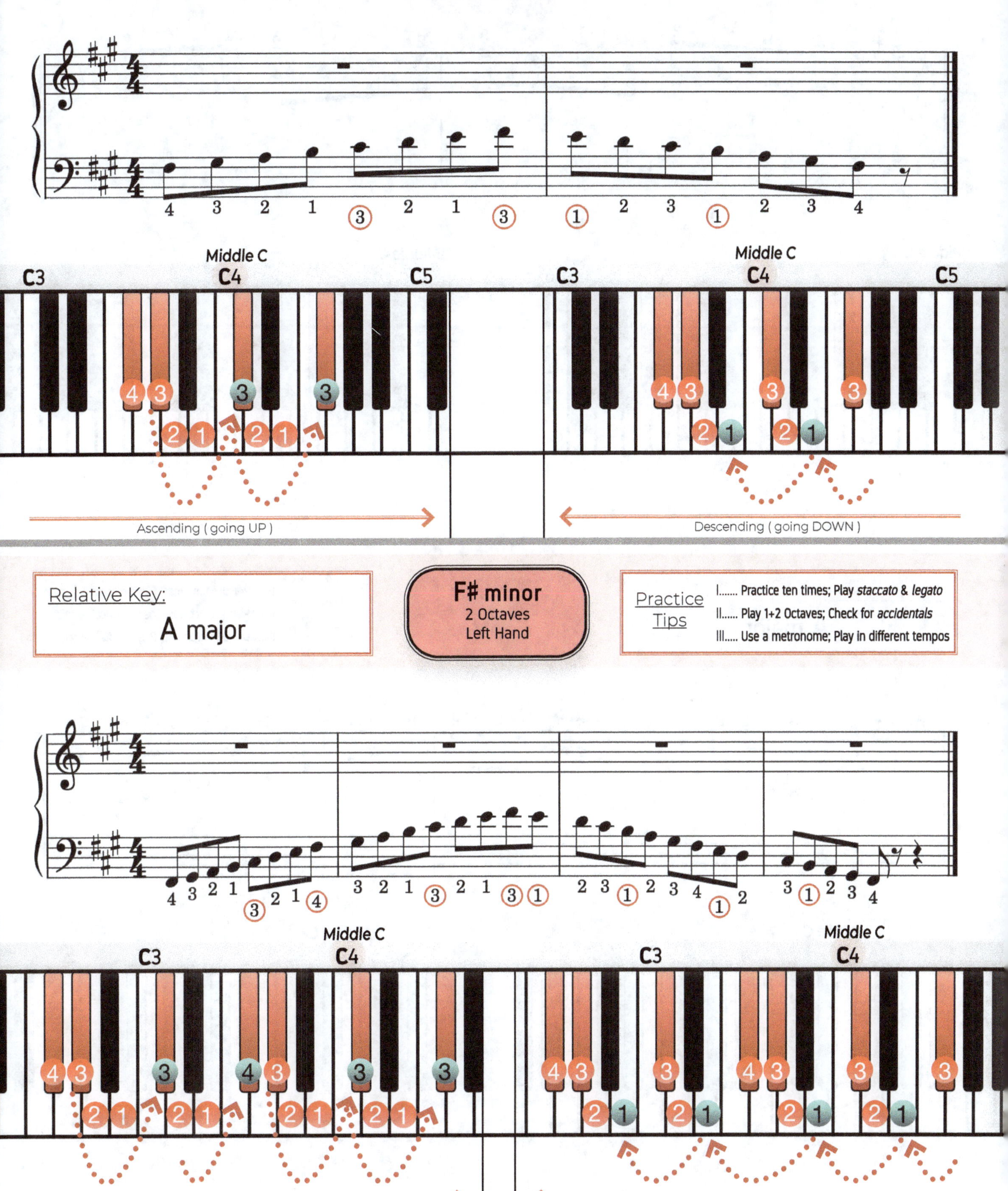
Notes of the Scale:
F#, G#, A, B, C#, D, E
F# minor
1 Octave
Left Hand
Key Signature:
Three Sharps (F#, C#, G#)
Middle C
C3
C4
C5
Middle C
C3
C4
C5
4 3 2 1 3 2 1 3
1 2 3 1 2 3 4
4 3 3 3
2 1 2 1
Ascending (going UP)
4 3 3 3
2 1 2 1
Descending (going DOWN)
Relative Key:
A major
F# minor
2 Octaves
Left Hand
Practice Tips
I....... Practice ten times; Play staccato & legato
II....... Play 1+2 Octaves; Check for accidentals
III..... Use a metronome; Play in different tempos
4 3 2 1 3 2 1 3 1 2 3 1 2 3 4 1 3 1 2 3 4
3 2 1 4
Middle C
C3
Middle C
C4
Middle C
C3
Middle C
C4
4 3 3 4 3 3 3
2 1 2 1 2 1 2 1
Ascending (going UP)
4 3 3 4 3 3 3
2 1 2 1 2 1 2 1
Descending (going DOWN)

Notes of the Scale:
F#, G#, A, B, C#, D, E
F# minor
1 Octave
Right Hand
Key Signature:
Three Sharps (F#,C#,G#) 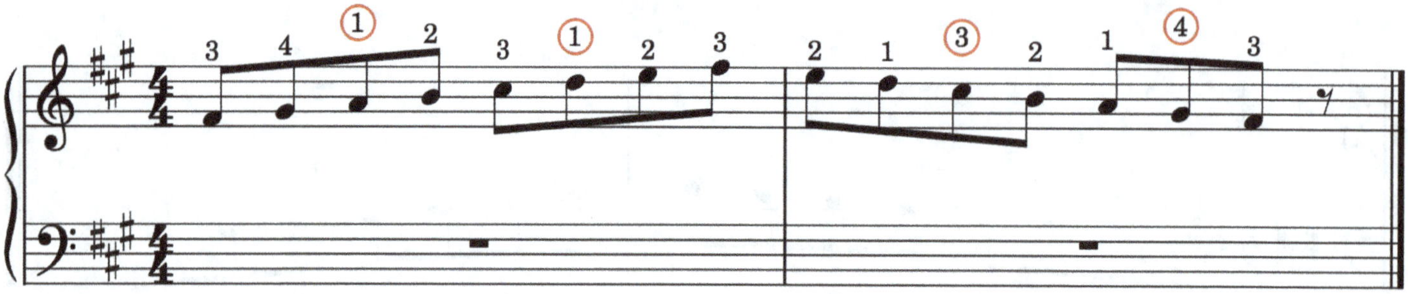 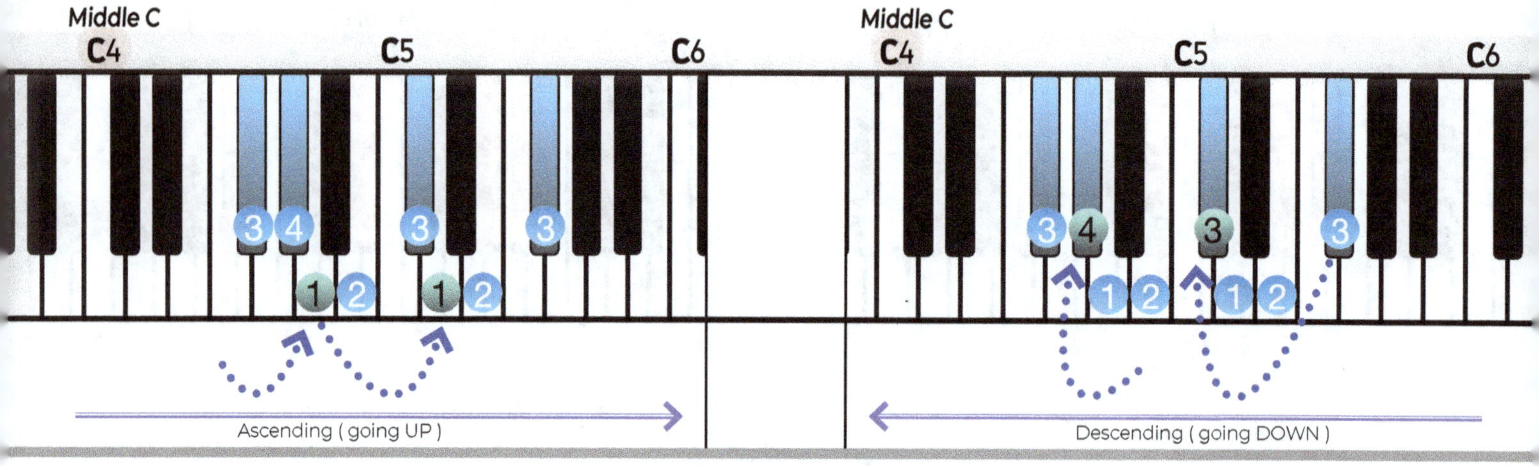
3 4 1 2 3 1 2 3 2 1 3 2 1 4 3
Middle C
C4
C5
C6
Middle C
C4
C5
C6
3 4 1 2 1 2 3 3
3 4 1 2 1 2 3 3
Ascending (going UP)
Descending (going DOWN)
Relative Key:
A major
F# minor
2 Octaves
Right Hand
Practice Tips
I....... Practice ten times; Play staccato & legato
II...... Play 1+2 Octaves; Check for accidentals
III..... Use a metronome; Play in different tempos
3 4 1 2 3 1 2 3 4 1 2 3 1 2 3 2 1 3 2 1 4 3 2 1 3 2 1 4 3
Middle C
C4
C5
Middle C
C4
C5
3 4 1 2 3 1 2 3 4 1 2 1 2 3 3 4 3 3 4 3 3
Ascending (going UP)
Descending (going DOWN)

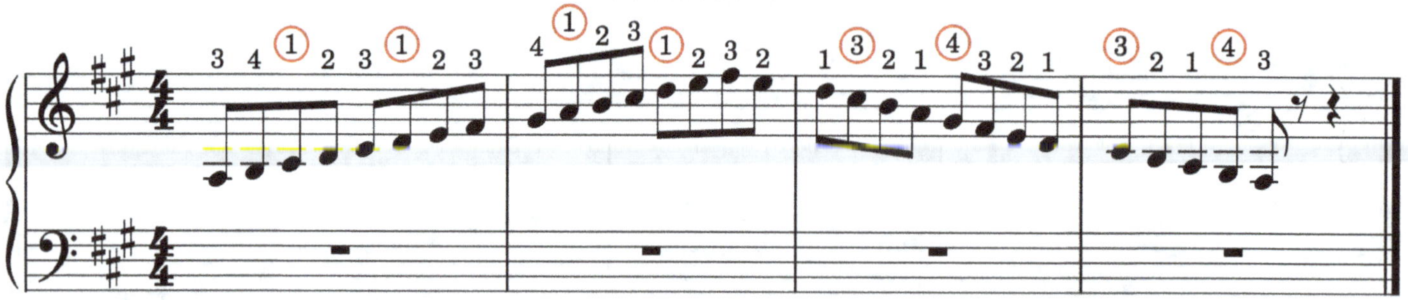

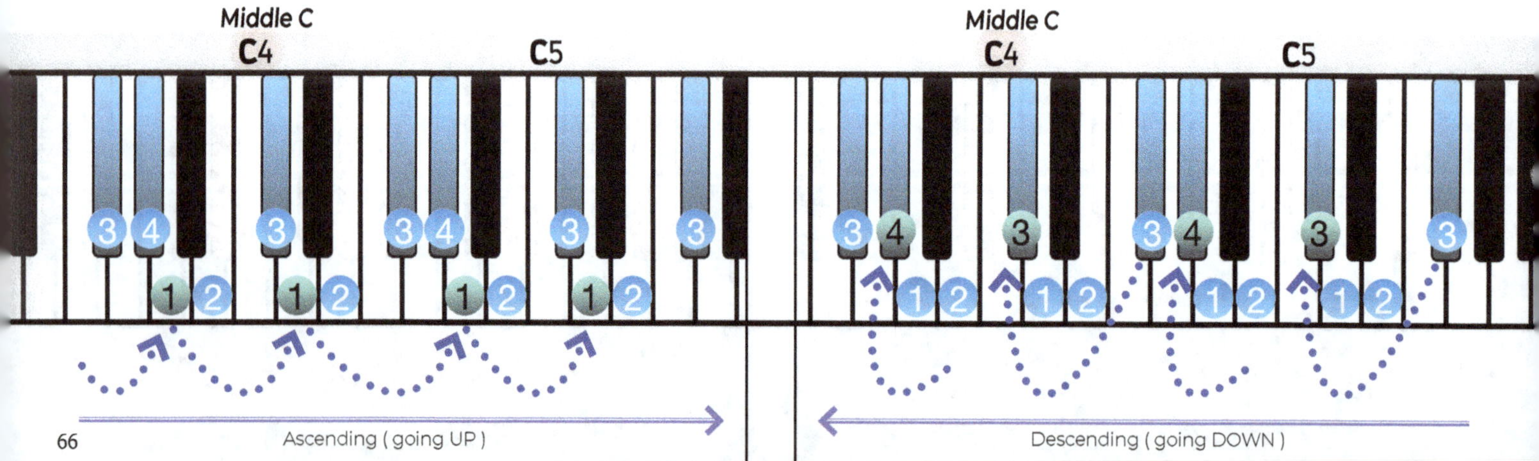

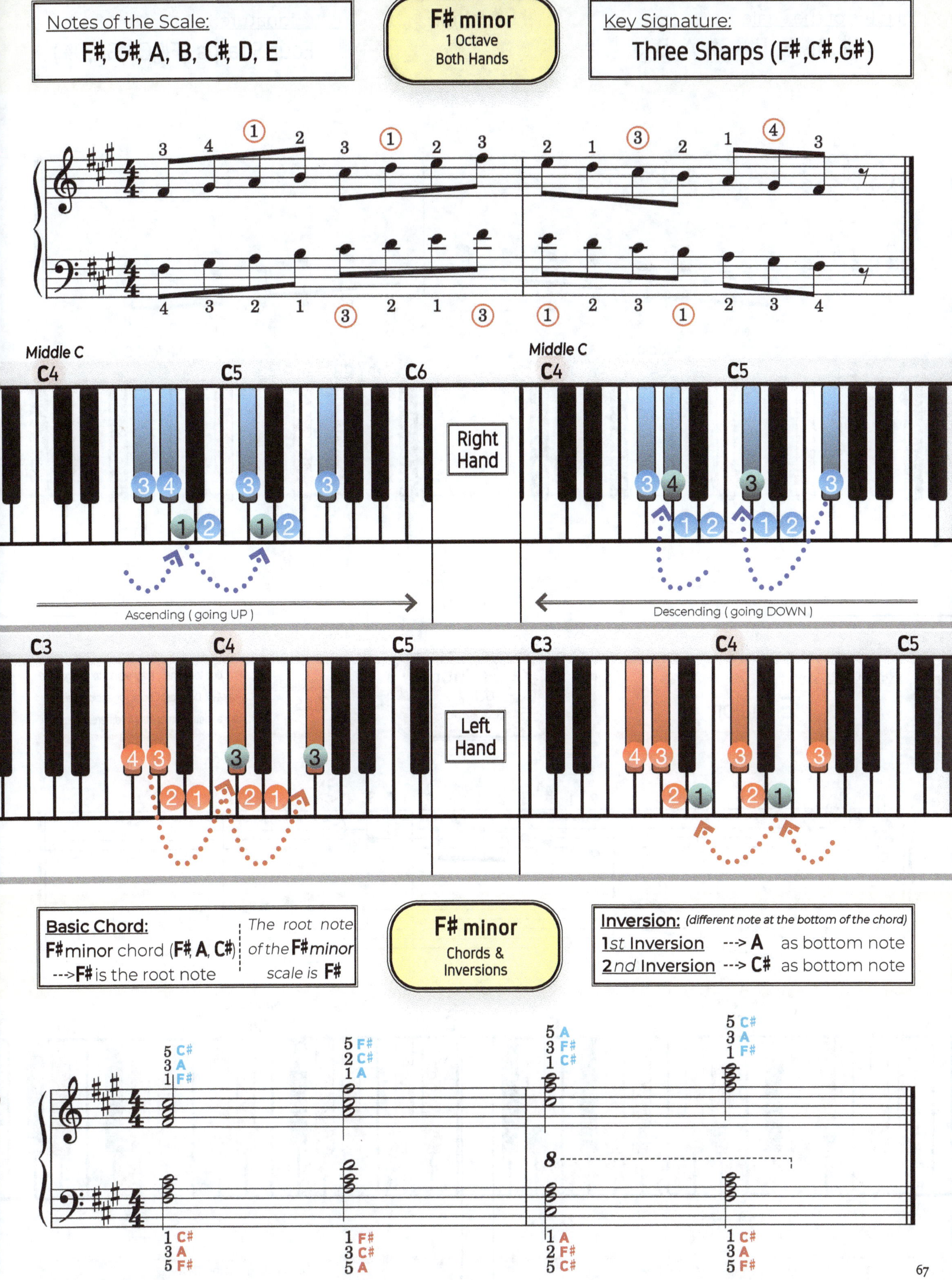

Notes of the Scale:
F#, G#, A, B, C#, D, E
F# minor
1 Octave
Both Hands
Key Signature:
Three Sharps (F#,C#,G#)
Middle C
C4
C5
C6
Right Hand
Ascending (going UP)
Middle C
C4
C5
Descending (going DOWN)
C3
C4
C5
Left Hand
C3
C4
C5
Basic Chord:
F# minor chord (F#, A, C#)
--->F# is the root note
The root note of the F# minor scale is F#
F# minor
Chords & Inversions
Inversion: (different note at the bottom of the chord)
1st Inversion ---> A as bottom note
2nd Inversion ---> C# as bottom note
5 C#
3 A
1 F#
5 F#
2 C#
1 A
5 A
3 F#
1 C#
5 C#
3 A
1 F#
1 C#
3 A
5 F#
1 F#
3 C#
5 A
1 A
2 F#
5 C#
1 C#
3 A
5 F#

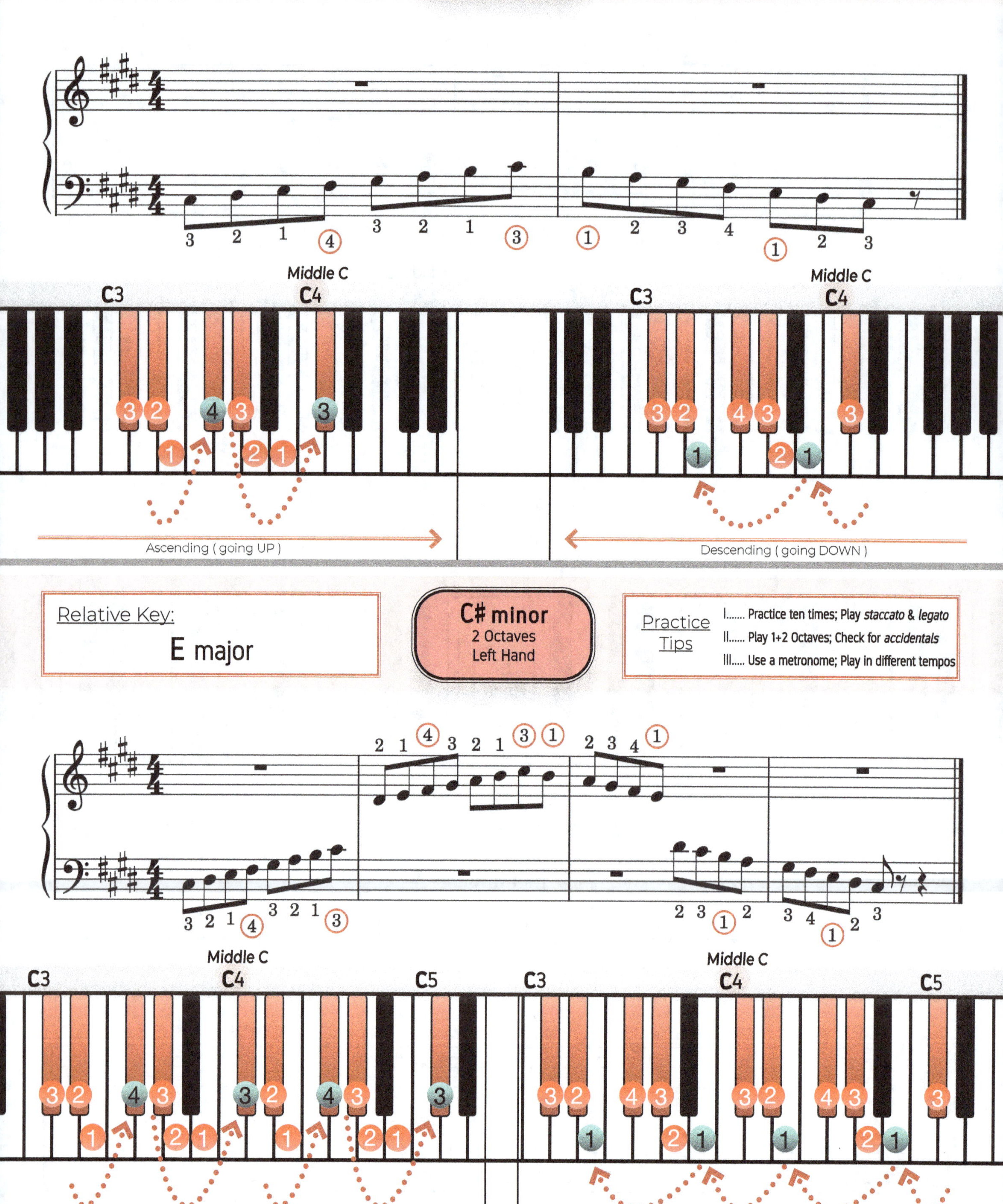

Notes of the Scale:
C#, D#, E, F#, G#, A, B

C# minor
1 Octave
Left Hand

Key Signature:
Four Sharps (F#, C#, G#, D#)

Middle C
C3
C4
3 2 1 4 3 2 1 3
Ascending (going UP)

Middle C
C3
C4
3 2 4 3 3
Descending (going DOWN)

Relative Key:
E major

C# minor
2 Octaves
Left Hand

Practice Tips
I....... Practice ten times; Play staccato & legato
II...... Play 1+2 Octaves; Check for accidentals
III..... Use a metronome; Play in different tempos

Middle C
C3
C4
C5
3 2 1 4 3 3 2 4 3 3
Ascending (going UP)

Middle C
C3
C4
C5
3 2 4 3 3 2 4 3 3
Descending (going DOWN)

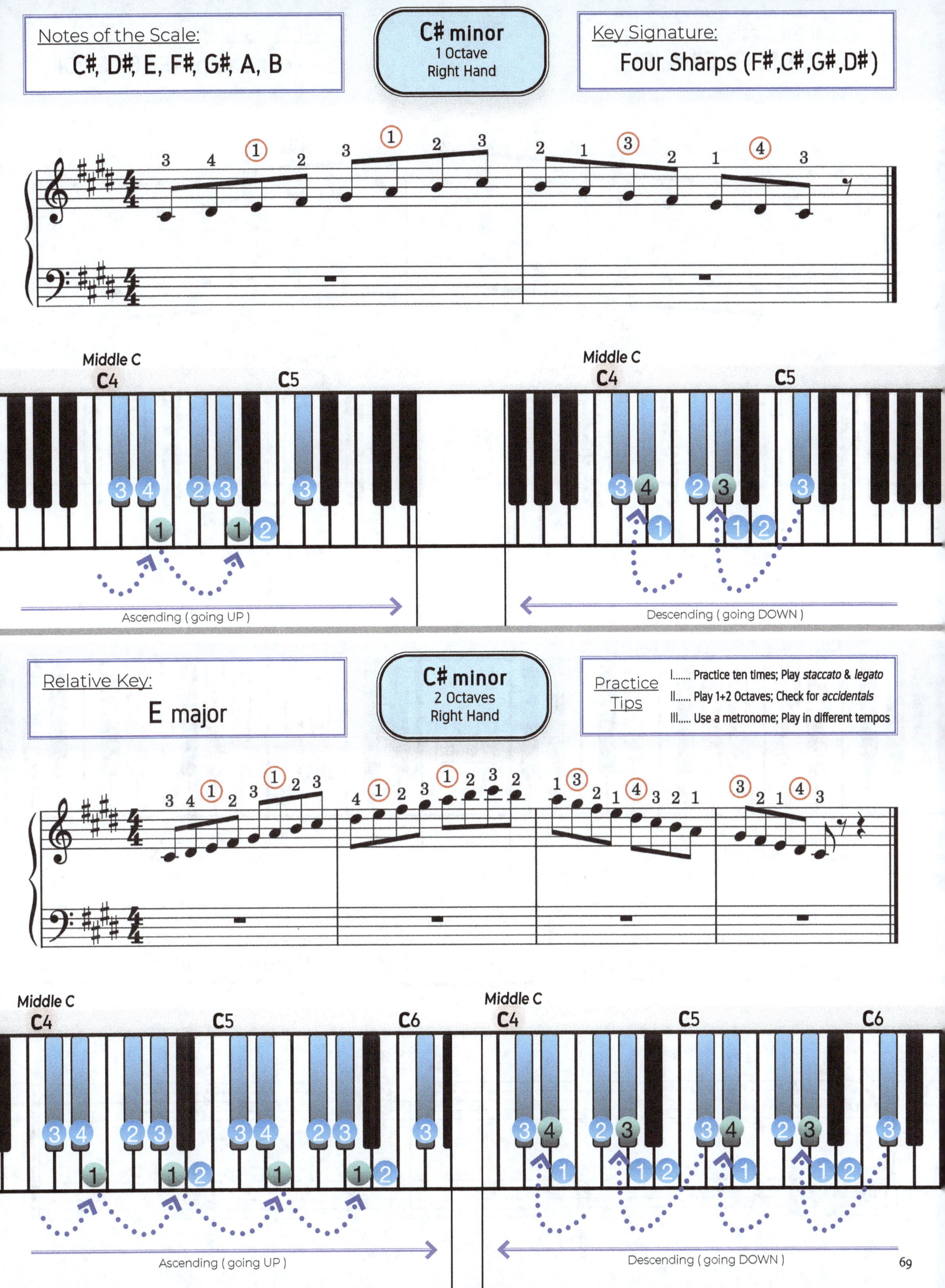

Notes of the Scale:
C#, D#, E, F#, G#, A, B
C# minor
1 Octave
Right Hand
Key Signature:
Four Sharps (F#, C#, G#, D#)
Middle C
C4
C5
Ascending (going UP)
Middle C
C4
C5
Descending (going DOWN)
Relative Key:
E major
C# minor
2 Octaves
Right Hand
Practice Tips
I....... Practice ten times; Play staccato & legato
II...... Play 1+2 Octaves; Check for accidentals
III..... Use a metronome; Play in different tempos
Middle C
C4
C5
C6
Ascending (going UP)
Middle C
C4
C5
C6
Descending (going DOWN)

Notes of the Scale:
C#, D#, E, F#, G#, A, B

C# minor
1 Octave
Both Hands

Key Signature:
Four Sharps (F#, C#, G#, D#)

Middle C
C4
C5
Right Hand
Ascending (going UP)
Descending (going DOWN)

C3
C4
Left Hand

Basic Chord:
C# minor chord (C#, E, G#)
--> C# is the root note
The root note of the C# minor scale is C#

C# minor
Chords &
Inversions

Inversion: (different note at the bottom of the chord)
1st Inversion ---> E as bottom note
2nd Inversion ---> G# as bottom note

5 G#
3 E
1 C#

5 C#
2 G#
1 E

5 E
3 C#
1 G#

5 G#
3 E
1 C#

1 G#
3 E
5 C#

1 C#
3 G#
5 E

1 E
2 C#
5 G#

1 G#
3 E
5 C#

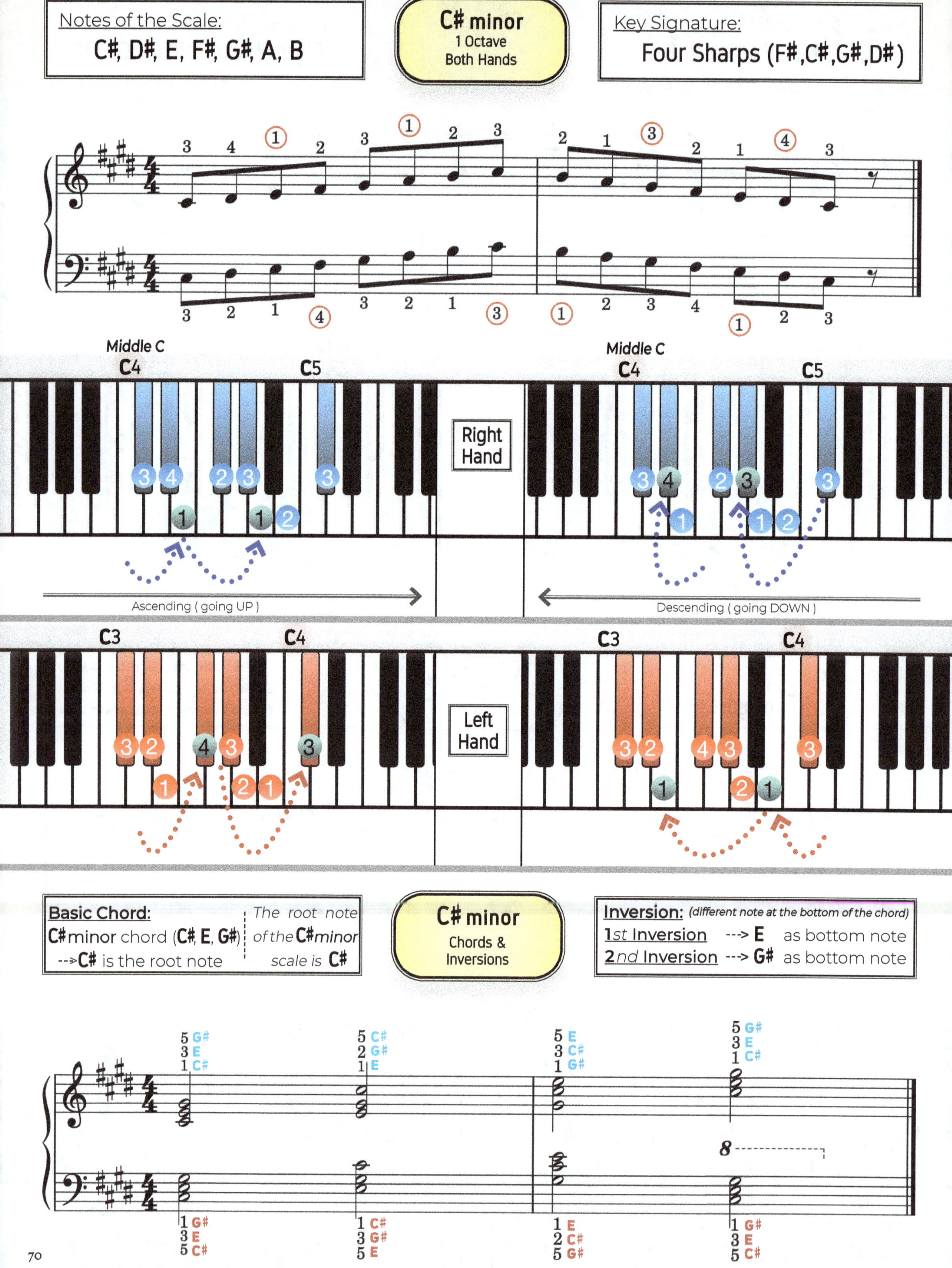

70

Notes of the Scale:
G#, A#, B, C#, D#, E, F#

G# minor
1 Octave
Left Hand

Key Signature:
Five Sharps (F#,C#,G#,D#,A#)

Middle C
C3
C4
Middle C
C3
C4

3 2 1 3 2 1 4 3 4 1 2 3 1 2 3

3 2 1 3 2 4 3
Ascending (going UP)

3 2 3 2 4 3
1 1
Descending (going DOWN)

Relative Key:
B major

G# minor
2 Octaves
Left Hand

Practice Tips
I...... Practice ten times; Play staccato & legato
II..... Play 1+2 Octaves; Check for accidentals
III.... Use a metronome; Play in different tempos

2 1 3 2 1 4 3 4 1 2 3 1

3 2 1 3 2 1 4 3 2 1 3 2 1 4 2 3 4 1 2 3

Middle C
C3
C4
Middle C
C3
C4

3 2 3 2 4 3 2 3 2 4 3
1 1 1 1
Ascending (going UP)

3 2 3 2 4 3 2 3 2 4 3
1 1 1 1
Descending (going DOWN)

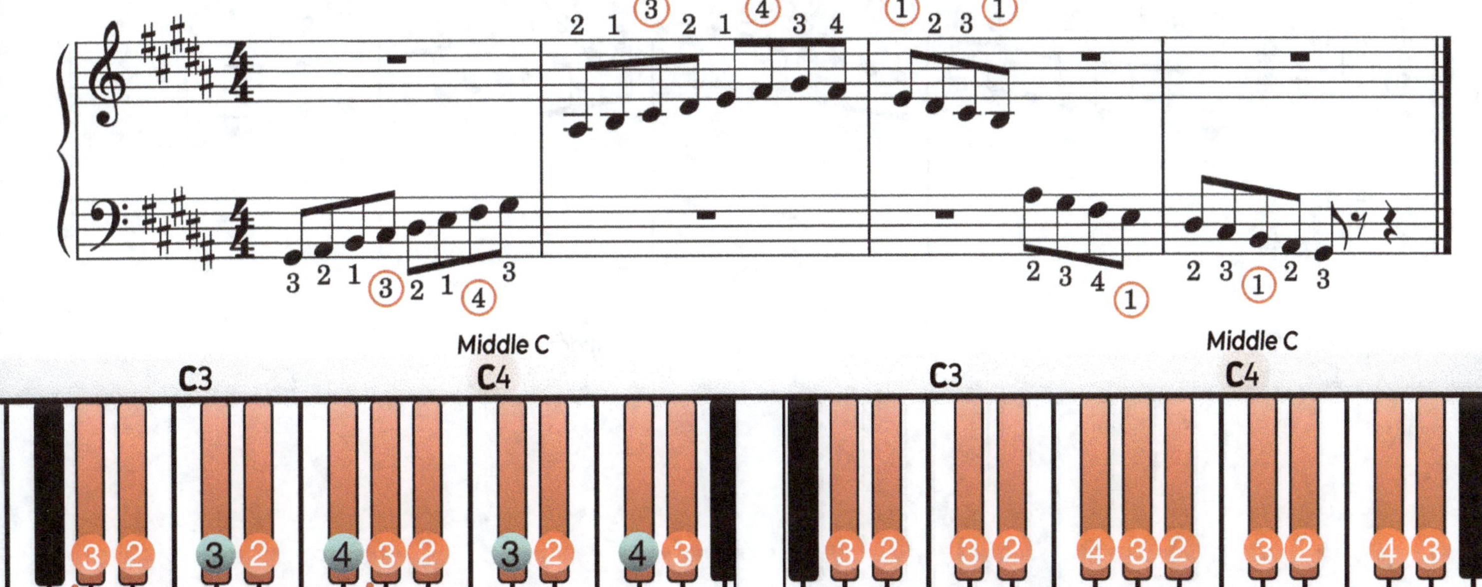

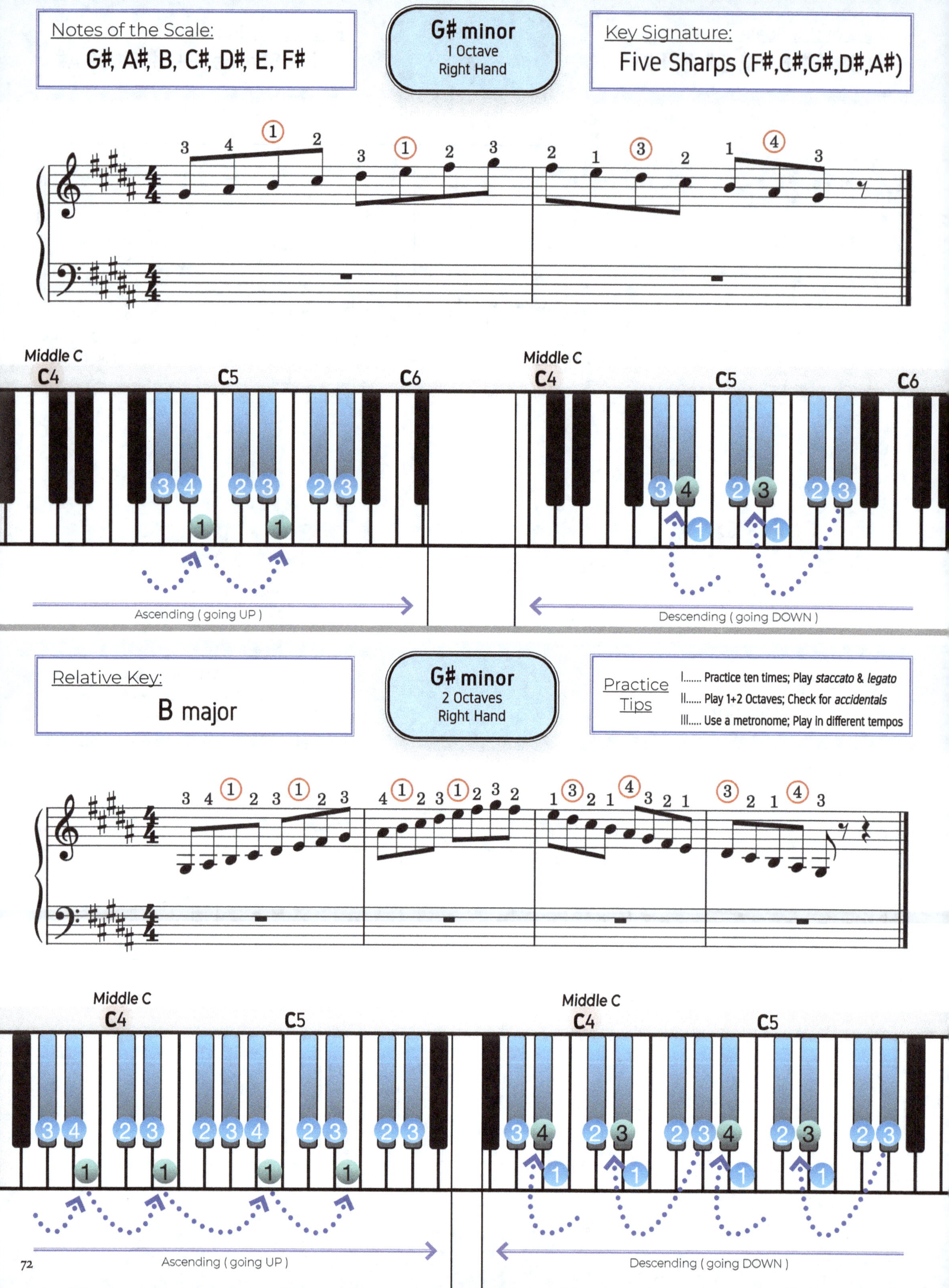

Notes of the Scale:
G#, A#, B, C#, D#, E, F#
G# minor
1 Octave
Right Hand
Key Signature:
Five Sharps (F#,C#,G#,D#,A#)
Middle C
C4
C5
C6
Middle C
C4
C5
C6
3 4 2 3 2 3
1 1
1 1
3 4 2 3 2 3
Ascending (going UP)
Descending (going DOWN)
Relative Key:
B major
G# minor
2 Octaves
Right Hand
Practice Tips
I....... Practice ten times; Play staccato & legato
II...... Play 1+2 Octaves; Check for accidentals
III..... Use a metronome; Play in different tempos
Middle C
C4
C5
Middle C
C4
C5
3 4 2 3 2 3 4 2 3 2 3
1 1 1 1
3 4 2 3 2 3 4 2 3 2 3
1 1 1 1
Ascending (going UP)
Descending (going DOWN)

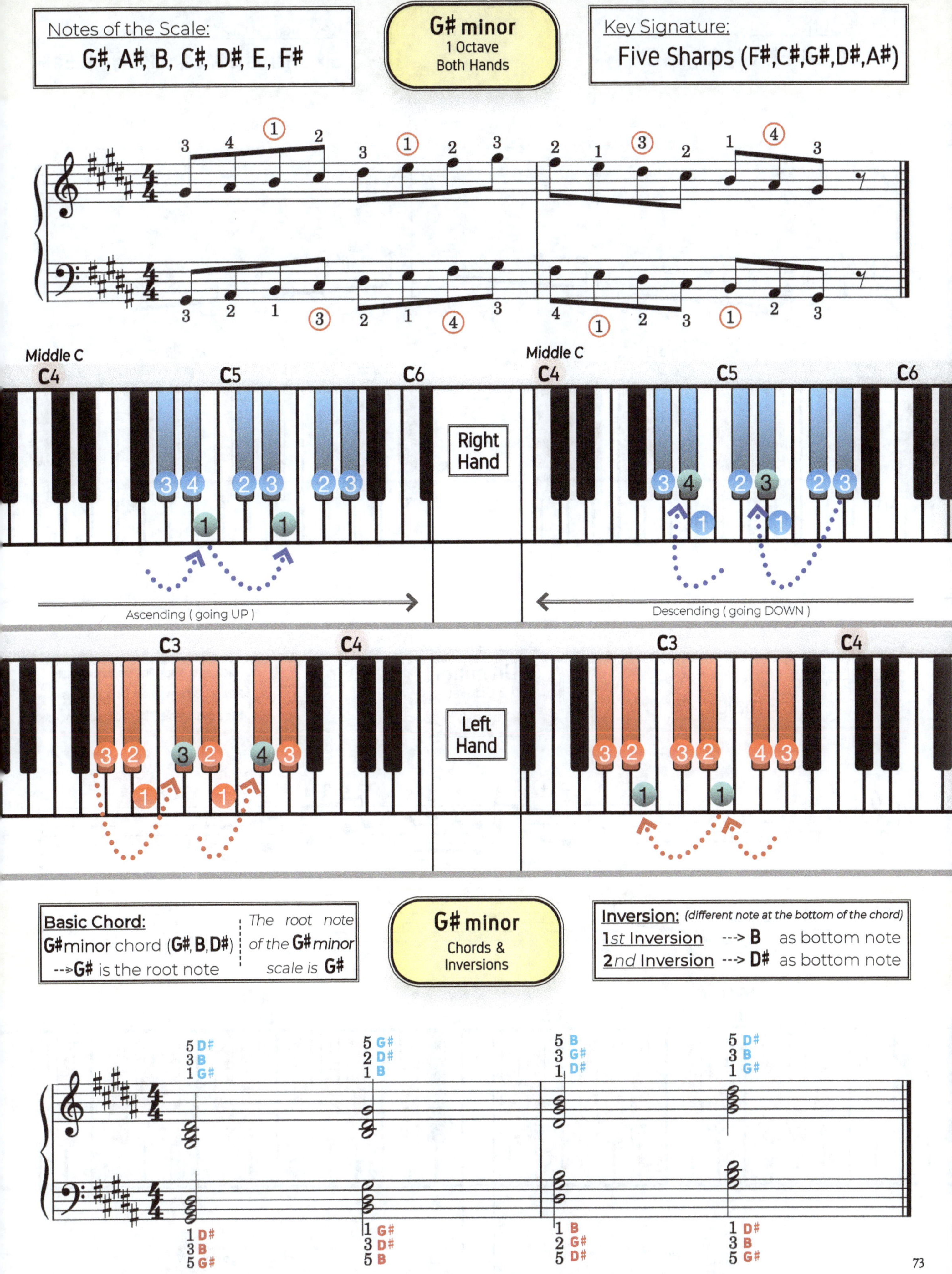

Notes of the Scale:
G#, A#, B, C#, D#, E, F#
G# minor
1 Octave
Both Hands
Key Signature:
Five Sharps (F#,C#,G#,D#,A#)
Middle C
C4
C5
C6
Right Hand
Ascending (going UP)
Middle C
C4
C5
C6
Descending (going DOWN)
C3
C4
Left Hand
C3
C4
Basic Chord:
G# minor chord (G#, B, D#)
--> G# is the root note
The root note of the G# minor scale is G#
G# minor
Chords & Inversions
Inversion: (different note at the bottom of the chord)
1st Inversion ---> B as bottom note
2nd Inversion ---> D# as bottom note
5 D#
3 B
1 G#
5 G#
2 D#
1 B
5 B
3 G#
1 D#
5 D#
3 B
1 G#
1 D#
3 B
5 G#
1 G#
3 D#
5 B
1 B
2 G#
5 D#
1 D#
3 B
5 G#

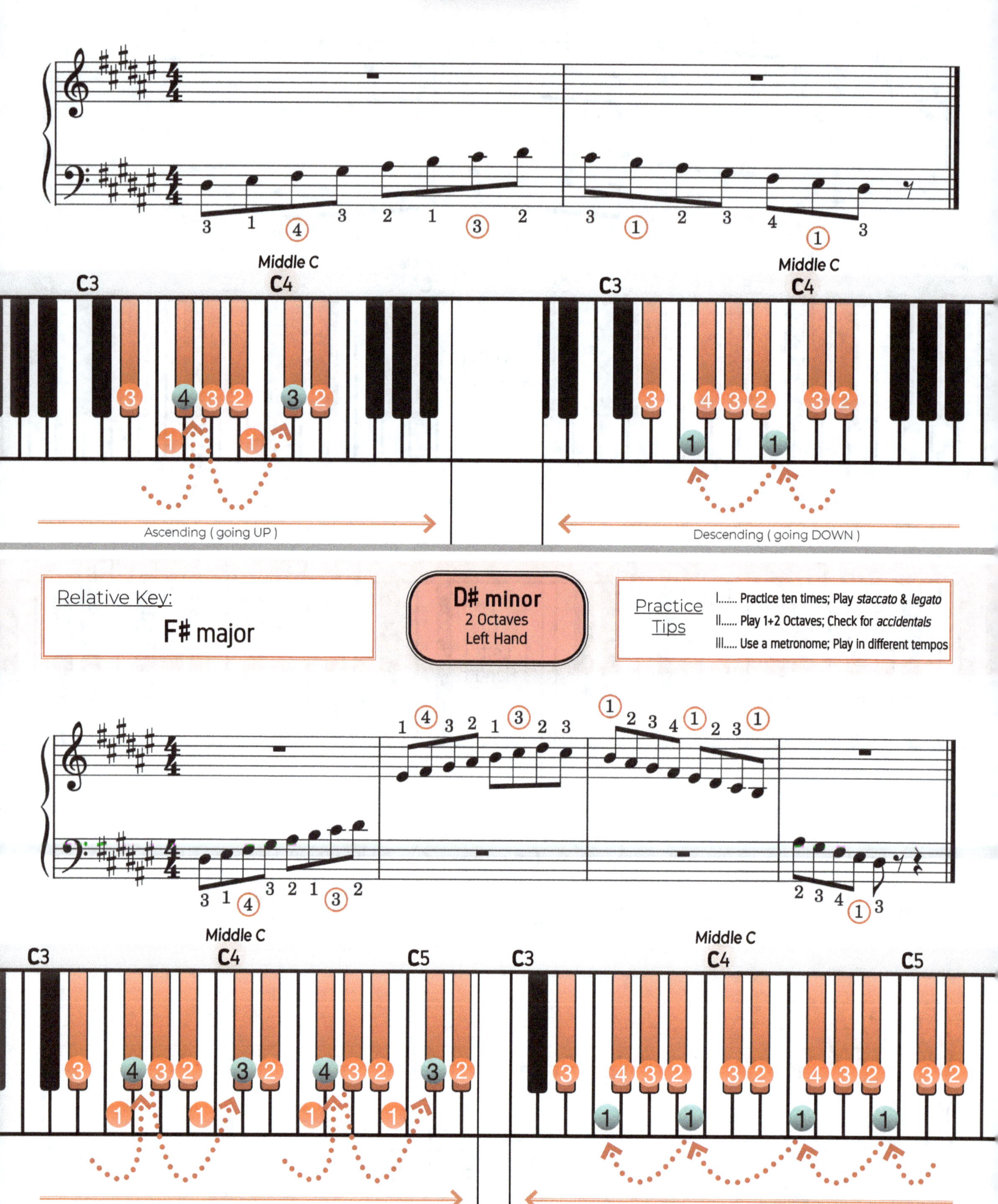

Notes of the Scale:
D#, E#, F#, G#, A#, B, C#
D# minor
1 Octave
Left Hand
Key Signature:
Six Sharps (F#, C#, G#, D#, A#, E#)
Middle C
C3
C4
Middle C
C3
C4
Ascending (going UP)
Descending (going DOWN)
Relative Key:
F# major
D# minor
2 Octaves
Left Hand
Practice Tips
I....... Practice ten times; Play staccato & legato
II...... Play 1+2 Octaves; Check for accidentals
III..... Use a metronome; Play in different tempos
Middle C
C3
C4
C5
C3
Middle C
C4
C5
Ascending (going UP)
Descending (going DOWN)

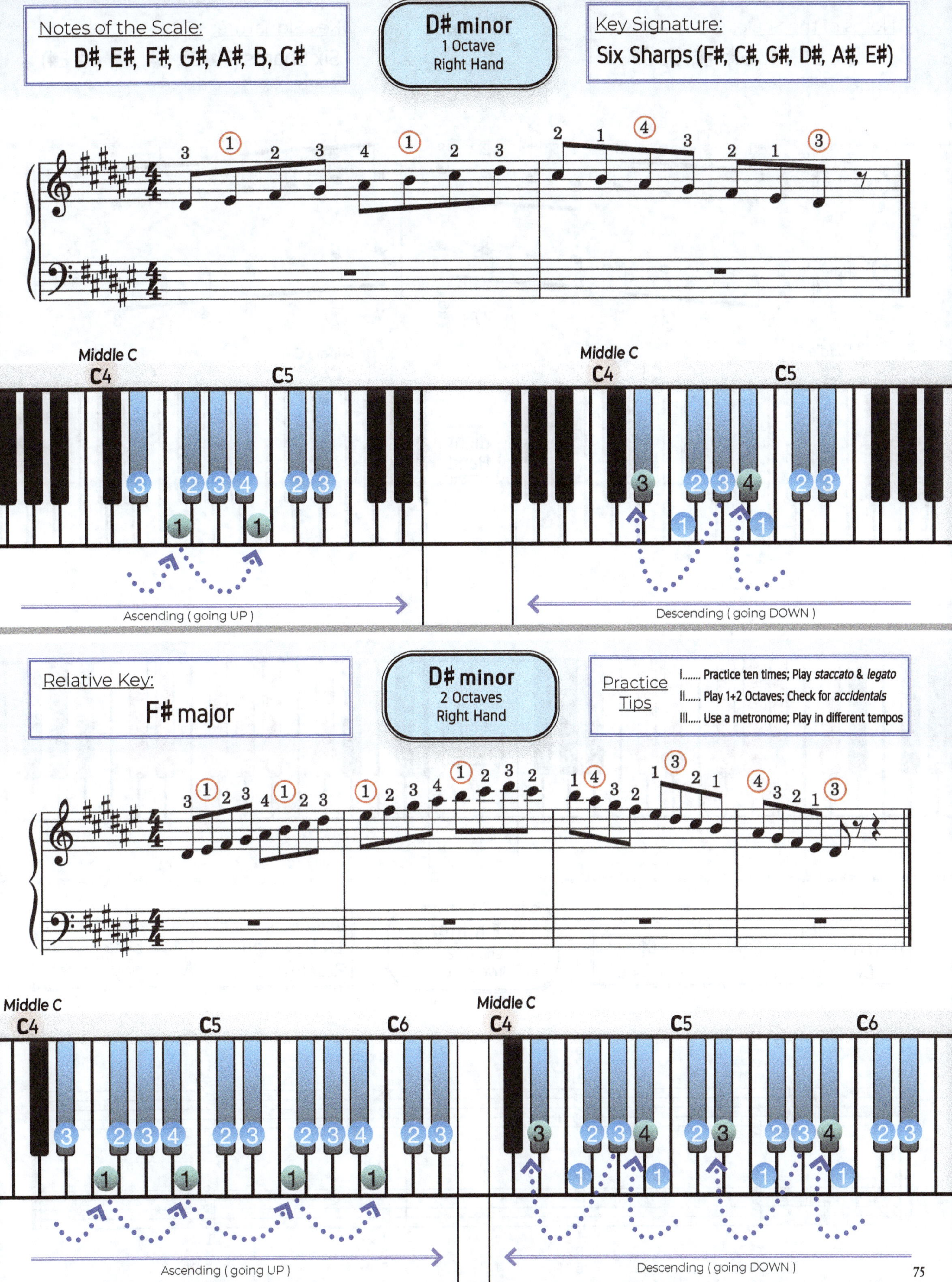

Notes of the Scale:
D#, E#, F#, G#, A#, B, C#
D# minor
1 Octave
Right Hand
Key Signature:
Six Sharps (F#, C#, G#, D#, A#, E#)
Middle C
C4
C5
3 1 2 3 4 1 2 3
2 1 4 3 2 1 3
Middle C
C4
C5
Ascending (going UP)
Descending (going DOWN)
Relative Key:
F# major
D# minor
2 Octaves
Right Hand
Practice Tips
I....... Practice ten times; Play staccato & legato
II...... Play 1+2 Octaves; Check for accidentals
III..... Use a metronome; Play in different tempos
Middle C
C4
C5
C6
Middle C
C4
C5
C6
Ascending (going UP)
Descending (going DOWN)
75

Notes of the Scale:
D#, E#, F#, G#, A#, B, C#

D# minor
1 Octave
Both Hands

Key Signature:
Six Sharps (F#, C#, G#, D#, A#, E#)

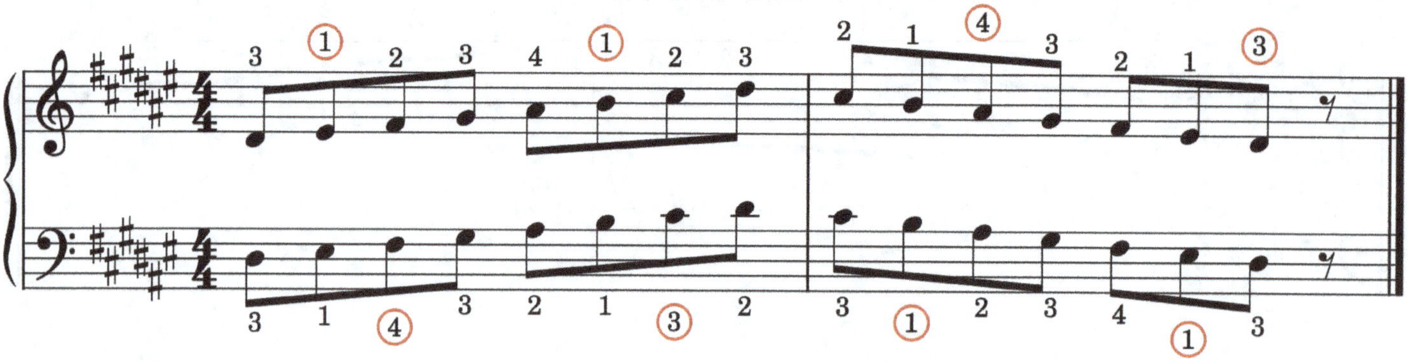

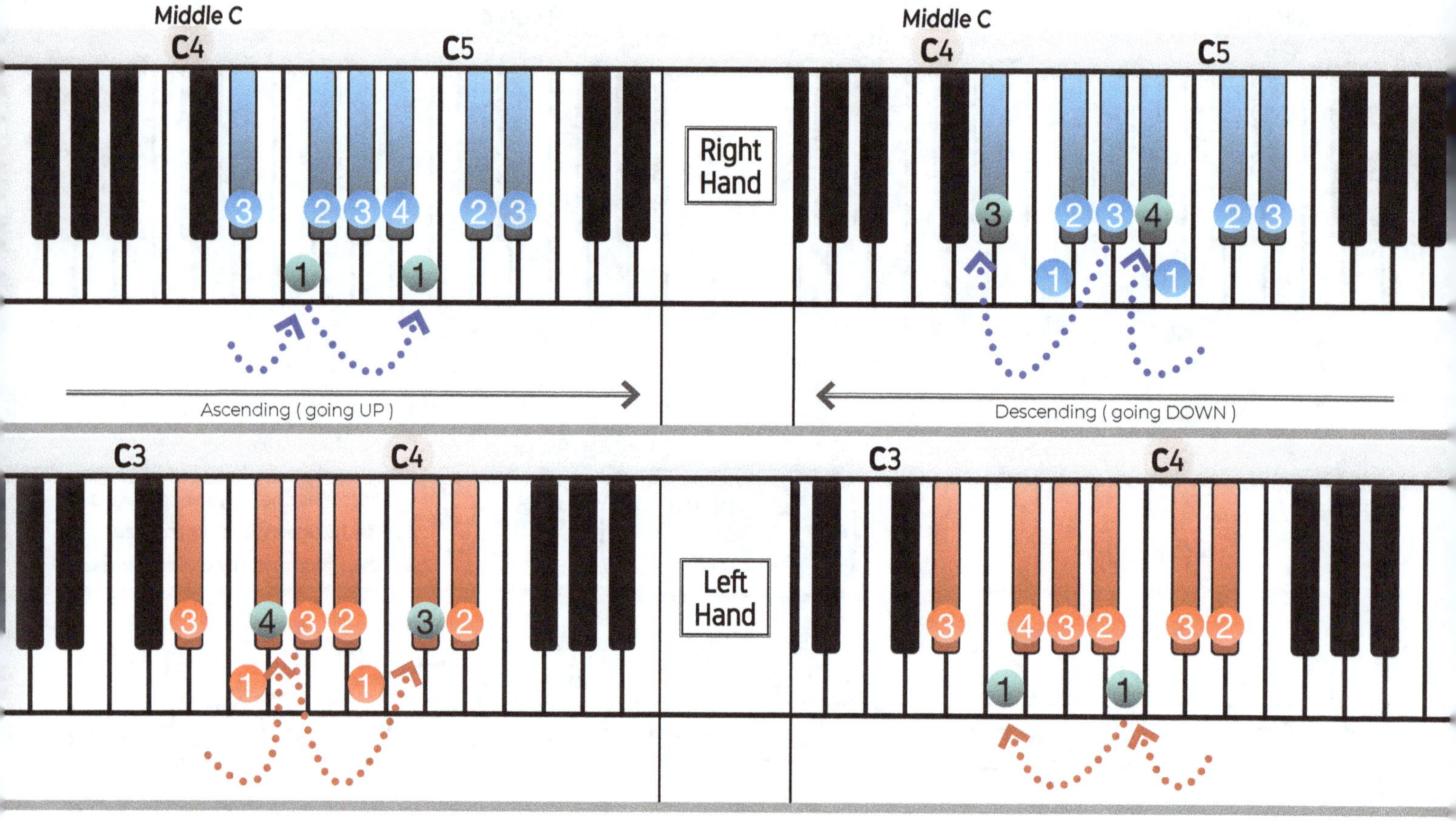

Middle C
C4
C5
Right Hand
Ascending (going UP)
Descending (going DOWN)

C3
C4
Left Hand

Basic Chord:
D# minor chord (D#, F#, A#)
---> D# is the root note
The root note of the D# minor scale is D#

D# minor
Chords &
Inversions

Inversion: (different note at the bottom of the chord)
1st Inversion ---> F# as bottom note
2nd Inversion ---> A# as bottom note

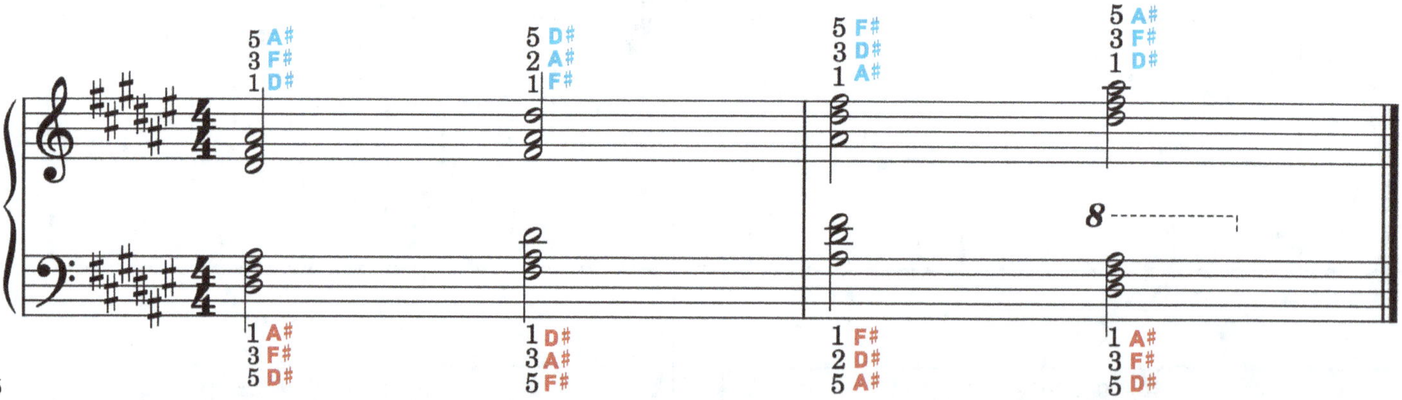

5 A#
3 F#
1 D#

5 D#
2 A#
1 F#

5 F#
3 D#
1 A#

5 A#
3 F#
1 D#

1 A#
3 F#
5 D#

1 D#
3 A#
5 F#

1 F#
2 D#
5 A#

1 A#
3 F#
5 D#

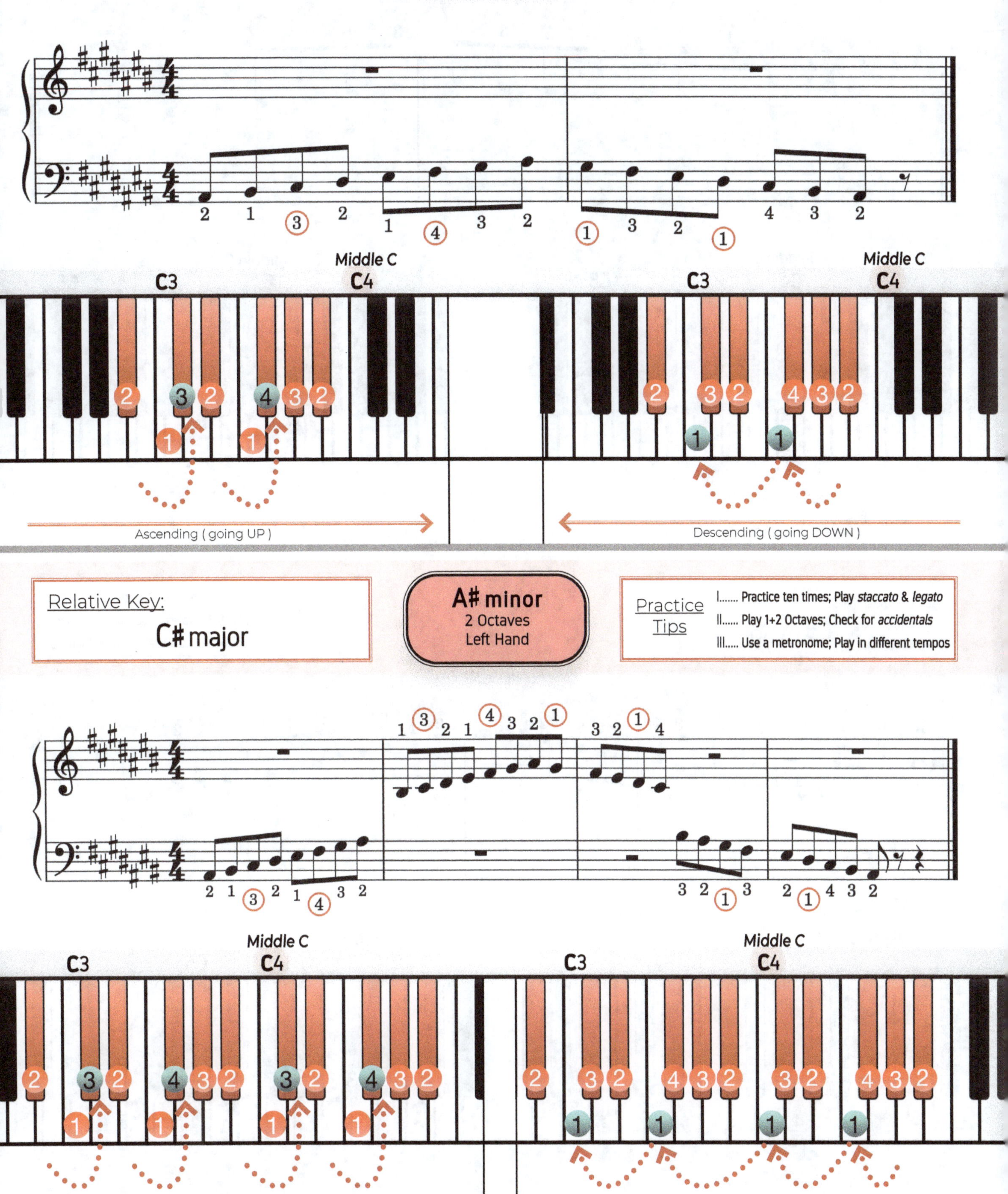

Notes of the Scale:
A#, B#, C#, D#, E#, F#, G#

A# minor
1 Octave
Left Hand

Key Signature:
Seven Sharps (F#, C#, G#, D#, A#, E#, B#)

2 1 3 2 1 4 3 2 1 3 2 1 4 3 2

Middle C
C4
C3

Middle C
C4
C3

2 3 2 4 3 2
1 1

2 3 2 4 3 2
1 1

Ascending (going UP)
Descending (going DOWN)

Relative Key:
C# major

A# minor
2 Octaves
Left Hand

Practice Tips
I....... Practice ten times; Play staccato & legato
II...... Play 1+2 Octaves; Check for accidentals
III..... Use a metronome; Play in different tempos

1 3 2 1 4 3 2 1 3 2 1 4

2 1 3 2 1 4 3 2
3 2 1 3 2 1 4 3 2

Middle C
C4
C3

Middle C
C4
C3

2 3 2 4 3 2 3 2 4 3 2
1 1 1 1

2 3 2 4 3 2 3 2 4 3 2
1 1 1 1

Ascending (going UP)
Descending (going DOWN)

Notes of the Scale:
A#, B#, C#, D#, E#, F#, G#

A# minor
1 Octave
Right Hand

Key Signature:
Seven Sharps (F#, C#, G#, D#, A#, E#, B#)

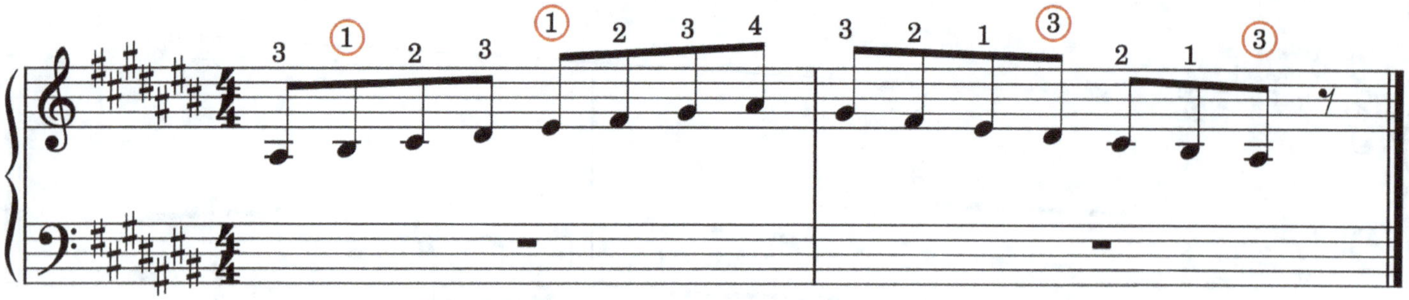

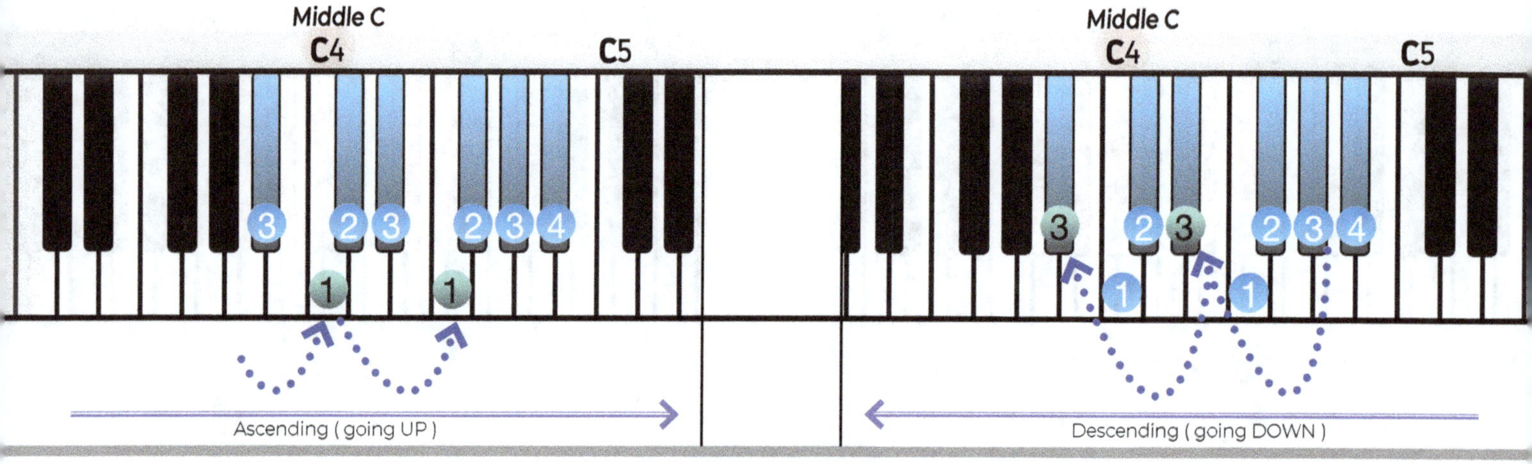

Middle C
C4
C5
Ascending (going UP)
Descending (going DOWN)

Relative Key:
C# major

A# minor
2 Octaves
Right Hand

Practice Tips
I...... Practice ten times; Play staccato & legato
II...... Play 1+2 Octaves; Check for accidentals
III..... Use a metronome; Play in different tempos

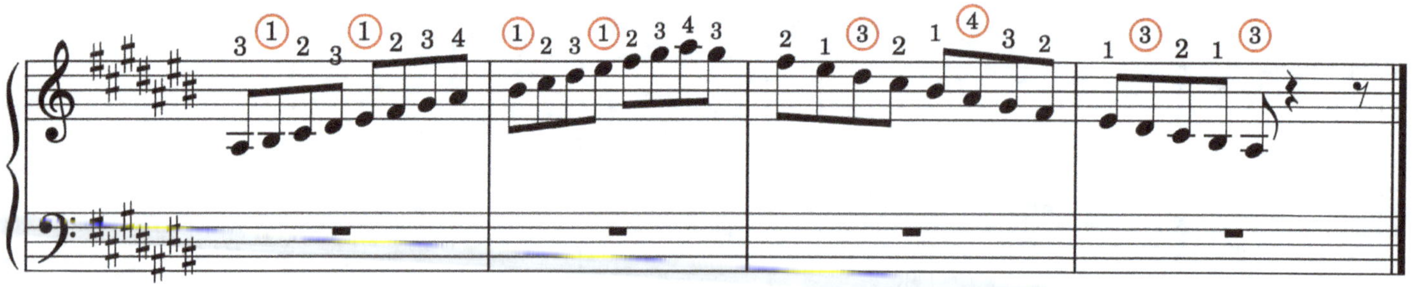

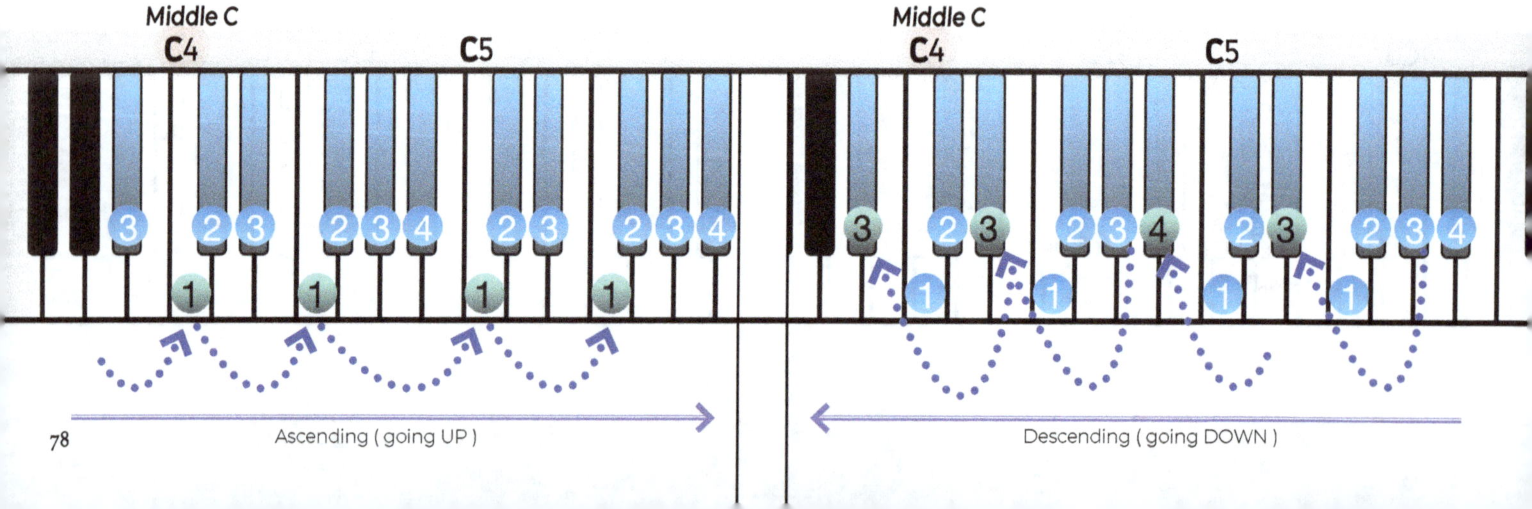

Middle C
C4
C5
Ascending (going UP)
Descending (going DOWN)

Notes of the Scale:
A#, B#, C#, D#, E#, F#, G#

A# minor
1 Octave
Both Hands

Key Signature:
Seven Sharps (F#, C#, G#, D#, A#, E#, B#)

Middle C
C4
C5
Right Hand
Ascending (going UP)
Descending (going DOWN)

C3
C4
Left Hand

Basic Chord:
A#minor chord (A#,C#,E#)
-->A# is the root note
The root note of the A#minor scale is A#

A# minor
Chords & Inversions

Inversion: (different note at the bottom of the chord)
1st Inversion ---> C# as bottom note
2nd Inversion ---> E# as bottom note

5E#
3C#
1A#

5A#
2E#
1C#

5C#
3A#
1E#

5E#
3C#
1A#

1E#
3C#
5A#

1A#
3E#
5C#

1C#
2A#
5E#

1E#
3C#
5A#

MINOR SCALES

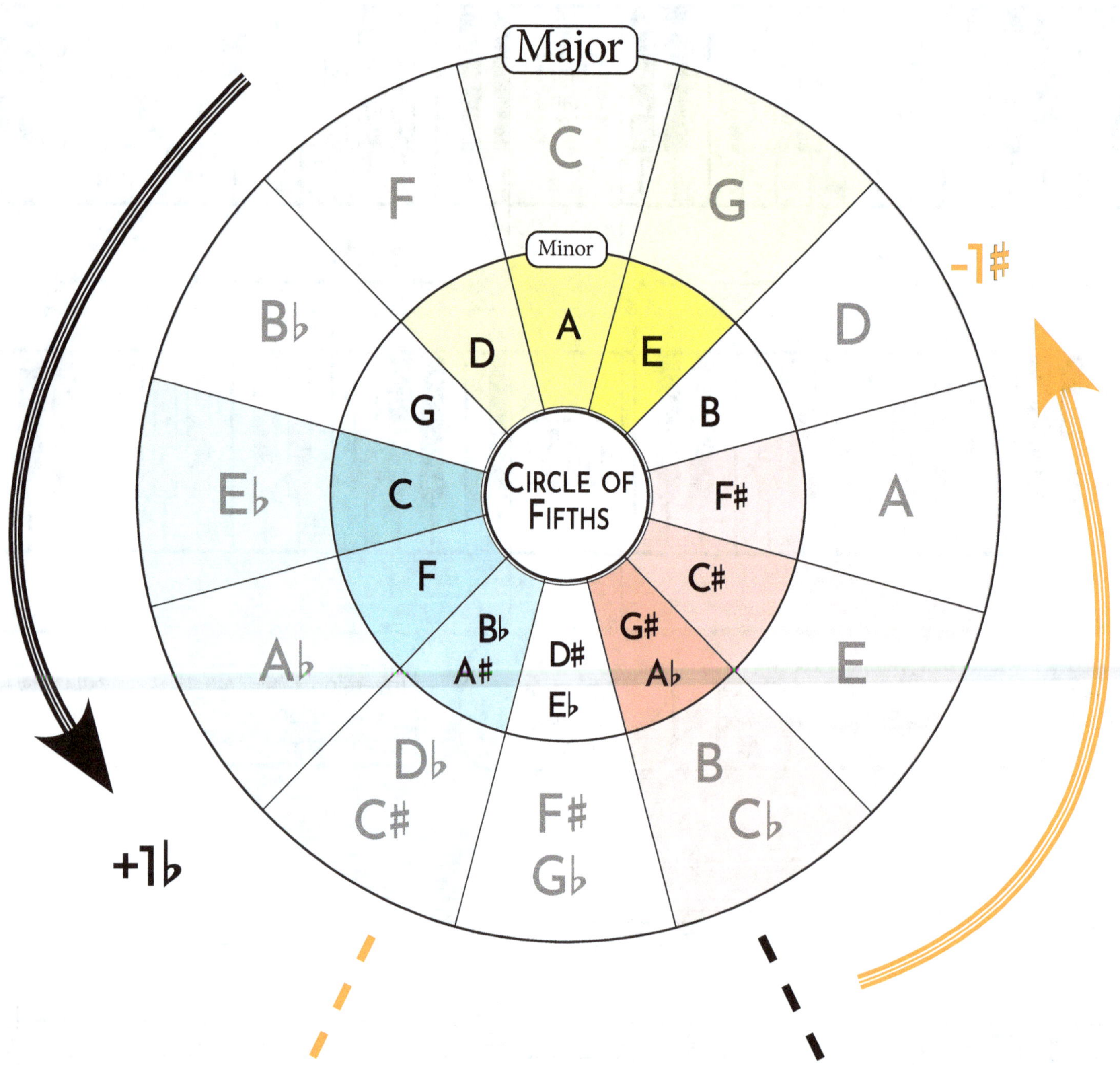

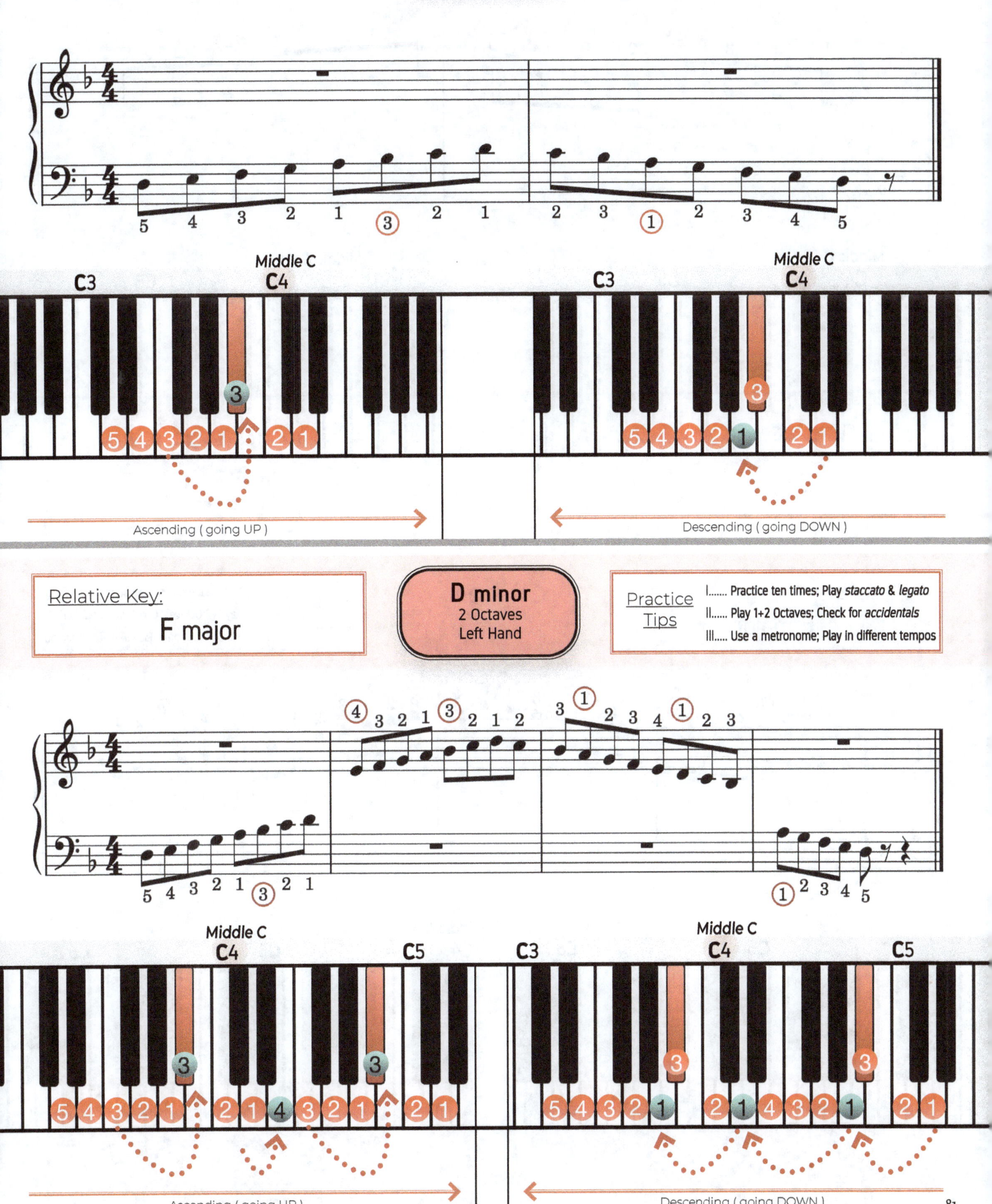

Notes of the Scale:
D, E, F, G, A, B♭, C

D minor
1 Octave
Left Hand

Key Signature:
One Flat (B♭)

C3
Middle C
C4
5 4 3 2 1   2 1
3
Ascending (going UP)

C3
Middle C
C4
5 4 3 2 1
3
2 1
Descending (going DOWN)

Relative Key:
F major

D minor
2 Octaves
Left Hand

Practice Tips
I....... Practice ten times; Play staccato & legato
II...... Play 1+2 Octaves; Check for accidentals
III..... Use a metronome; Play in different tempos

Middle C
C4
C5
C3
Middle C
C4
C5

5 4 3 2 1   2 1 4 3 2 1   2 1
3   3
Ascending (going UP)

5 4 3 2 1   2 1 4 3 2 1   2 1
3   3
Descending (going DOWN)

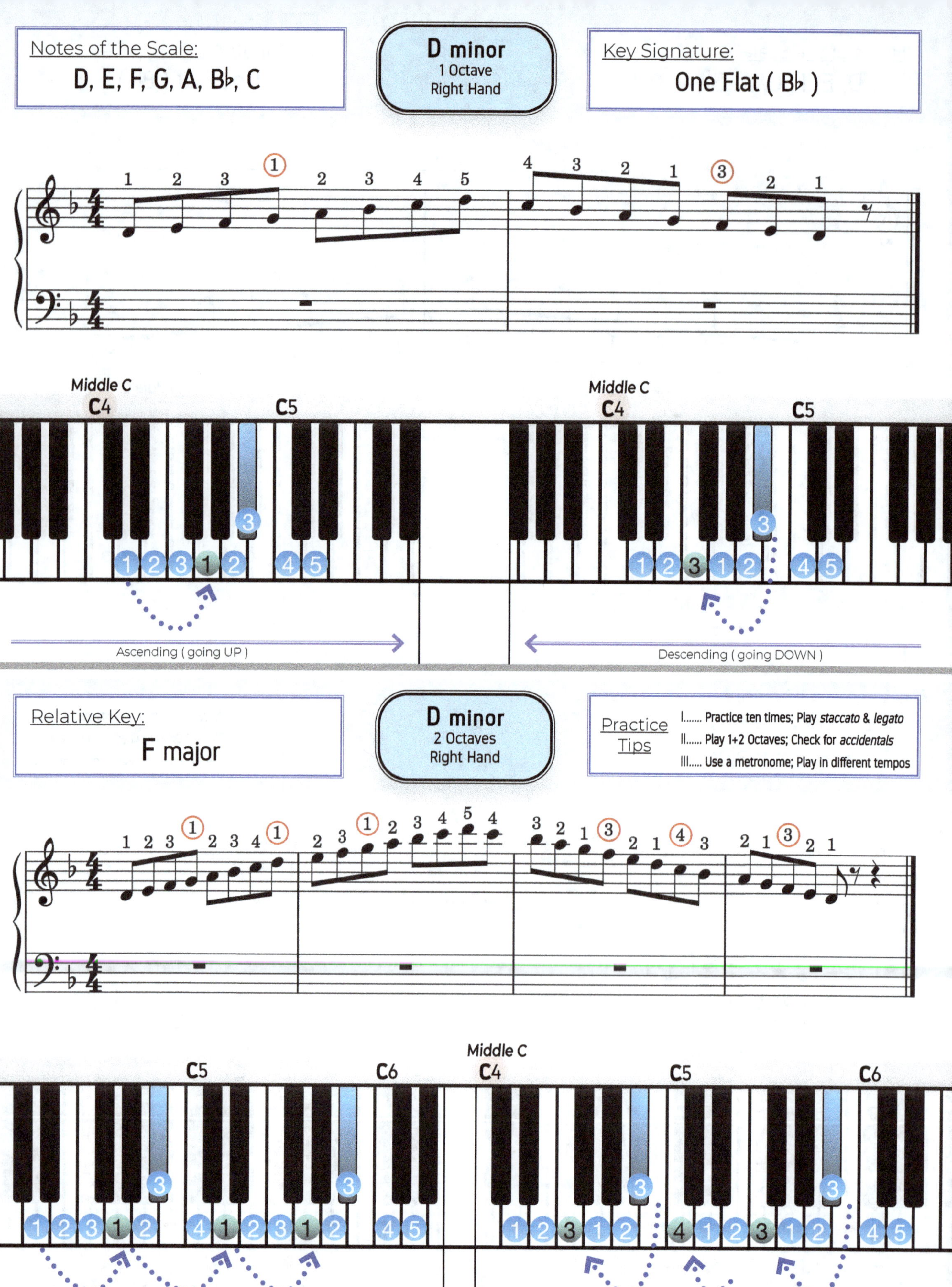

Notes of the Scale:
D, E, F, G, A, B♭, C
D minor
1 Octave
Right Hand
Key Signature:
One Flat (B♭)
Middle C
C4
C5
3
1 2 3 1 2 4 5
Ascending (going UP)
Middle C
C4
C5
3
1 2 3 1 2 4 5
Descending (going DOWN)
Relative Key:
F major
D minor
2 Octaves
Right Hand
Practice Tips
I....... Practice ten times; Play staccato & legato
II...... Play 1+2 Octaves; Check for accidentals
III..... Use a metronome; Play in different tempos
C5
C6
3
3
1 2 3 1 2 4 1 2 3 1 2 4 5
Ascending (going UP)
Middle C
C4
C5
C6
3
3
1 2 3 1 2 4 1 2 3 1 2 4 5
Descending (going DOWN)
82

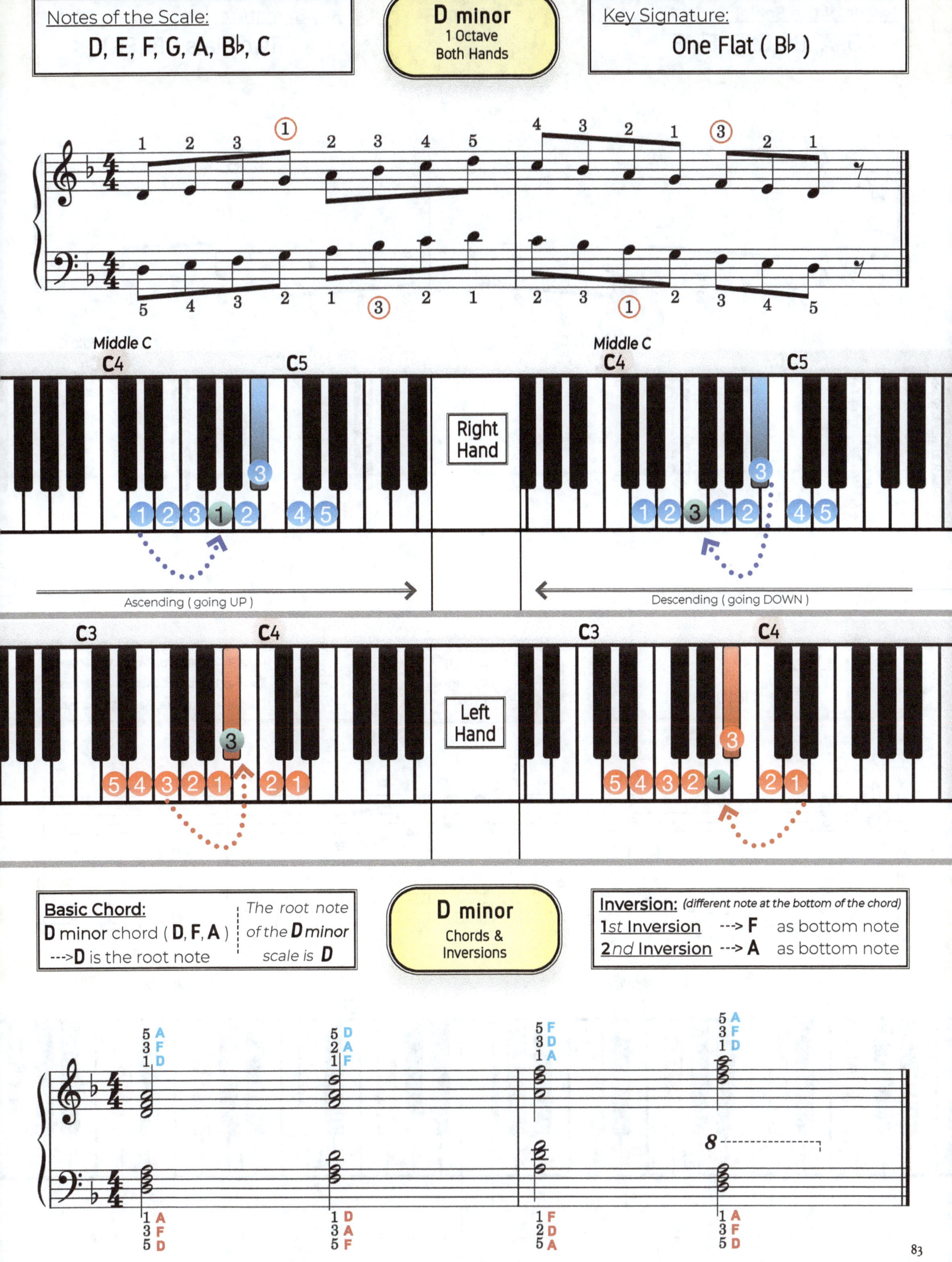

Notes of the Scale:
D, E, F, G, A, B♭, C

D minor
1 Octave
Both Hands

Key Signature:
One Flat (B♭)

Middle C
C4
C5
Right Hand
Ascending (going UP)

Middle C
C4
C5
Descending (going DOWN)

C3
C4

C3
C4
Left Hand

Basic Chord:
D minor chord (D, F, A)
---> D is the root note

The root note of the D minor scale is D

D minor
Chords &
Inversions

Inversion: (different note at the bottom of the chord)
1st Inversion ---> F as bottom note
2nd Inversion ---> A as bottom note

5 A
3 F
1 D

5 D
2 A
1 F

5 F
3 D
1 A

5 A
3 F
1 D

8

1 A
3 F
5 D

1 D
3 A
5 F

1 F
2 D
5 A

1 A
3 F
5 D

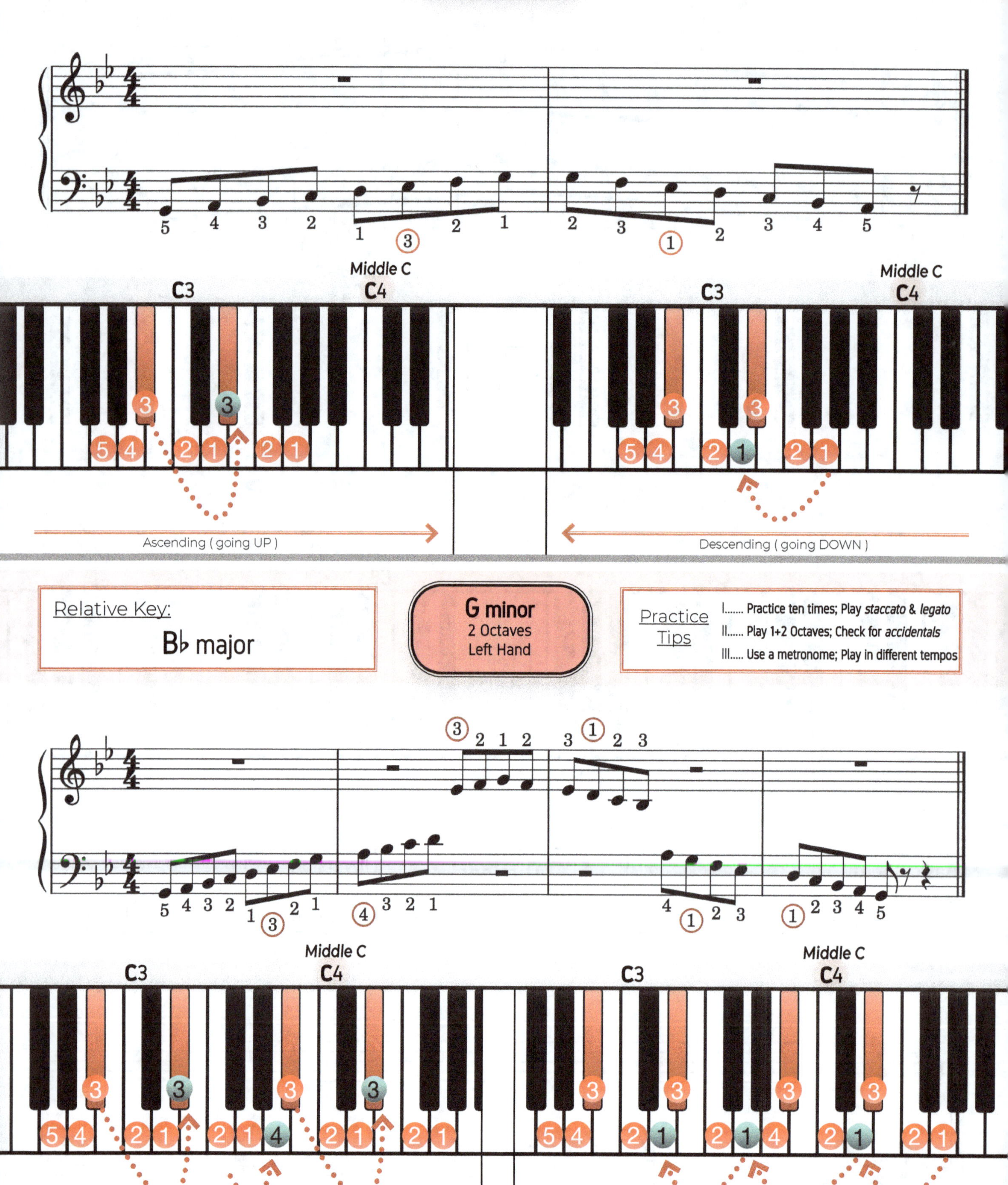

Notes of the Scale:
G, A, B♭, C, D, E♭, F

G minor
1 Octave
Left Hand

Key Signature:
Two Flats (B♭, E♭)

C3
Middle C
C4
C3
Middle C
C4

Ascending (going UP)
Descending (going DOWN)

Relative Key:
B♭ major

G minor
2 Octaves
Left Hand

Practice Tips
I....... Practice ten times; Play staccato & legato
II..... Play 1+2 Octaves; Check for accidentals
III..... Use a metronome; Play in different tempos

C3
Middle C
C4
C3
Middle C
C4

Ascending (going UP)
Descending (going DOWN)

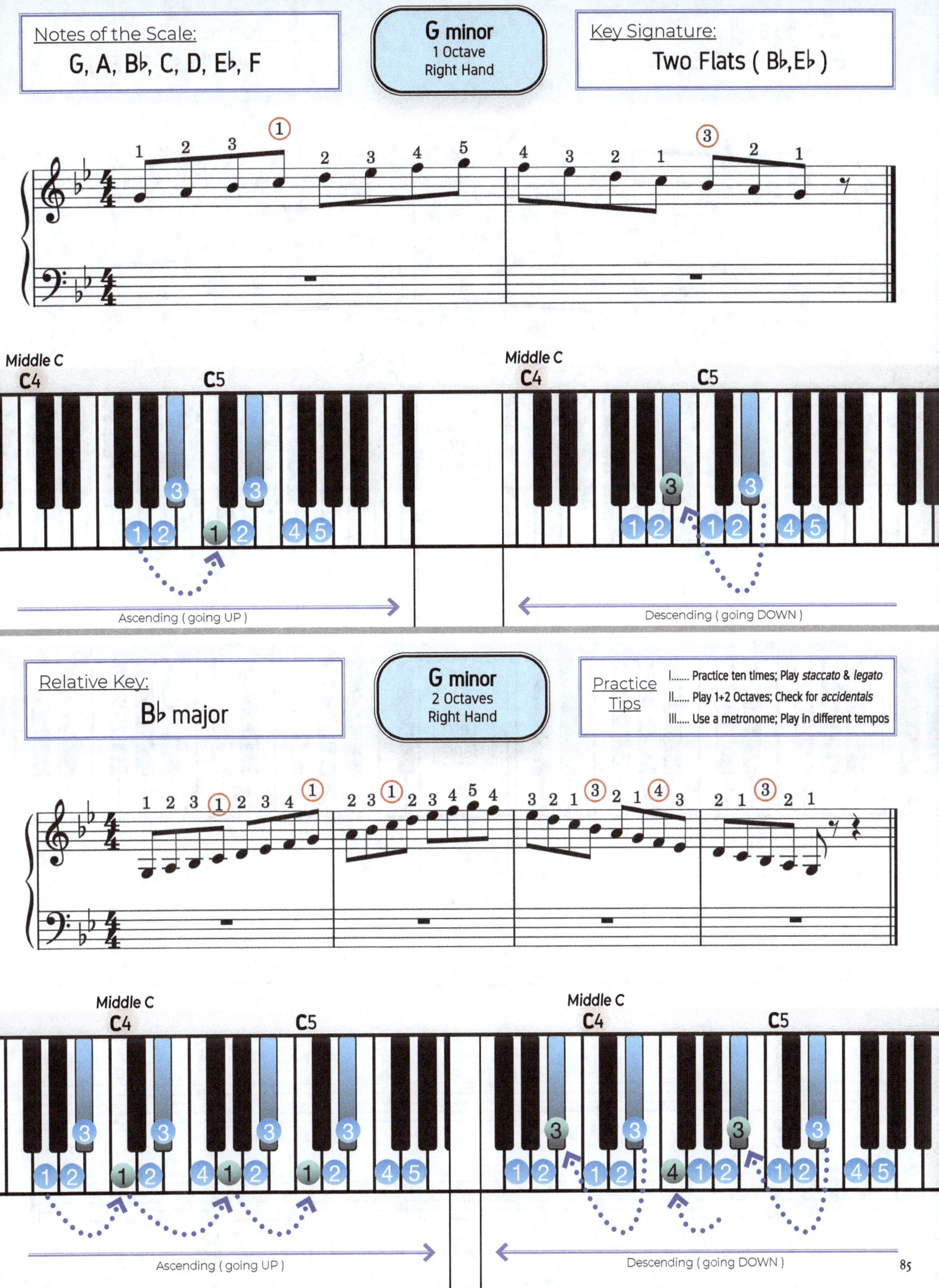

Notes of the Scale:
G, A, B♭, C, D, E♭, F
G minor
1 Octave
Right Hand
Key Signature:
Two Flats (B♭, E♭)
Middle C
C4
C5
Middle C
C4
C5
Ascending (going UP)
Descending (going DOWN)
Relative Key:
B♭ major
G minor
2 Octaves
Right Hand
Practice Tips
I....... Practice ten times; Play staccato & legato
II....... Play 1+2 Octaves; Check for accidentals
III..... Use a metronome; Play in different tempos
Middle C
C4
C5
Middle C
C4
C5
Ascending (going UP)
Descending (going DOWN)
85

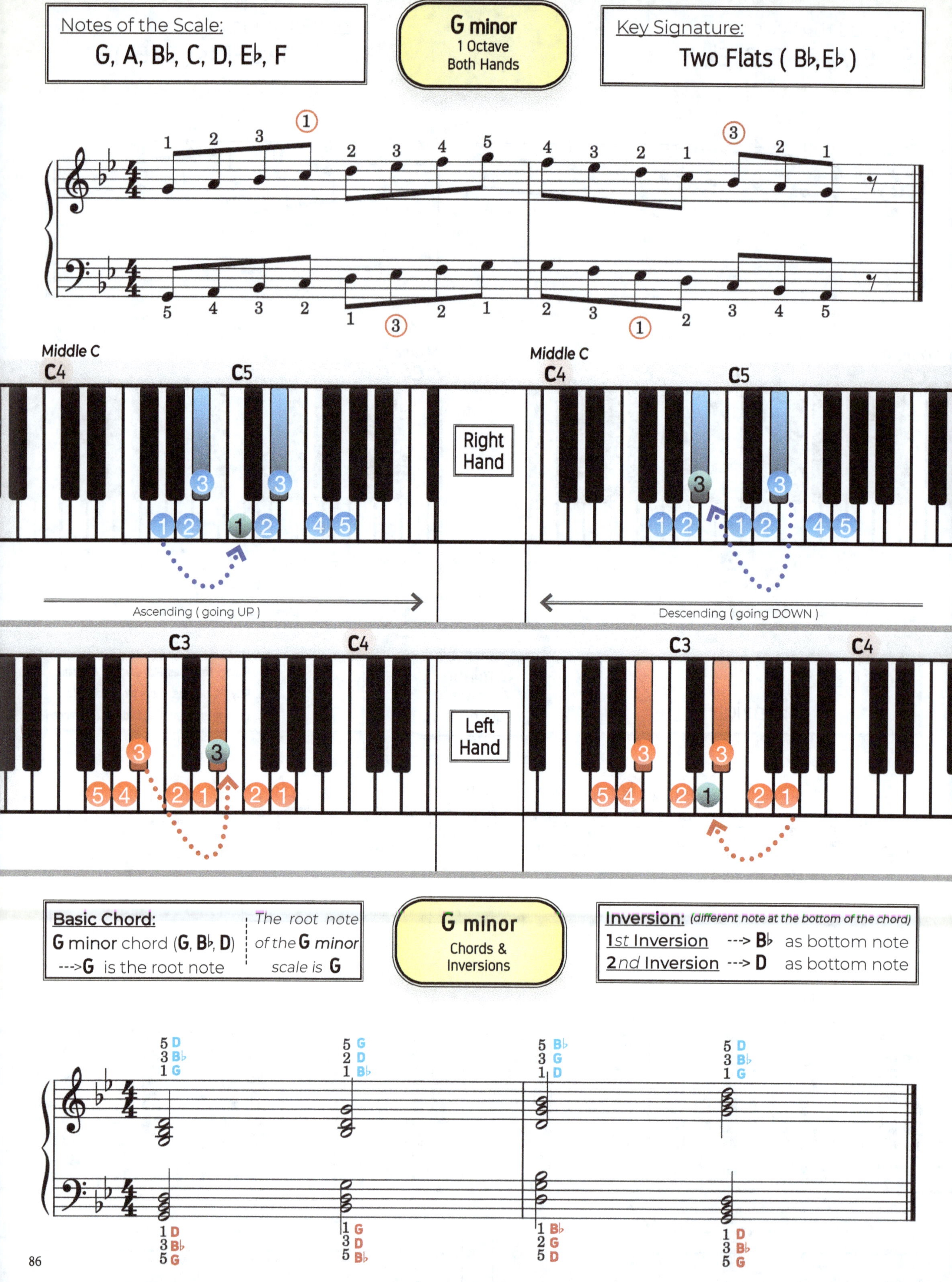

Notes of the Scale:
G, A, B♭, C, D, E♭, F
G minor
1 Octave
Both Hands
Key Signature:
Two Flats (B♭, E♭)
Middle C
C4
C5
Right Hand
Ascending (going UP)
Middle C
C4
C5
Descending (going DOWN)
C3
C4
Left Hand
C3
C4
Basic Chord:
G minor chord (G, B♭, D)
--->G is the root note
The root note of the G minor scale is G
G minor
Chords & Inversions
Inversion: (different note at the bottom of the chord)
1st Inversion ---> B♭ as bottom note
2nd Inversion ---> D as bottom note
5 D
3 B♭
1 G
5 G
2 D
1 B♭
5 B♭
3 G
1 D
5 D
3 B♭
1 G
1 D
3 B♭
5 G
1 G
3 D
5 B♭
1 B♭
2 G
5 D
1 D
3 B♭
5 G
86

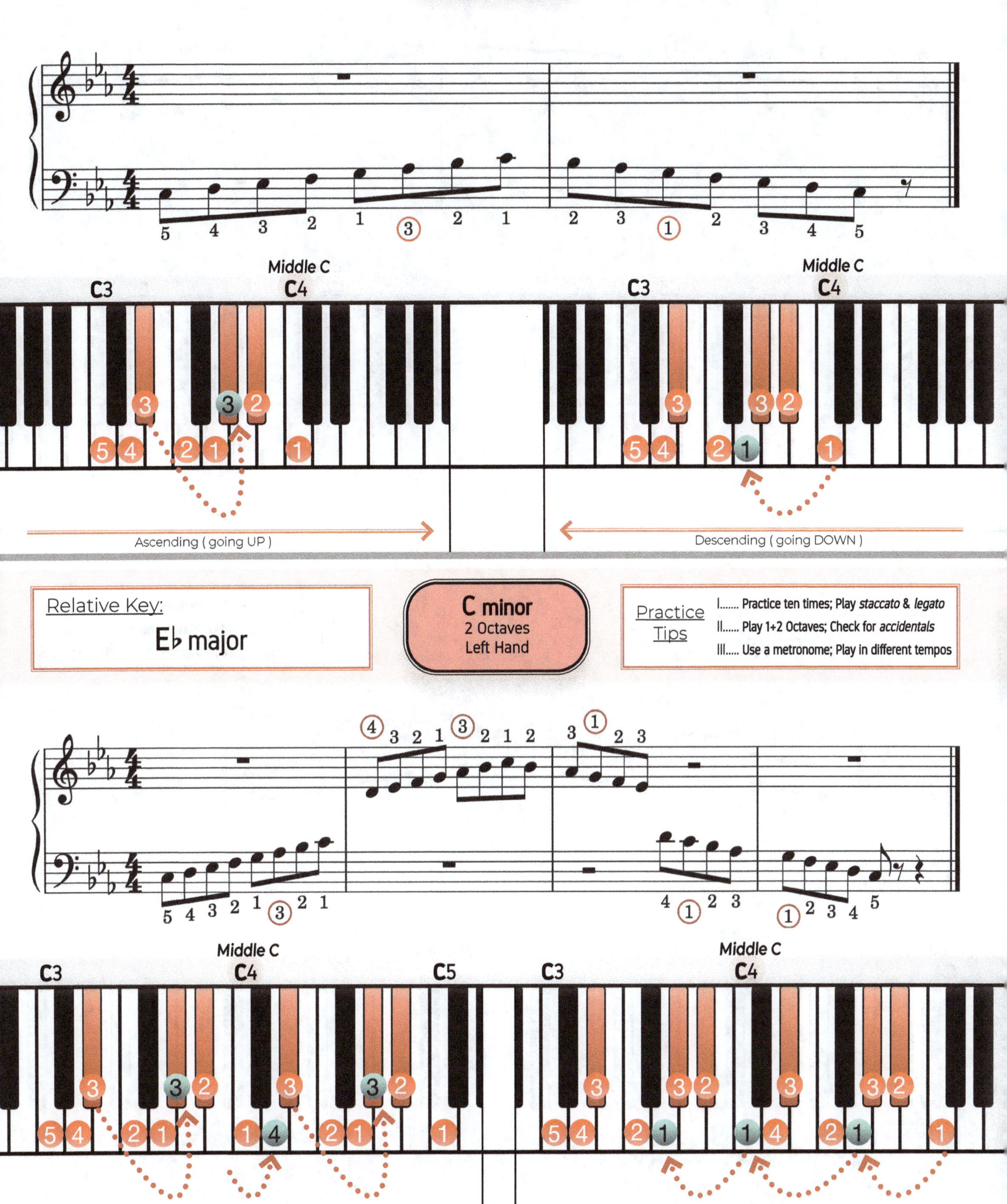
Notes of the Scale:
C, D, E♭, F, G, A♭, B♭
C minor
1 Octave
Left Hand
Key Signature:
Three Flats (B♭, E♭, A♭)
Middle C
C3
C4
Middle C
C3
C4
Ascending (going UP)
Descending (going DOWN)
Relative Key:
E♭ major
C minor
2 Octaves
Left Hand
Practice Tips
I....... Practice ten times; Play staccato & legato
II...... Play 1+2 Octaves; Check for accidentals
III..... Use a metronome; Play in different tempos
Middle C
C3
C4
C5
C3
C4
Middle C
Ascending (going UP)
Descending (going DOWN)
87

Notes of the Scale:

C, D, Eb, F, G, Ab, Bb

C minor
1 Octave
Right Hand

Key Signature:

Three Flats (Bb, Eb, Ab)

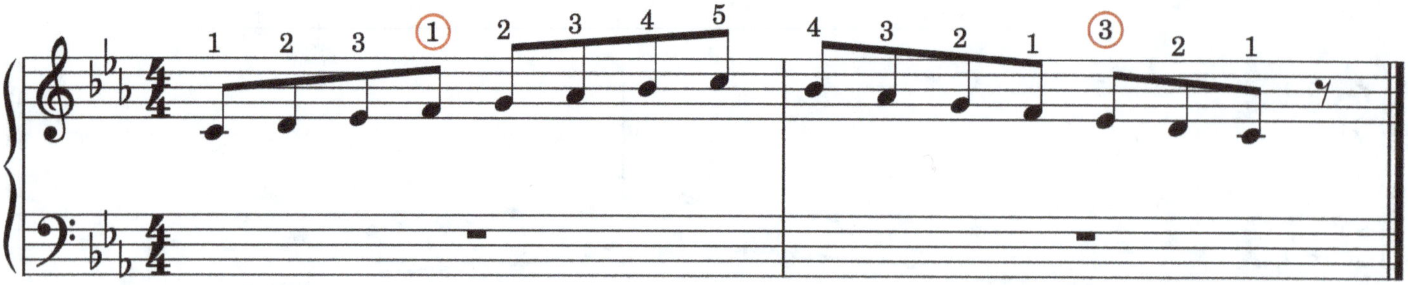

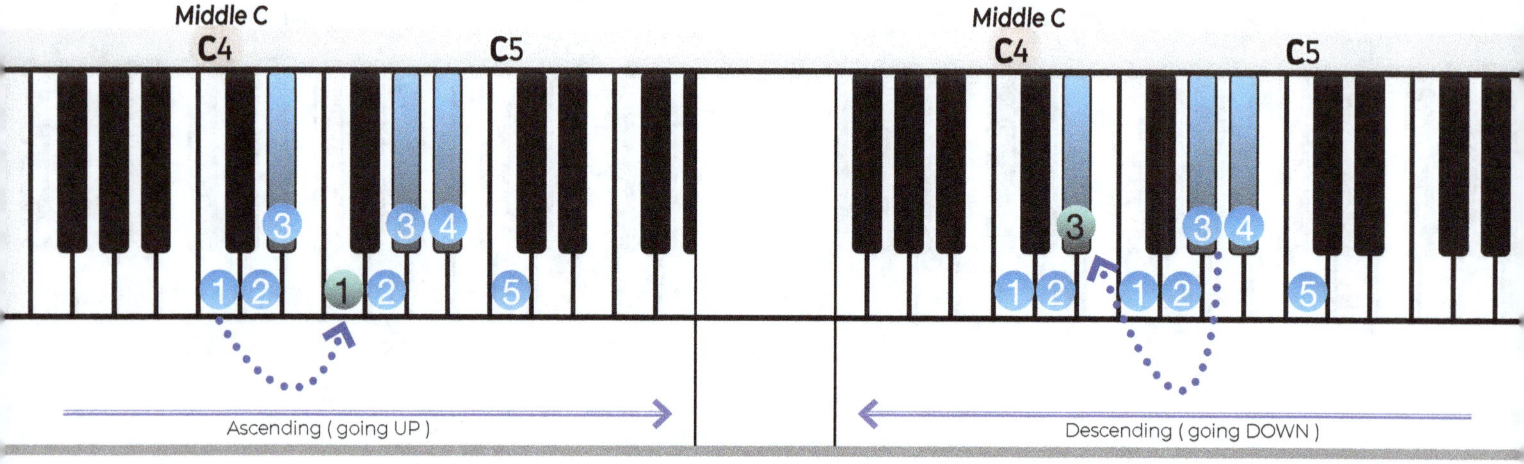

Middle C
C4   C5

Ascending (going UP)

Middle C
C4   C5

Descending (going DOWN)

Relative Key:

Eb major

C minor
2 Octaves
Right Hand

Practice Tips

I....... Practice ten times; Play *staccato* & *legato*

II..... Play 1+2 Octaves; Check for *accidentals*

III..... Use a metronome; Play in different tempos

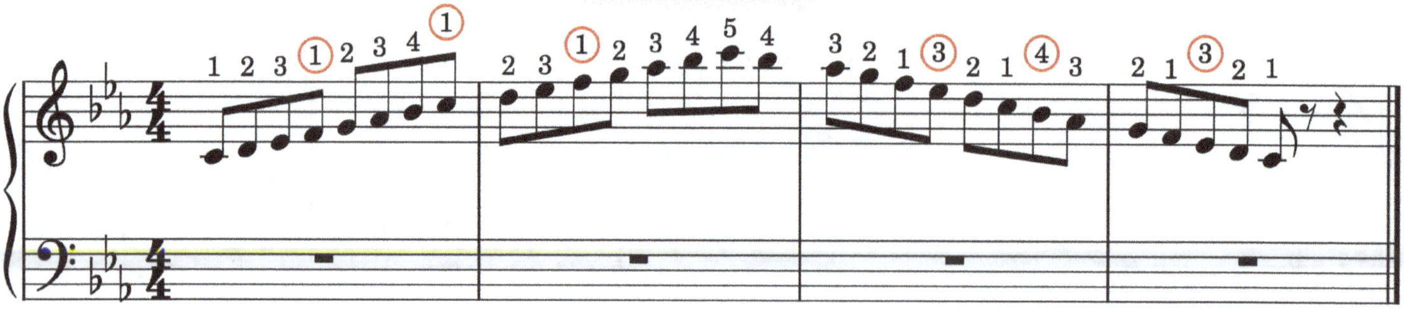

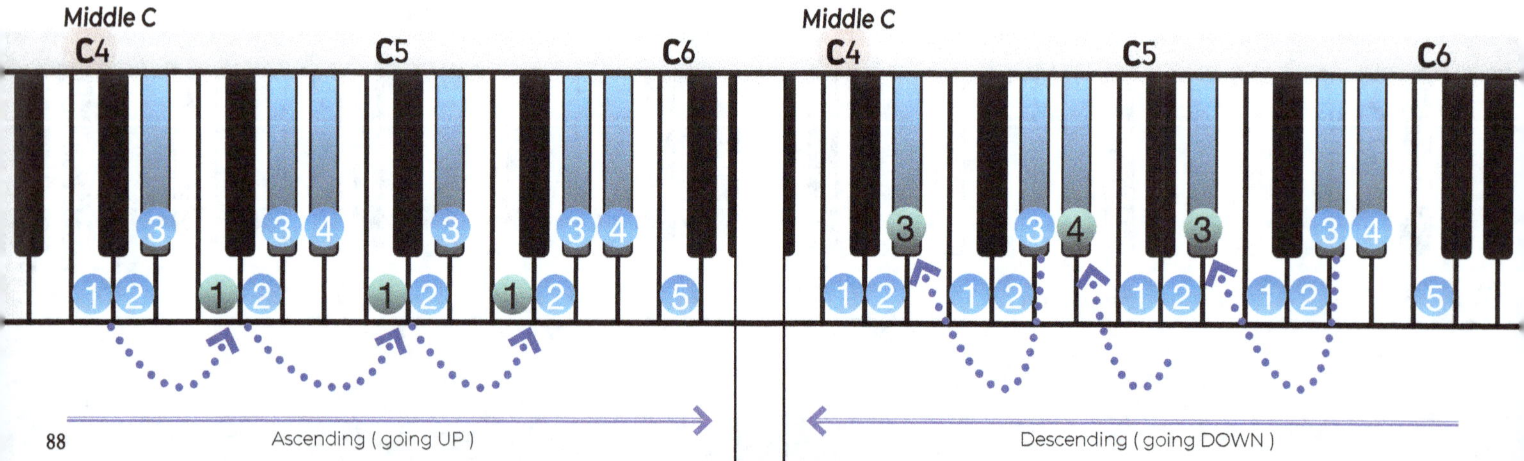

Middle C
C4   C5   C6

Ascending (going UP)

Middle C
C4   C5   C6

Descending (going DOWN)

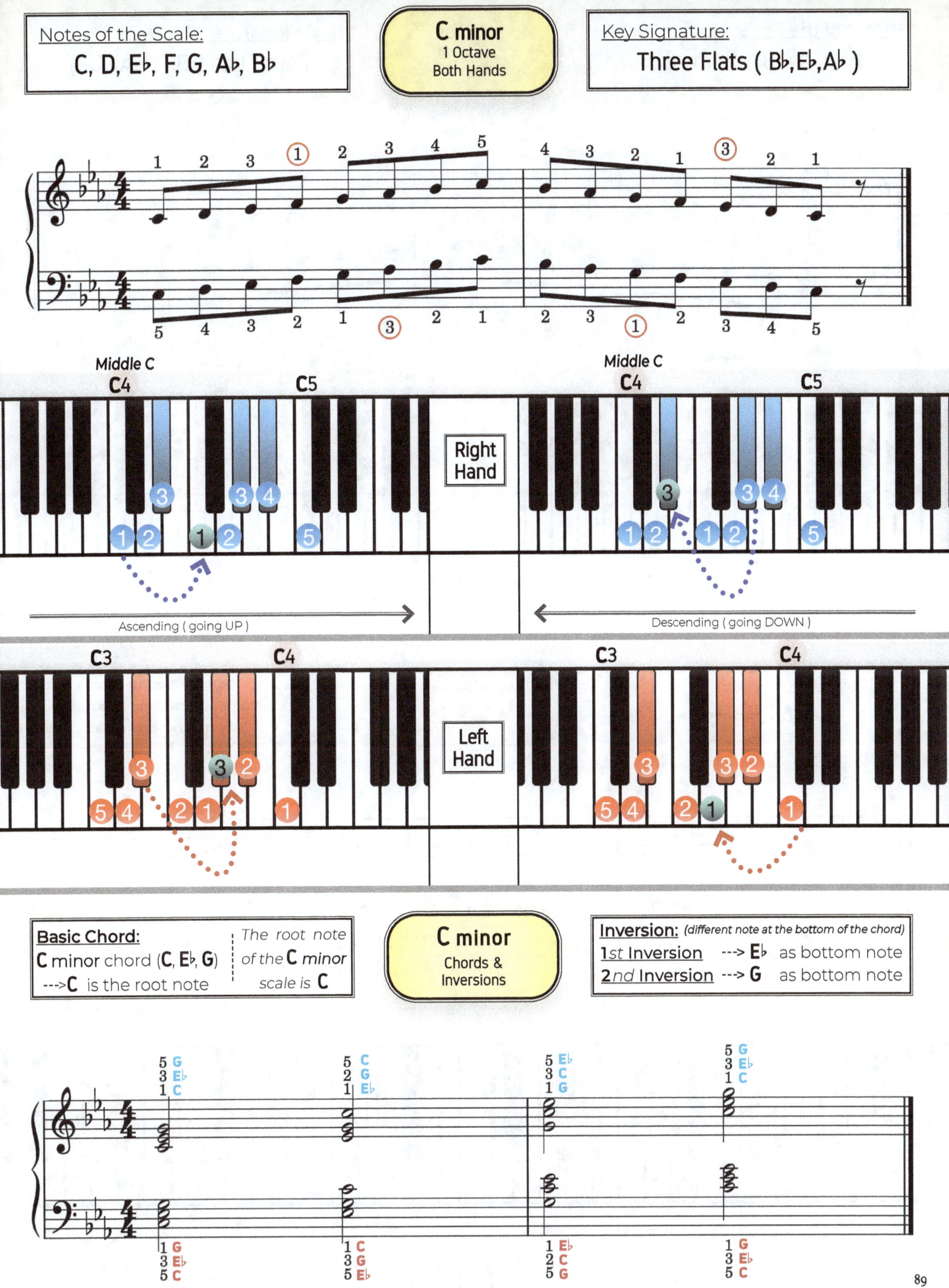

Notes of the Scale:
C, D, E♭, F, G, A♭, B♭

C minor
1 Octave
Both Hands

Key Signature:
Three Flats (B♭, E♭, A♭)

Middle C
C4
C5
Right Hand
Ascending (going UP)
Descending (going DOWN)

Middle C
C4
C5

C3
C4
Left Hand

C3
C4

Basic Chord:
C minor chord (C, E♭, G)
---> C is the root note

The root note of the C minor scale is C

C minor
Chords & Inversions

Inversion: (different note at the bottom of the chord)
1st Inversion ---> E♭ as bottom note
2nd Inversion ---> G as bottom note

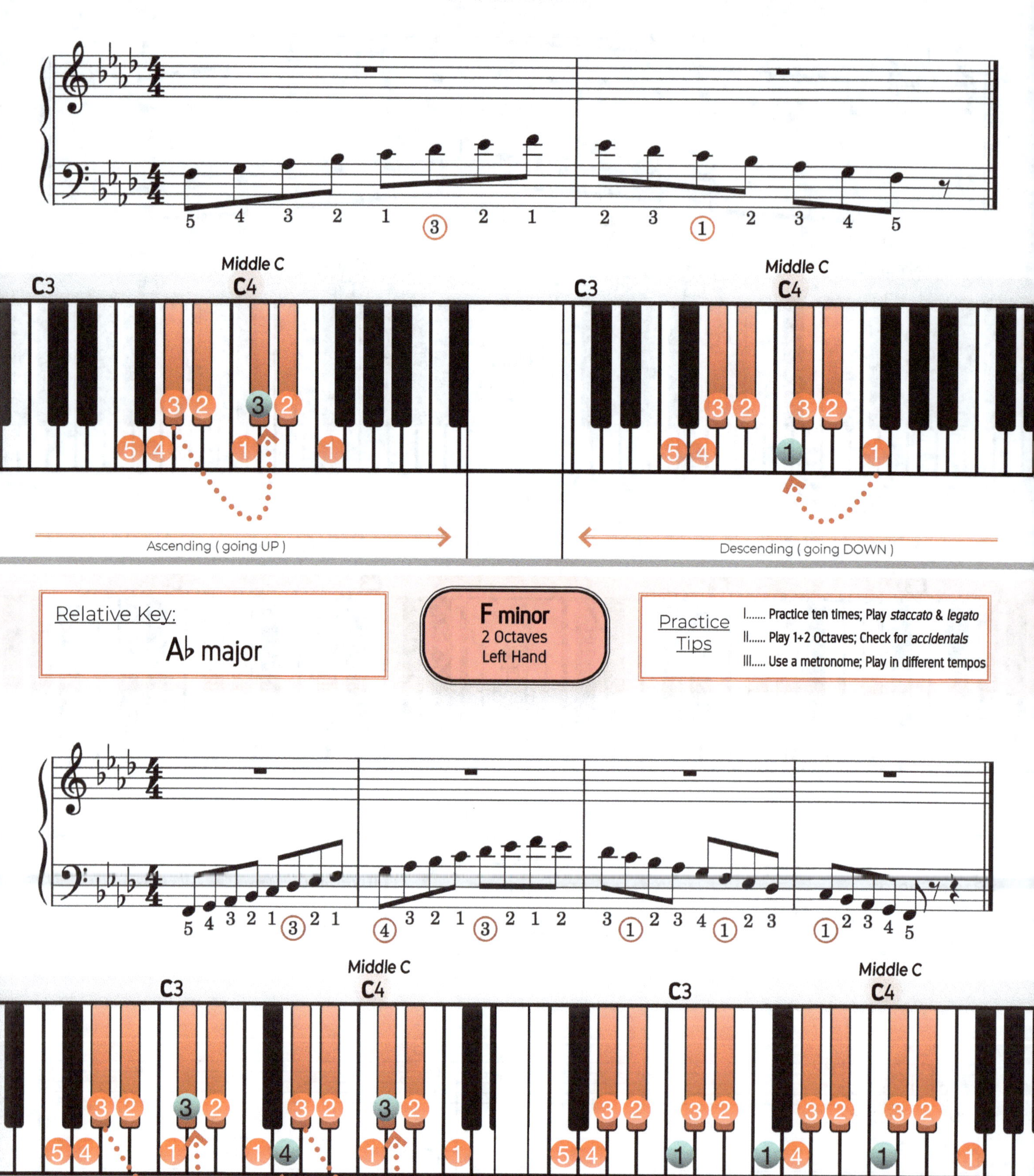

Notes of the Scale:
F, G, A♭, B♭, C, D♭, E♭
F minor
1 Octave
Left Hand
Key Signature:
Four Flats (B♭, E♭, A♭, D♭)
Middle C
C3
C4
5 4 3 2 1 3 2 1
2 3 1 2 3 4 5
Ascending (going UP)
Descending (going DOWN)
Relative Key:
A♭ major
F minor
2 Octaves
Left Hand
Practice Tips
I....... Practice ten times; Play staccato & legato
II...... Play 1+2 Octaves; Check for accidentals
III..... Use a metronome; Play in different tempos
5 4 3 2 1 3 2 1
4 3 2 1 3 2 1 2
3 1 2 3 4 1 2 3
1 2 3 4 5
Middle C
C3
C4
C3
Middle C
C4
Ascending (going UP)
Descending (going DOWN)

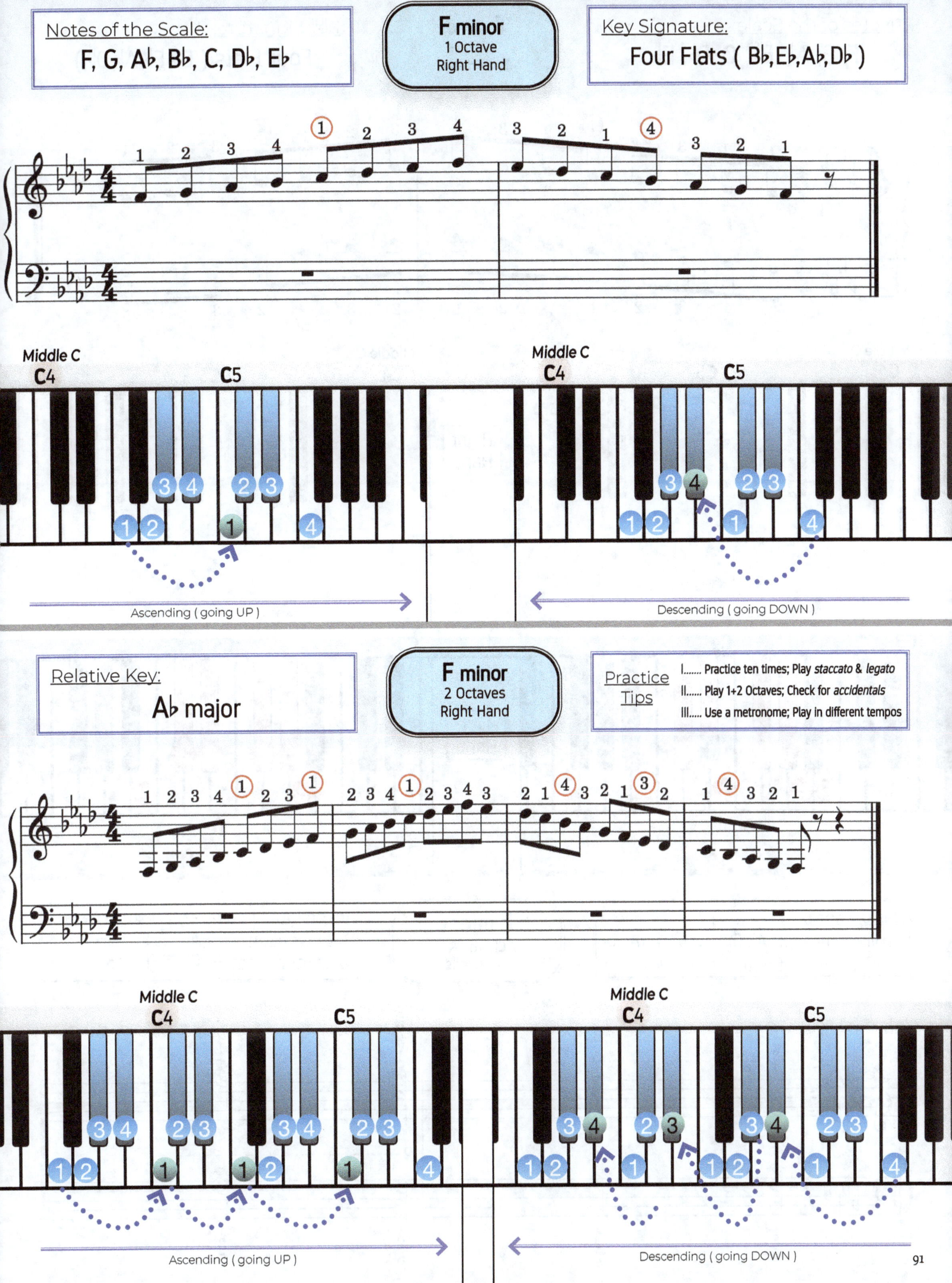

Notes of the Scale:
F, G, Ab, Bb, C, Db, Eb

F minor
1 Octave
Right Hand

Key Signature:
Four Flats (Bb, Eb, Ab, Db)

Middle C
C4
C5
3 4 2 3
1 2 1 4
Ascending (going UP)

Middle C
C4
C5
3 4 2 3
1 2 1 4
Descending (going DOWN)

Relative Key:
Ab major

F minor
2 Octaves
Right Hand

Practice Tips
I....... Practice ten times; Play staccato & legato
II...... Play 1+2 Octaves; Check for accidentals
III..... Use a metronome; Play in different tempos

Middle C
C4
C5
3 4 2 3 3 4 2 3
1 2 1 2 1 4
Ascending (going UP)

Middle C
C4
C5
3 4 2 3 3 4 2 3
1 2 1 1 2 1 4
Descending (going DOWN)

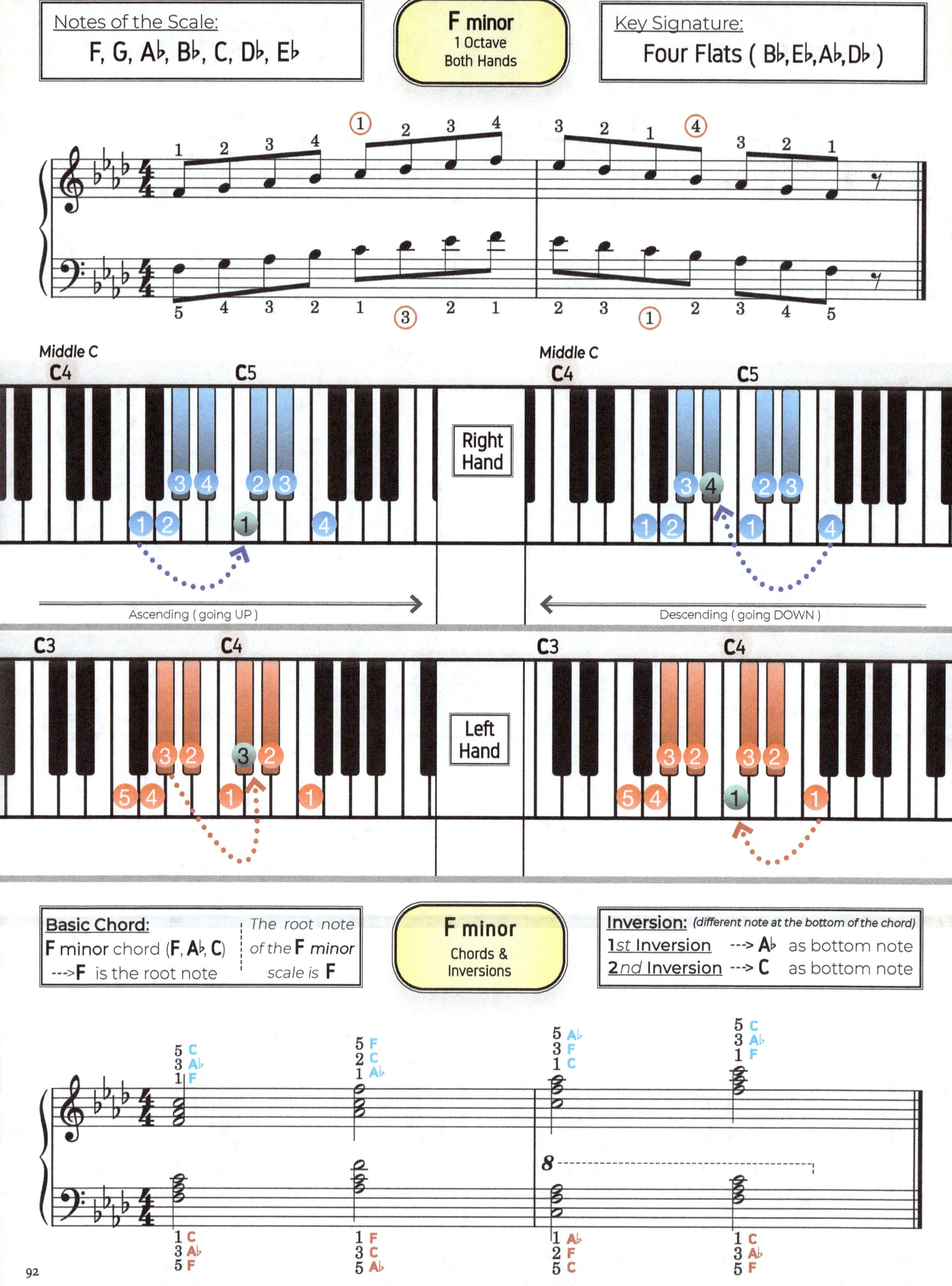

Notes of the Scale:
F, G, A♭, B♭, C, D♭, E♭

F minor
1 Octave
Both Hands

Key Signature:
Four Flats (B♭, E♭, A♭, D♭)

Middle C
C4
C5
Right Hand
Ascending (going UP)
Descending (going DOWN)
Middle C
C4
C5

C3
C4
Left Hand
C3
C4

Basic Chord:
F minor chord (F, A♭, C)
---> F is the root note
The root note of the F minor scale is F

F minor
Chords & Inversions

Inversion: (different note at the bottom of the chord)
1st Inversion ---> A♭ as bottom note
2nd Inversion ---> C as bottom note

5 C
3 A♭
1 F

5 F
2 C
1 A♭

5 A♭
3 F
1 C

5 C
3 A♭
1 F

1 C
3 A♭
5 F

1 F
3 C
5 A♭

1 A♭
2 F
5 C

1 C
3 A♭
5 F

92

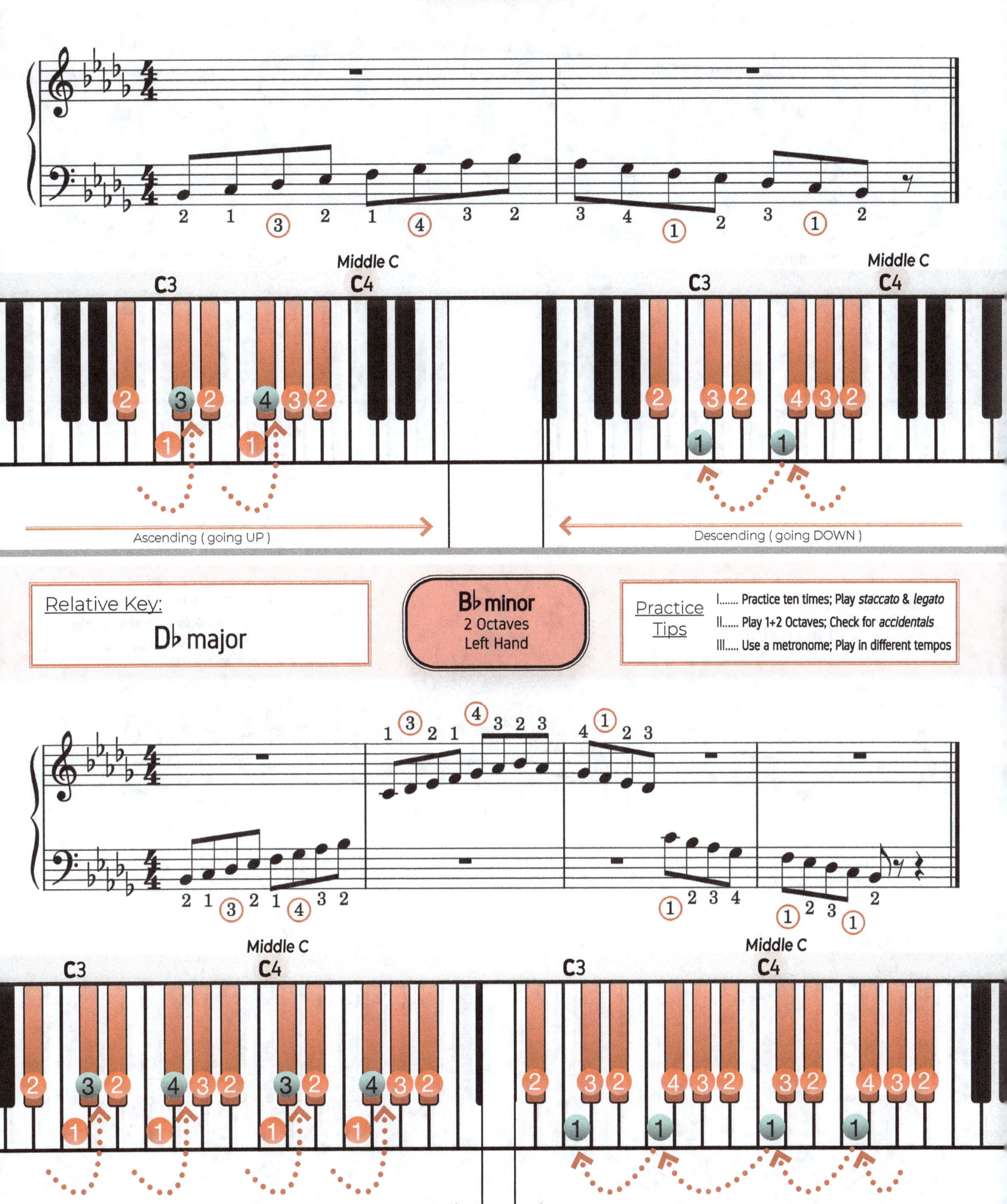

Notes of the Scale:
Bb, C, Db, Eb, F, Gb, Ab

Bb minor
1 Octave
Left Hand

Key Signature:
Five Flats (Bb, Eb, Ab, Db, Gb)

Middle C
C3
C4

2 1 3 2 1 4 3 2   3 4 1 2 3 1 2

Ascending (going UP)

Descending (going DOWN)

Relative Key:
Db major

Bb minor
2 Octaves
Left Hand

Practice Tips
I....... Practice ten times; Play staccato & legato
II...... Play 1+2 Octaves; Check for accidentals
III..... Use a metronome; Play in different tempos

Middle C
C3   C4

1 3 2 1 4 3 2 3   4 1 2 3

2 1 3 2 1 4 3 2   1 2 3 4   1 2 3 1

Middle C
C3   C4

Ascending (going UP)

Descending (going DOWN)

Notes of the Scale:
Bb, C, Db, Eb, F, Gb, Ab
Bb minor
1 Octave
Right Hand
Key Signature:
Five Flats (Bb, Eb, Ab, Db, Gb)
3 1 2 3 1 2 3 4 3 2 1 3 2 1 3
Middle C
C4
C5
3 2 3 2 3 4
1 1
Ascending (going UP)
Middle C
C4
C5
3 2 3 2 3 4
1 1
Descending (going DOWN)
Relative Key:
Db major
Bb minor
2 Octaves
Right Hand
Practice Tips
I....... Practice ten times; Play staccato & legato
II...... Play 1+2 Octaves; Check for accidentals
III..... Use a metronome; Play in different tempos
3 1 2 3 1 2 3 4 1 2 3 1 2 3 4 3 2 1 3 2 1 4 3 2 1 3 2 1 3
Middle C
C4
C5
3 2 3 2 3 4 2 3 2 3 4
1 1 1 1
Ascending (going UP)
Middle C
C4
C5
3 2 3 2 3 4 2 3 2 3 4
1 1 1 1
Descending (going DOWN)

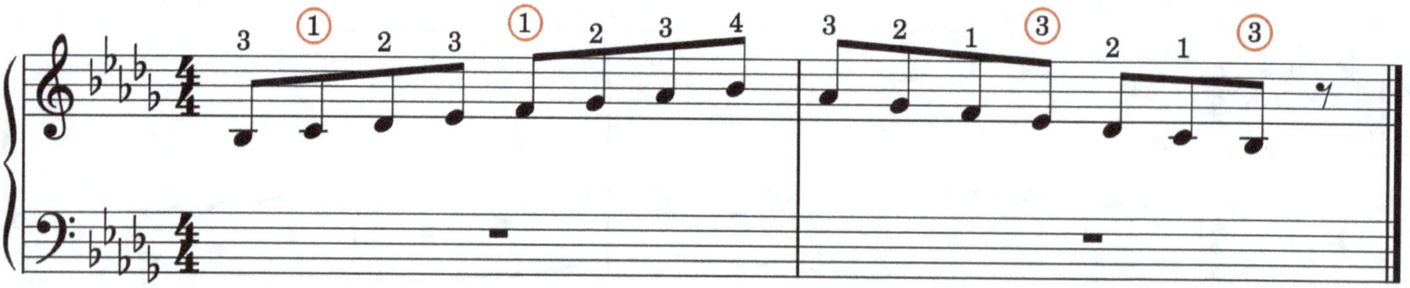

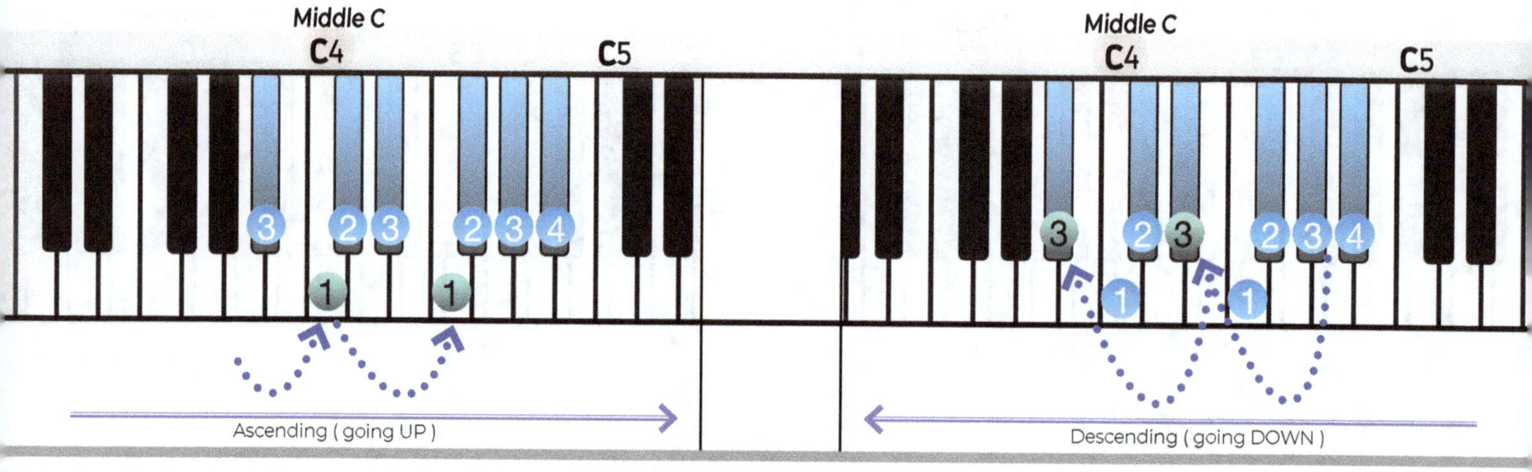

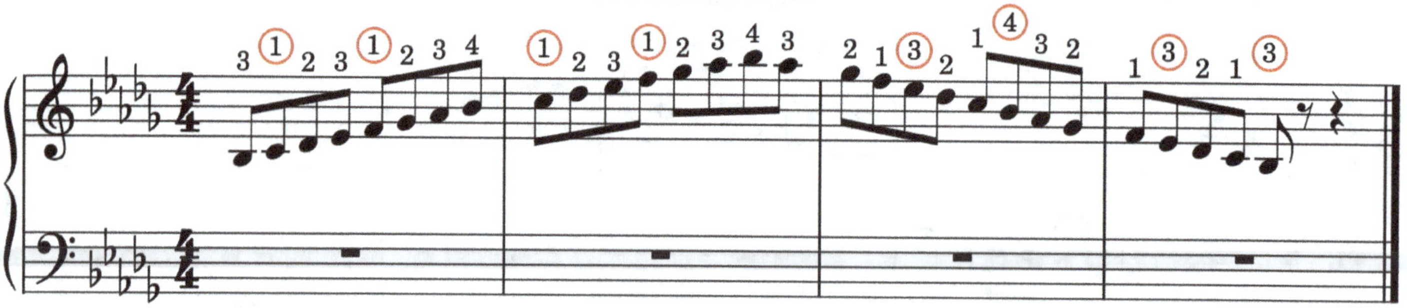

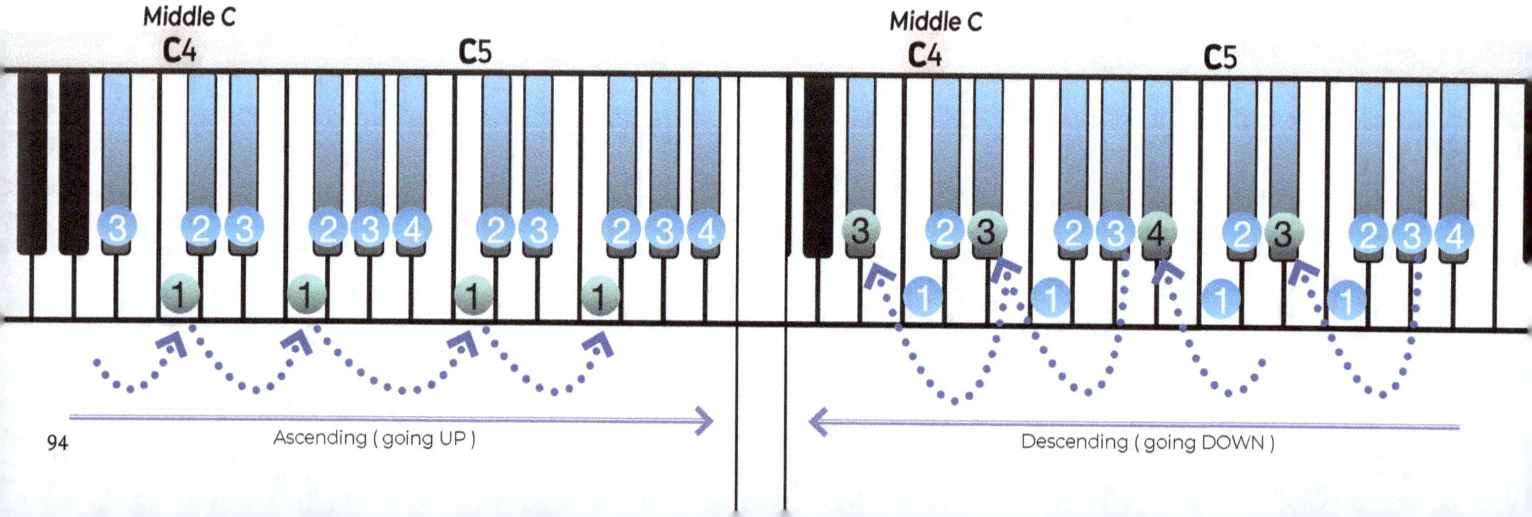

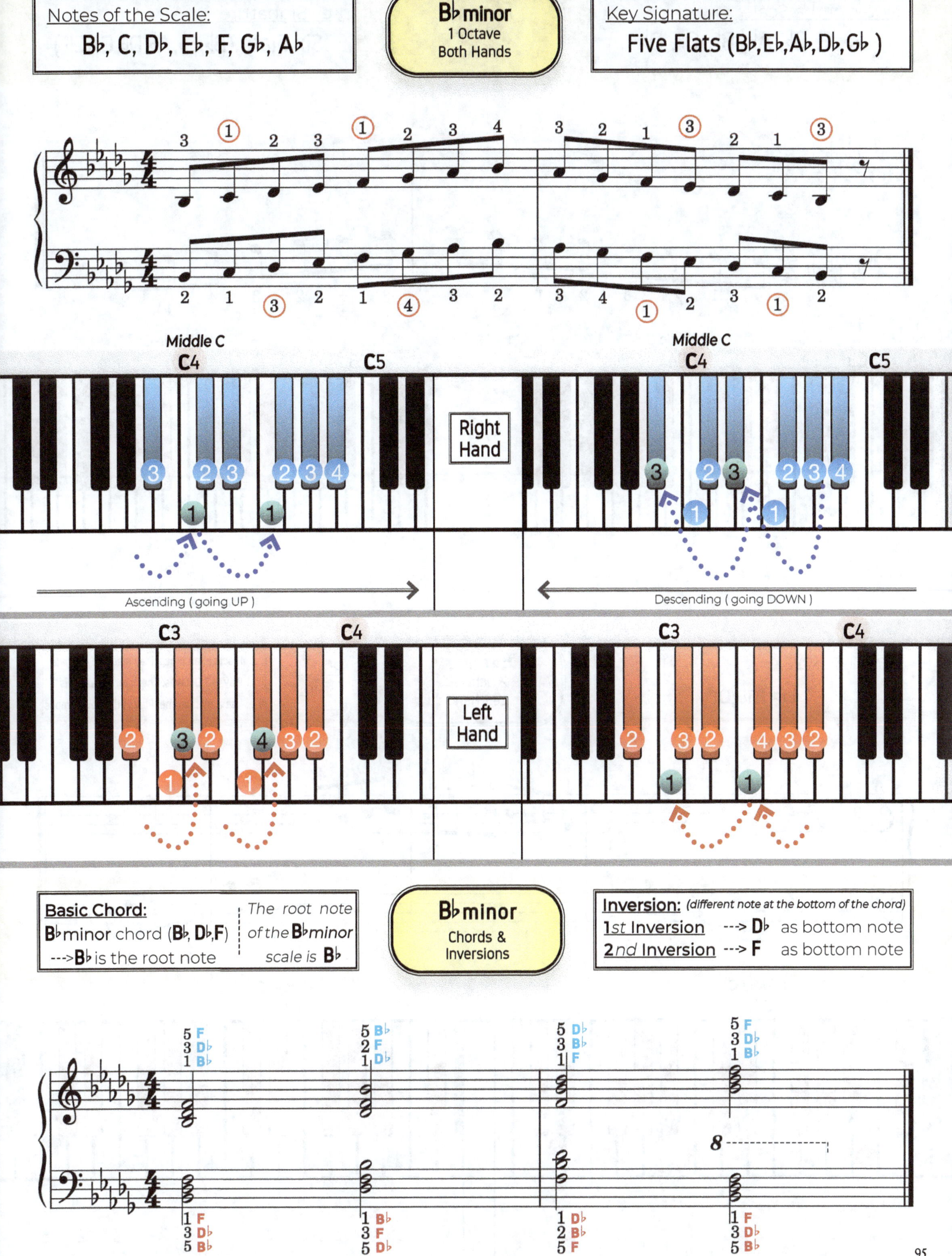

Notes of the Scale:
B♭, C, D♭, E♭, F, G♭, A♭

B♭ minor
1 Octave
Both Hands

Key Signature:
Five Flats (B♭,E♭,A♭,D♭,G♭)

Middle C
C4
C5
Right Hand
Ascending (going UP)
Descending (going DOWN)

C3
C4
Left Hand

Basic Chord:
B♭ minor chord (B♭, D♭, F)
---> B♭ is the root note
The root note of the B♭ minor scale is B♭

B♭ minor
Chords &
Inversions

Inversion: (different note at the bottom of the chord)
1st Inversion ---> D♭ as bottom note
2nd Inversion ---> F as bottom note

5 F
3 D♭
1 B♭

5 B♭
2 F
1 D♭

5 D♭
3 B♭
1 F

5 F
3 D♭
1 B♭

8

1 F
3 D♭
5 B♭

1 B♭
3 F
5 D♭

1 D♭
2 B♭
5 F

1 F
3 D♭
5 B♭

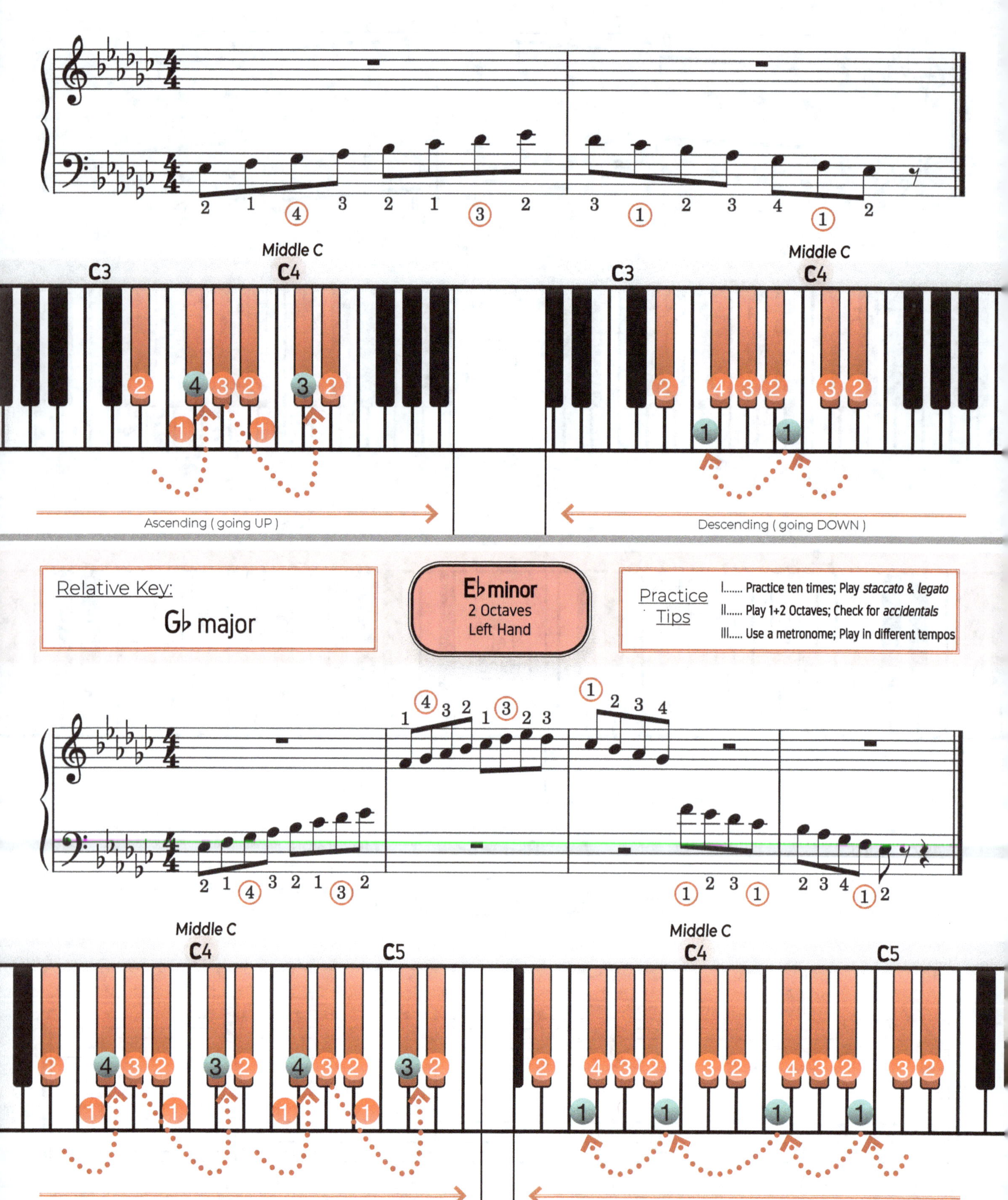

Notes of the Scale:
Eb, F, Gb, Ab, Bb, Cb, Db

Eb minor
1 Octave
Left Hand

Key Signature:
Six Flats (Bb, Eb, Ab, Db, Gb, Cb)

Middle C
C4
C3
2 1 4 3 2 1 3 2 3 1 2 3 4 1 2

Middle C
C4
C3
2 4 3 2 3 2 1 1

Ascending (going UP)
Descending (going DOWN)

Relative Key:
Gb major

Eb minor
2 Octaves
Left Hand

Practice Tips
I....... Practice ten times; Play staccato & legato
II...... Play 1+2 Octaves; Check for accidentals
III..... Use a metronome; Play in different tempos

4 3 2 1 3 2 3 1 2 3 4
2 1 4 3 2 1 3 2 1 2 3 1 2 3 4 1 2

Middle C
C4
C5
2 4 3 2 3 2 4 3 2 3 2

Middle C
C4
C5
2 4 3 2 3 2 4 3 2 3 2
1 1 1 1 1 1 1 1

Ascending (going UP)
Descending (going DOWN)

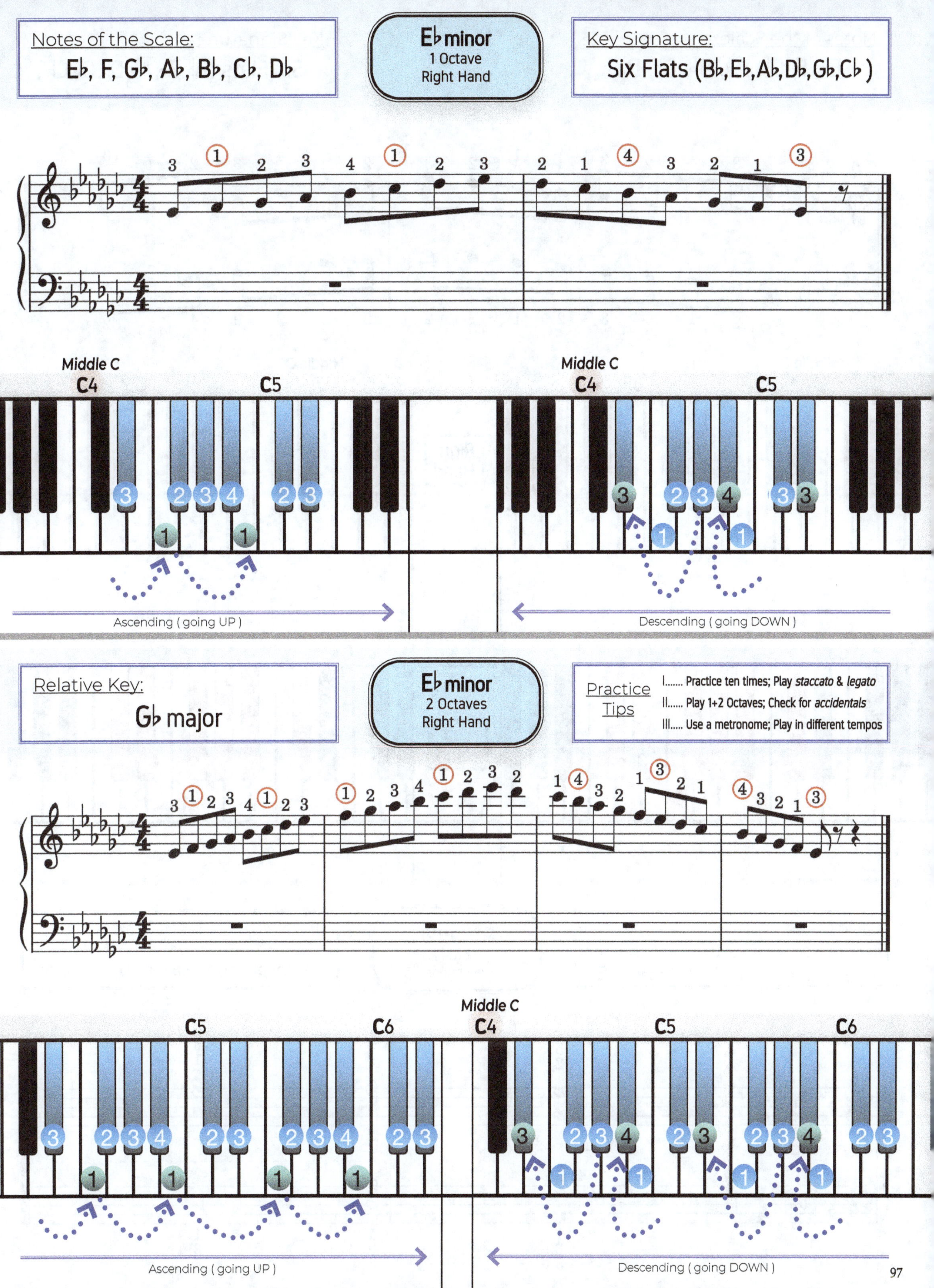

Notes of the Scale:
Eb, F, Gb, Ab, Bb, Cb, Db
Eb minor
1 Octave
Right Hand
Key Signature:
Six Flats (Bb, Eb, Ab, Db, Gb, Cb)
Middle C
C4
C5
Middle C
C4
C5
Ascending (going UP)
Descending (going DOWN)
Relative Key:
Gb major
Eb minor
2 Octaves
Right Hand
Practice Tips
I....... Practice ten times; Play staccato & legato
II...... Play 1+2 Octaves; Check for accidentals
III..... Use a metronome; Play in different tempos
C5
C6
Middle C
C4
C5
C6
Ascending (going UP)
Descending (going DOWN)

Notes of the Scale:
E♭, F, G♭, A♭, B♭, C♭, D♭

E♭ minor
1 Octave
Both Hands

Key Signature:
Six Flats (B♭, E♭, A♭, D♭, G♭, C♭)

Middle C
C4
C5
Right Hand
Ascending (going UP)
Descending (going DOWN)

Middle C
C4
C5

C3
C4
Left Hand

C3
C4

Basic Chord:
E♭ minor chord (E♭, G♭, B♭)
---> E♭ is the root note
The root note of the E♭ minor scale is E♭

E♭ minor
Chords &
Inversions

Inversion: (different note at the bottom of the chord)
1st Inversion ---> G♭ as bottom note
2nd Inversion ---> B♭ as bottom note

5 B♭
3 G♭
1 E♭

5 E♭
2 B♭
1 G♭

5 G♭
3 E♭
1 B♭

5 B♭
3 G♭
1 E♭

1 B♭
3 G♭
5 E♭

1 E♭
3 B♭
5 G♭

1 G♭
2 E♭
5 B♭

1 B♭
3 G♭
5 E♭

Notes of the Scale:
Ab, Bb, Cb, Db, Eb, Fb, Gb

Ab minor
1 Octave
Left Hand

Key Signature:
Seven Flats (Bb, Eb, Ab, Db, Gb, Cb , Fb)

Middle C
C3   C4
Middle C
C3   C4

Ascending (going UP)
Descending (going DOWN)

Relative Key:
Cb major

Ab minor
2 Octaves
Left Hand

Practice Tips
I....... Practice ten times; Play staccato & legato
II...... Play 1+2 Octaves; Check for accidentals
III..... Use a metronome; Play in different tempos

Middle C
C3   C4
Middle C
C3   C4

Ascending (going UP)
Descending (going DOWN)

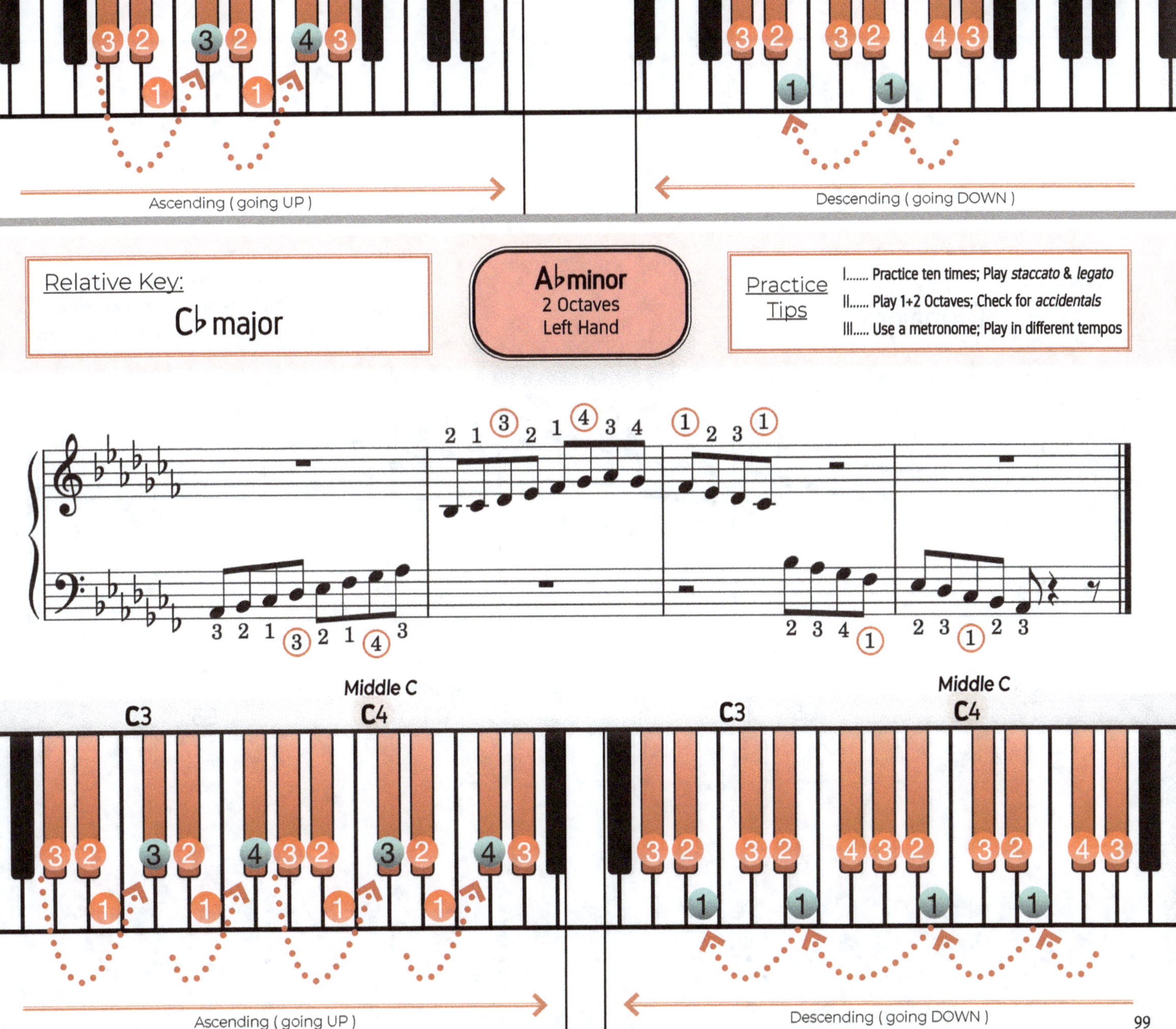

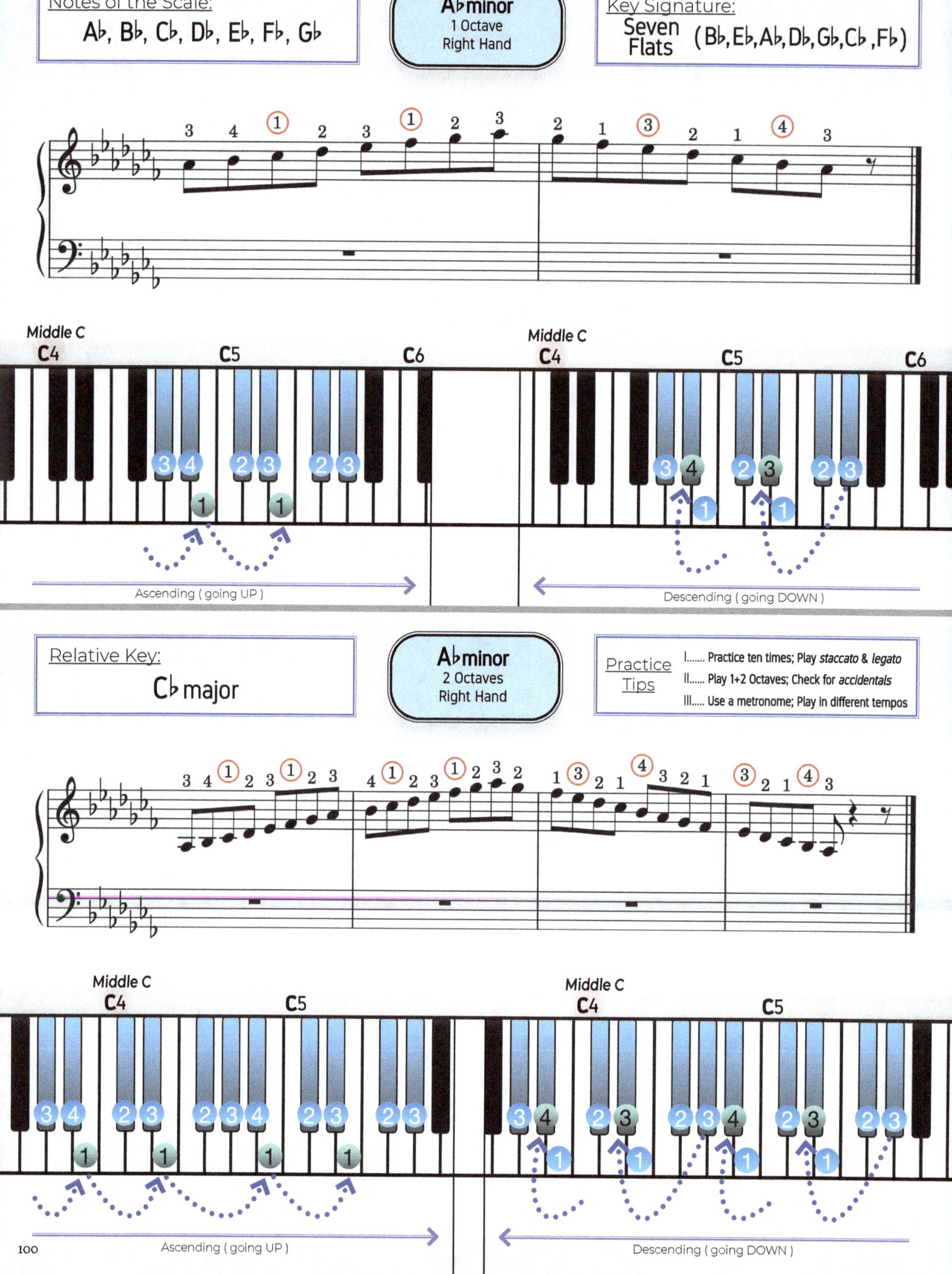

Notes of the Scale:
Ab, Bb, Cb, Db, Eb, Fb, Gb

Ab minor
1 Octave
Right Hand

Key Signature:
Seven Flats (Bb, Eb, Ab, Db, Gb, Cb, Fb)

Middle C
C4
C5
C6
Middle C
C4
C5
C6

Ascending (going UP)
Descending (going DOWN)

Relative Key:
Cb major

Ab minor
2 Octaves
Right Hand

Practice Tips
I....... Practice ten times; Play staccato & legato
II...... Play 1+2 Octaves; Check for accidentals
III..... Use a metronome; Play in different tempos

Middle C
C4
C5
Middle C
C4
C5

Ascending (going UP)
Descending (going DOWN)

100

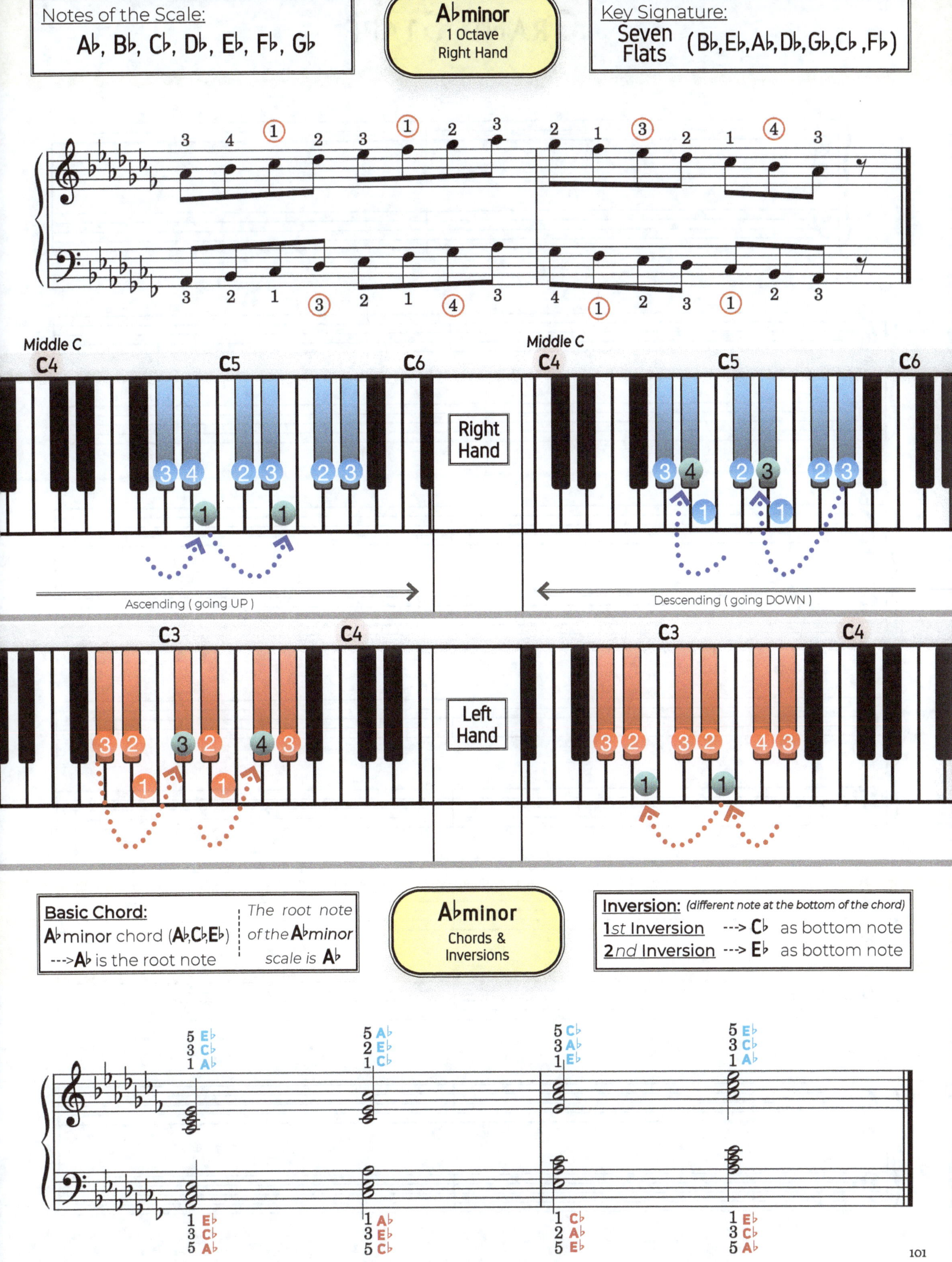

Notes of the Scale:
Ab, Bb, Cb, Db, Eb, Fb, Gb

Ab minor
1 Octave
Right Hand

Key Signature:
Seven Flats (Bb, Eb, Ab, Db, Gb, Cb, Fb)

3 4 1 2 3 1 2 3   2 1 3 2 1 4 3
3 2 1 3 2 1 4 3   4 1 2 3 1 2 3

Middle C
C4   C5   C6
3 4   2 3   2 3
1   1
Ascending (going UP)

Middle C
C4   C5   C6
3 4   2 3   2 3
1   1
Descending (going DOWN)

Right Hand

C3   C4
3 2   3 2   4 3
1   1
Left Hand

C3   C4
3 2   3 2   4 3
1   1

Basic Chord:
Ab minor chord (Ab,Cb,Eb)
---> Ab is the root note

The root note of the Ab minor scale is Ab

Ab minor
Chords &
Inversions

Inversion: (different note at the bottom of the chord)
1st Inversion ---> Cb as bottom note
2nd Inversion ---> Eb as bottom note

5 Eb   5 Ab   5 Cb   5 Eb
3 Cb   2 Eb   3 Ab   3 Cb
1 Ab   1 Cb   1 Eb   1 Ab

1 Eb   1 Ab   1 Cb   1 Eb
3 Cb   3 Eb   2 Ab   3 Cb
5 Ab   5 Cb   5 Eb   5 Ab

GRAND STAFF

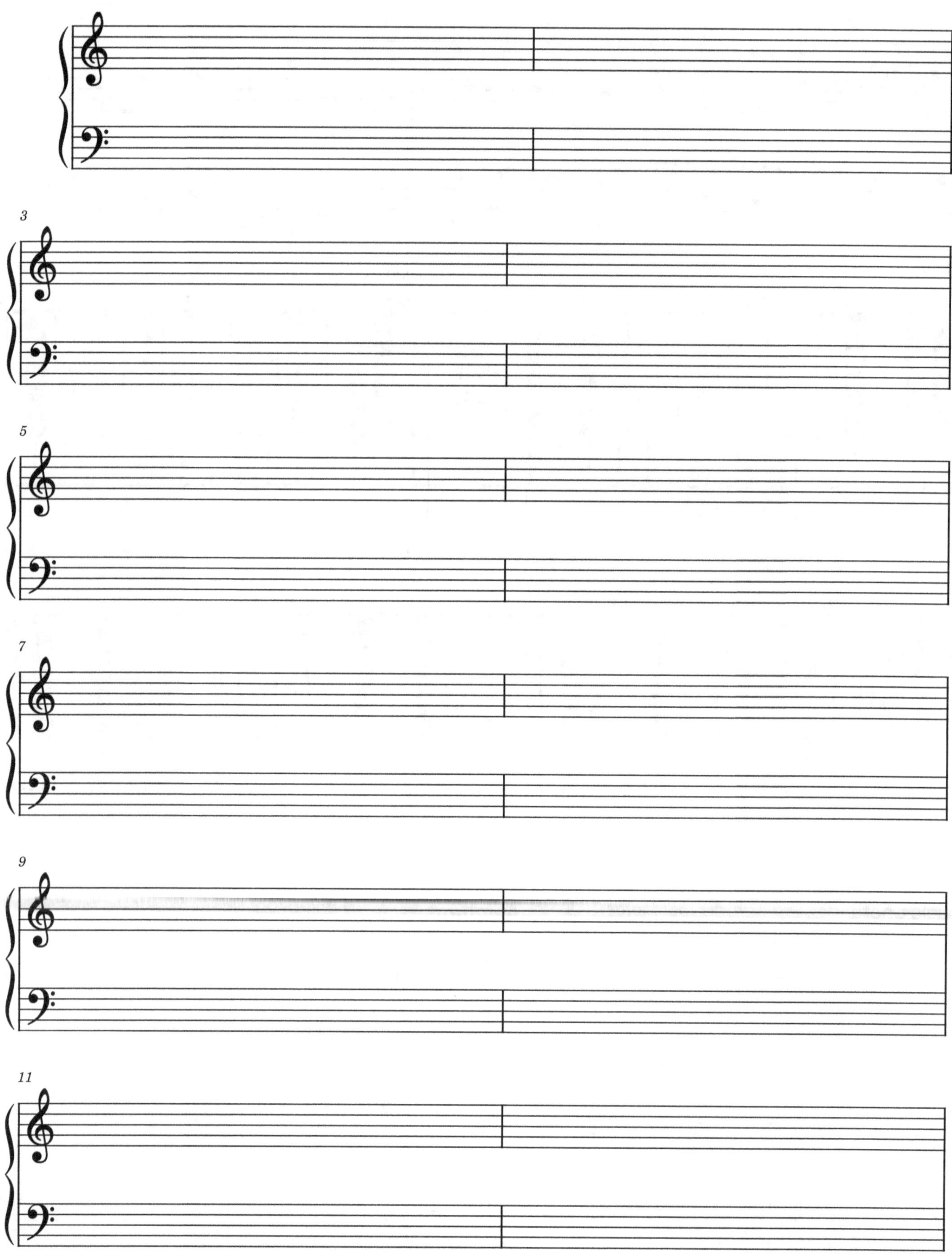

SOLUTION TO EXERCISES

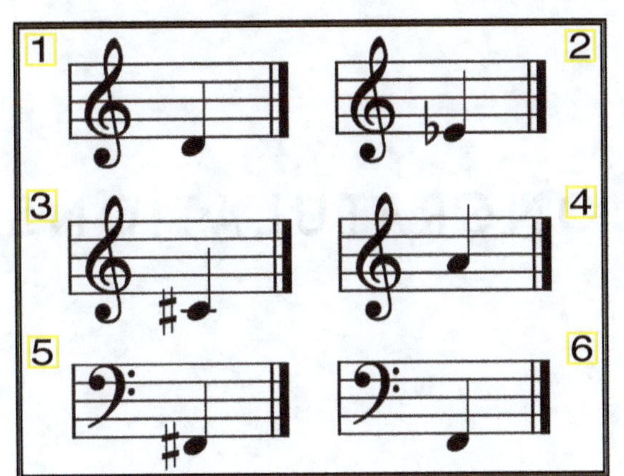

Exercise I

Rewrite each scale fom the Figure as an <u>ascending</u> natural minor scale.

Exercise II

Rewrite each scale fom the Figure as a <u>descending</u> major scale..

Solutions:

You can either write the accidentals in front of each note(*see below*), or write the key signature after the clef-symbol as shown in our pages for the scales.

1. D natural minor --> *see p. 83*

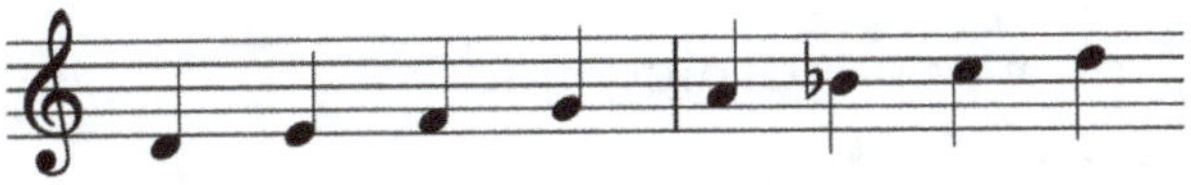

2. E♭ natural minor --> *see p. 98*

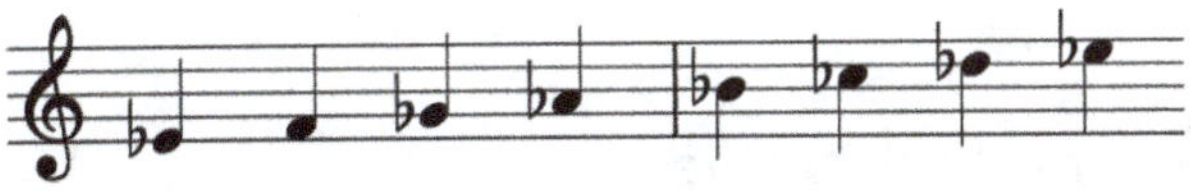

3. C# natural minor --> *see p. 68*

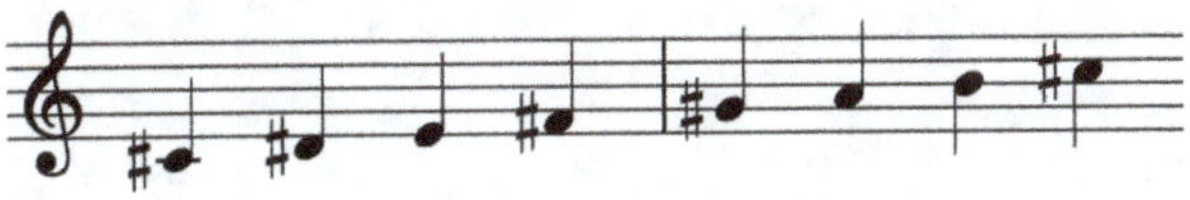

4. A natural minor --> *see p. 58*

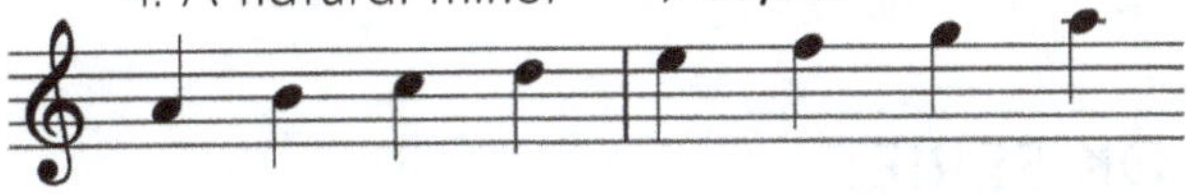

5. F# natural minor --> *see p. 67*

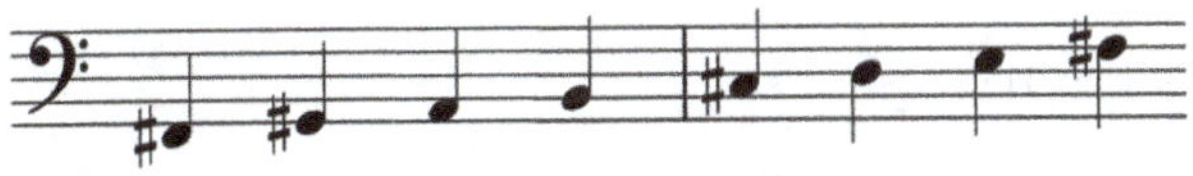

6. F natural minor --> *see p. 92*

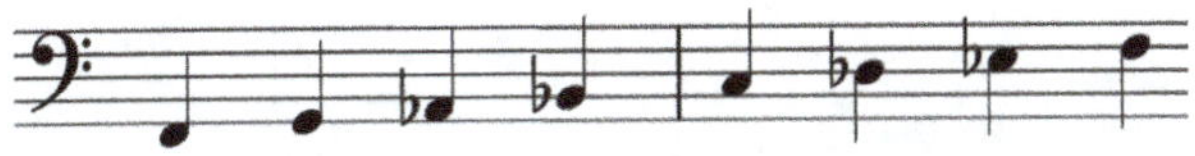

1. D natural major --> *see p. 17*

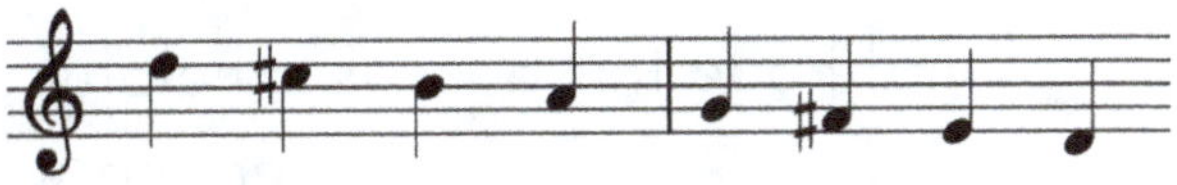

2. E♭ natural major --> *see p. 42*

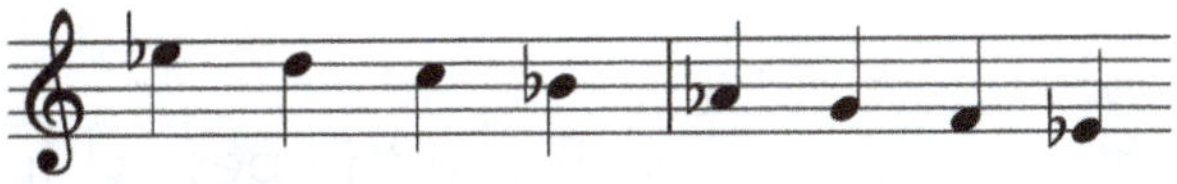

3. C# natural major --> *see p. 32*

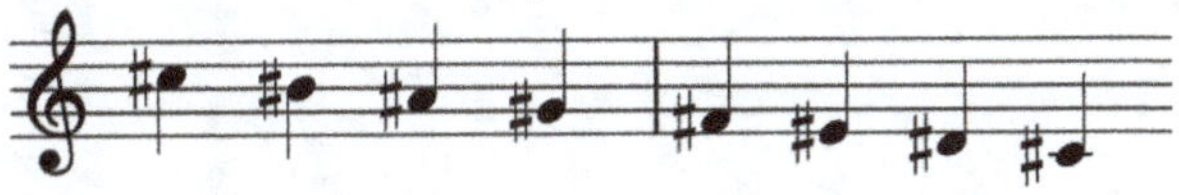

4. A natural major --> *see p. 20*

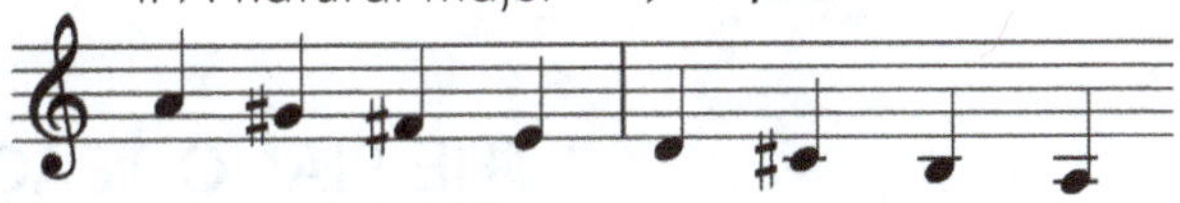

5. F# natural major --> *see p. 29*

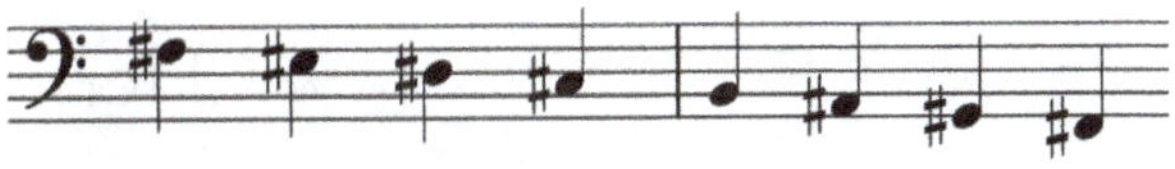

6. F natural major --> *see p. 36*

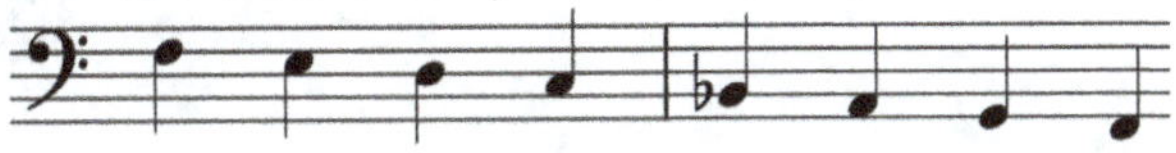

A key signature is important because it gives you information about the music, related notes, how it might sound, and a guideline when composing, since the Circle of Fifths tells you the close related keys. It is commonly written at the beginning of the music.

Congratulations!

You've made it to the end of this book.

Just keep in mind, 'Repetition is the mother of all Learning'.

I hope this book is a helpful guide for you when learning and creating wonderful music.

I wish you the best of luck on your musical journey.

Cheers.

THE PIANO TEACHER BOOK SERIES:

www.HermannPress.com